It's So Easy!

Comments from the Village People

Linda's life story reads like a modern day "Alice in Wonderland." It's like a fairy tale where she has made the impossible come true. She reminds me of a performer who will never grow old. She's like a young girl, who in the span of a very few years has run the gamut. Being a multitalented performer, you never know what to expect from her . . .

— ALEX BRILEY
The G.I.

Fanáticos de "La Linda Ronstadt," como yo, le van a divertir este libro de el Señor Bego, como la música de ella. En mi opinión, ella conveniente tiene el titulo, "La Paloma de la primera voz."

Fans of Linda Ronstadt, like I am, will love this book by Mr. Bego as much as they love her music. In my mind, she befits the title of "beautiful voice of a dove."

— FELIPE ROSE
El Indio
The Indian

I've known Mark Bego for nearly a dozen years now, and I've watched him take the life stories of people like Madonna and Michael Jackson and turn them into engrossing best-selling biographies. Well, he's done it again with *Linda Ronstadt: It's So Easy*. I've been in love with Linda's music since she was a country and folk singer. I've watched her develop into one of the most versatile contemporary singers in the history of the record business. Her story is filled with exciting career moves, unpredictable stylistic shifts, and twenty years of great music. Mark has covered every aspect of Linda's life, and it's all here in this book!

— RANDY JONES
The Cowboy

Linda Ronstadt: what a talented beauty! With her dark silky hair, big incredible eyes, and clear-cut confidence, there's no stopping her: she's always Linda. She does what she wants to do, and takes chances that other people don't. I think she's hot stuff!

— RAY SIMPSON
The Police Officer

I've been a Linda Ronstadt fan from the very first moment I ever heard her. I bought the sheet music for "Different Drum" in the '60s, and I've used that song for countless auditions. She has an incredible sense of what songs to record. If you take a beautiful song and put her voice to it, she creates that Linda Ronstadt magic!

Linda's working relationship with Peter Asher has yielded some of the greatest music ever recorded. I completely wore out my copy of "You're No Good!" *Hasten Down the Wind* and *Heart Like a Wheel* are two of my all-time favorite albums. I'm crazy about *Cry Like a Rainstorm, Howl Like the Wind,* and I think that Linda Ronstadt still has a lot of surprises for us. I love reading biographies, and her story is one of the most fascinating and insightful looks into a phenomenal talent.

— DAVID HODO
The Construction Worker

One of my ways of coping with the complexities of the music business is to read biographies, to see how others handle it. Many of the books that I have read were written by Mark Bego, and he was the first journalist to interview Village People . . .

Mark takes the reader from adorable, simple, naive Linda — through the experimentation, the high sexuality, the performers and people in her life — to the controlled adventurous artist we adore. He has not only given us a thorough, concise history of Linda's career, but also insightful quotes and references to the person she was in each of the phases. Mark's extensive knowledge of music styles and artists has added an incredible depth to this book, and an understanding of the influences that shaped the growth of Linda Ronstadt.

Linda started with a musical family background and the raw materials, but her dissatisfaction with her own work has her constantly striving for growth and improvement . . . She is a basic person who lives by her feelings, and some of those feelings allow her to take what others would call "risks." The casual jeans and halter tops wasn't a created image, it was just Linda. Linda has no "star ego" and definitely credits all the people who contribute to her success . . .

Mark captures this shy, multitalented person, and shows us that the drastic stylistic changes in her career have not been changes in her — just different views of the wholly talented Linda Ronstadt.

— GLENN HUGHES
The Leatherman

Linda Ronstadt
It's So Easy!

By
Mark Bego

EAKIN PRESS ★ Austin, Texas

ISBN 0-89015-775-8

Library of Congress Cataloging-in-Publication Data

Bego, Mark.
    Linda Ronstadt, it's so easy/by Mark Bego.
        p.   cm.
    Includes bibliographical references.
    ISBN 0-89015-775-8   : $12.95
    1. Ronstadt, Linda.   2. Singers – United States – Biography.
    I. Title.
ML420.R8753B45   1990
782.42164'092 – dc20
[B]   90-36152
                                                                    CIP
                                                                    MN

To Sindi Markoff:
You're such a "Party Girl"!

Acknowledgments

The author would like to thank:

Jim Bessman
Fran Boyar
Jimmy Greenspoon
Karen Greenspoon
Will Grega
Virginia Lohle
Walter McBride
Marcy MacDonald

Terrance Morgan
Robin Platzer
David Salidor
Tony Seidl
Russell Turiak
Mitchell Weiss
Beth Wernick

"Special thanks" to my friends the Village People:

Alex Briley
David Hodo
Glenn Hughes

Randy Jones
Felipe Rose
Ray Simpson

"Extra special thanks" to Brad DeMeulenaere for all of your research assistance — you're wonderful!

— MARK BEGO

Contents

Introduction   3
1. Tucson, Arizona   9
2. The Stone Poneys   20
3. Flying Solo   31
4. Heart Like a Wheel   43
5. Ronstadt: Rock Star   66
6. From New Wave To Broadway   105
7. A Sentimental Journey   134
8. Viva Ronstadt!   160
9. Still Within the Sound of Her Voice   183
Discography   195
Bibliography   211

It's So Easy!

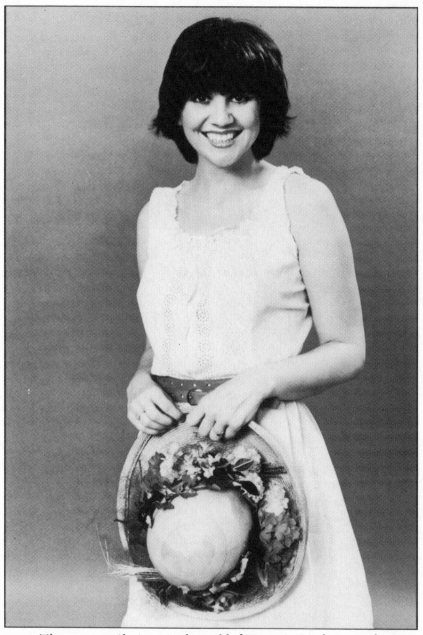

The most versatile singer in the world of pop music: Linda Ronstadt.
(Photo: Martha Swope/Mark Bego Archives)

Introduction

She stands in a spotlight on the stage of the Minskoff Theater on Broadway, surrounded by romantic blue light. She wears white gardenias in her braided hair and is dressed in a tailored black skirt and jacket, embroidered with silver threads in an elaborate Mexican design. Surrounded by an internationally famous mariachi band, she reaches the crescendo of a traditional South of the Border song. As she hits the final note of the song, two trained white *palomas* (doves) fly above the audience, to land on the outstretched fingers of the songstress. As a flock of *palomas* fly to the stage, the crowd is on its feet, shouting enthusiastic *"bravas"* to the spellbinding singing star standing center stage. Basking in the applause is the most versatile song stylist in the music business today — Linda Ronstadt.

Since she began her multifaceted singing career in the 1960s, Linda has become the most successful, most highly acclaimed, and best-selling female vocalist in the world of contemporary music. Although she achieved her first zenith of popularity as a rock and roll star, Ronstadt entered the 1990s as an accomplished Broadway star, a respected jazz and blues singer, a successful interpreter of classic Mexican folk songs, and an operatic performer as well. Over the last three decades, she has established a reputation for herself as the most unpredictable pop and rock superstar around. Having tallied seventeen Gold and

twelve Platinum albums since 1973, she has set an unsurpassed sales
record in the music industry.

With her piercing doelike brown eyes, and her naturally innocent
expression, she is arrestingly beautiful. Her rich and harmonious voice
can be lushly sensual on romantic ballads or strong and forceful when
she belts out unbridled rock and roll songs. As though these attributes
were not enough to sustain success in show business, she also has an un-
canny knack for setting amazingly unlikely goals for herself, and a glorious track record for attaining her dreams. It seems that there isn't a
musical style or a vocal range that can elude Ronstadt's resonant Midas
touch. Pop, country, rock, ethnic folk songs, jazz, and opera are all
within her grasp.

Linda Ronstadt is the only woman in the music business to have
been so successful at shifting musical gears without sacrificing any of
her established popularity. When she announced that she was going to
sing an operetta, record three albums of torch song standards, and release an entire album of Mexican mariachi music, skeptics — and her
record company — predicted that she would lose her fans. However,
everything she has touched has turned to gold. Much to the delight of
her followers, while her music has changed drastically, her penchant for
quality and her own vocal dexterity have grown with each move she has
made. Her singing on the *Canciones de mi Padre* album displays the wid-
est octave range and greatest vocal control of her career. The project
pushed her to achieve a new creative high point as a singer.

Certainly, other female pop performers in the rock and roll era
have recorded entire albums of material unrelated to their base of popularity. But none have attained the overwhelming degree of success that
Ronstadt has achieved. Albums by songbirds who branched out have
included Connie Francis' *Greatest American Waltzes, The Supremes Sing
and Perform "Funny Girl,"* Streisand's *Classical Barbra,* Carly Simon's
Torch, Joni Mitchell's jazzy *Mingus,* and even Annette Funicello's salute
to the fiftieth state: *Hawaiiannette.* These LPs went on to become
known as novelties, appealing mainly to die-hard fans.

Ronstadt's stylistic musical moves have all been quite unprecedented in terms of creativity and sales. Instead of becoming whim-
based collector's items, they have gone on to establish new vocal vistas,
increasing her audience with each new project. No one knows where
she'll turn for her next album.

Is she a rocker? . . . a Mexican folk singer? . . . a country and
western cowgirl? . . . a 1940s chanteuse? . . . an operatic diva? . . . or
a pop and rock singer-turned-actress? Actually, she is all of the above.
Through her many metamorphosis-like changes, Linda Ronstadt has
become as famous for her unpredictability as she has for her expressive

singing. When you begin to expect a particular type of music from her, she turns around and reinvents herself.

Her personal life has been as fascinating and as colorful as her ever-shifting career has been. Just as her musical persona has been shaped by the songs she has sung, her life offstage has often been directed and re-directed by her friends, lovers, and co-workers. The cast in the scenario of her life is as eclectic as her musical tastes. Her prestigious list of friends, influences, and compatriots includes James Taylor, Paul Simon, Peter Asher, Lowell George, Emmylou Harris, Kevin Kline, Angela Lansbury, Dolly Parton, Karla Bonoff, Gary Morris, Chuck Berry, Mick Jagger, Keith Richards, the Eagles, Nitty Gritty Dirt Band, Maria Muldaur, Bonnie Raitt, Andrew Gold, Joseph Papp, Wendy Waldman, Karla DeVito, James Ingram, Randy Newman, Nicolette Larson, Aaron Neville, and Phoebe Snow.

In 1977 Linda recorded a traditional folk song called "I Never Will Marry," which has become a philosophy that she lives by. Her list of famous "boyfriends" has kept her a hot topic in gossip columns for years. Singer/songwriter John David Souther, actor Steve Martin, co-median Albert Brooks, ex-Governor of California Jerry Brown, journalist Pete Hammel, and filmmaker George Lucas are among the celebrity beaux of La Ronstadt.

As headline-inspiring as her love affairs have been, her outspoken opinions and independent lifestyle have long been considered controversial and unique. Her 1970s "free love" philosophies, her reported drug experimentation, her self-professed stage fright, and her early career insecurities have all shared equal billing with her creative accomplishments. She is known to have a standoffish relationship with the press, and when she does grant interviews it is usually with one of her journalist friends.

"I've never understood all that," she said of her public image. "I think what happens is people hear you sing and they project their own yearnings onto you. They know a facet of you, and they think that's what you are. But they don't know anything about you. All they know is a print-and-paper person."

According to Linda, the stories she has read about her lovelife have often painted a more promiscuous picture than really exists. "I wish I had as much in bed as I get in the newspapers. Then I'd be real busy!" she joked. Although she has lived much of her life in the fast lane, she has a very serious nature. She is well-read, and proclaims that she feels like "an orphan without my books."

Standing only five feet, two inches tall, Linda claims that she has spent most of her life battling with her weight. The pressures of touring often lead to eating binges on the road. "I used to like to take speed, but food is my real addiction," she confessed.

As Paul Simon wrote about her in the lyrics of his *Graceland* album, Linda Ronstadt is a child from Tucson, Arizona, whose voice buoys her to the heavens. Musical memories of her childhood have influenced her musical taste as an adult. She grew up listening to traditional Mexican songs sung by her father, Gilbert Ronstadt. She sang to a recording of Gilbert and Sullivan's *H.M.S. Pinafore* as a child and was influenced at an early age by her father's Peggy Lee, Billie Holiday, and Ella Fitzgerald records. Songs on the radio and a collection of Hank Williams singles introduced her to the beat of rock and roll and the twang of country music. As a teenager, she performed in singing groups with her older brother and sister.

Linda attended a strict Catholic school as a child and dreamed of rebelling. In 1965, after rock and roll music and romantic dreams of California got into her blood, she dropped out of the University of Arizona and headed west for Los Angeles. From there the road has been rocky at times, but her maturity in the music business has been steadily successful — to the point of unprecedented stardom.

While her life continues to be one of exciting career challenges, dramatic artistic moves, and total unpredictability, the only thing that can be consistently counted upon is quality. When she jumps into a new arena — whether it is a new album, a movie, or a stage production — she dives into the deep end. If she needs a special vocal coach or the advice of a professional artist, she simply finds the best people for the job.

Since the 1970s, Linda has been joined by several other singers who have parlayed singing success into multimedia careers. Although she calls all of the shots on her projects, she has her own signature way of handling situations. She isn't brash like Madonna, overbearing like Streisand, outwardly aggressive like Cher, or bawdy like Bette Midler. But she has the same kind of drive that has made these women the prime decision-makers in their careers. So far, her instincts have served her well.

In spite of her international success, when it comes to her music, Linda remains self-critical and insecure about her own voice. "I don't like to listen to anything I've ever recorded. If it comes on the radio, I'll turn it off," she claimed. "I'd rather listen to someone else. Ella Fitzgerald, for example." However, she is quick to admit that she is consistent in her inconsistency. "I like to do what I feel — 'follow your bliss.' Like one morning I woke up and I *had* to paint my room purple. So I did. And some morning I'll want it yellow," she explained with equal amounts of seriousness and humor. She is as eclectic and unpredictable about her musical taste as she is about the color of her walls.

With her own trademark way of doing things, and a quiet but

forceful determination, Linda Ronstadt continues to seek new career challenges. She has maintained her vast popularity and her career momentum by consistently changing and adapting her talent to encompass new and exciting projects. Although she works very hard to achieve the resulting works of art, with her natural grace and style she makes it all appear so easy.

Producer, singer, songwriter, actress, rock and roller, Broadway star, operatic performer, and creative innovator — for Linda Ronstadt, this is just the beginning.

*When she was in high school in Tucson, Arizona, Linda was never the
cheerleader type. However, in later years she made up for lost time.*
(Photo: Arthur D'Amario/Retna Ltd.)

Tucson, Arizona

1

Bordered on the northeast by the Catalina Mountains, and on the southwest by an Indian reservation, Tucson is located in the lower part of Arizona, about an hour's drive north of the Mexican border. Although there are several major corporations with offices in Tucson, until the 1970s few buildings rose higher than the palm trees and saguaro cactus that grow abundantly in the surrounding desert.

Founded in 1775 by an Irishman who was exploring on behalf of the Spanish crown, Tucson is one of the oldest settlements in America. Its history is straight out of the western novels that Zane Grey made famous. Just south of town stands the majestic Mission San Xavier del Bac, representing the early Spanish influence that is characteristic of the American Southwest. Annual rodeos, a spring mariachi festival, and native crafts from several nearby Indian reservations indicate that Tucson is a city of many cultures. Mexican, Native American, Spanish, and frontier pioneer influences are abundant in the agriculture, clothes, food, lifestyle, and music of Tucson.

It was in this relaxed and charming Southwestern city on the Sonoran Desert that Linda Ronstadt was born and reared. Her father, Gilbert Ronstadt, was a native Tucsonian; her mother, Ruthmary Copeman, was the daughter of a wealthy Michigan family. It was while she was a college student in Tucson that Ruthmary met and was courted by Gilbert.

Much has been written about Linda's fascination with the culture of Mexico, but in reality her heritage is a combination of German, Dutch, English, *and* Mexican. Her maternal grandfather, Lloyd Copeman, was a famous inventor; her paternal grandfather, a successful rancher.

"My mom came from Michigan and my grandfather was a real well-known inventor. He invented things like the grease gun and the electric stove," Linda said. "My mother was not quite East Coast, but sort of 'Back East,' sort of DAR [Daughters of the American Revolution] . . . My mother was not a socially ambitious person. Her mom was DAR . . . They were millionaires and had been for generations.

". . . All the women in Holland are like my mother. Rigid. Straightforward. Earnest. Disarming. A cultural stubbornness," she explained. "Ours was the kind of family that belonged to the DAR, but my mother didn't equate that with snobbery so much as with grace, with a sense of style."

On her father's side of the family, she commented, "My grandfather was a rancher in Arizona . . . [he] had a ranch called Las Delicias, which means 'The Delights' . . . His father was the first mining engineer in the northern part of Mexico, and he was also in the Mexican army. He was born in Germany. My grandfather also owned a wagon-making shop which was eventually turned into a hardware store in Tucson. My dad grew up on the ranch, and in the hardware business."

When the Depression came in the 1930s, the Ronstadts were forced out of the cattle ranching business and into town. That's when Gilbert Ronstadt's Hardware Store got its start.

"The Ronstadts and a couple of other families were always the pillars of Tucson society," Linda claimed. With regard to her family tree, Linda has stated that she is "Mexican German on my father's side, and English also — he's Mexican, German and English. My mother's side is German, English and Dutch. In my heart I feel Mexican-German. I feel if I were to organize it correctly, I would try to sing like a Mexican person and think like a German. You know what I mean? I get it mixed up sometimes anyway, I sing like a Nazi, and I think like a Mexican . . . I can't get anything right."

Linda's lifelong fascination with music can be directly traced to her father's side of the family. "My grandfather used to have a band, the kind of band that plays in the middle of a public square. He used to play the flute, and he was the bandleader, and used to write a lot of marches and things like that. He was really a gas. Completely self-taught. He used to play the piano and everything. He also used to play guitar. I have his guitar, in fact. He had a real old beautiful Martin, with a rosewood back, ebony neckboard, things like that. I really love it. He taught my father how to play a guitar, and my father taught all of us how to play. We used to sing a lot together, all five of us," she said of her musically talented family. (Her brothers Mike and Pete sang with her on the *Canciones de mi Padre* album.)

"He also wanted to sing," she continued about her dad. "He was a wonderful singer. My father had a radio show when he was in his twenties. Oh, he was so dishy, so good-looking, the real dashing type. He rode his horse up the steps of my mother's sorority house. He was a real cowboy . . . She flipped out for him. How could she not? He was so dashing and romantic. And he had a gorgeous voice. He used to serenade her."

Ruthmary Copeman was so enthralled with handsome Gilbert Ronstadt that they married and made plans to live in Mexico. However, there was a slight problem: there just happened to be an untimely Mexican revolution under way at the time. Instead they settled north of the border.

Linda Marie Ronstadt was born on July 15, 1946, the third of four children. It seems that she was destined to become a singer or a musician: it was in her blood. Her Aunt Luisa Ronstadt, her father, her grandfather, and her brothers and sister were all responsible for her interest in music and her development as a performer.

Her aunt, who performed Mexican folk songs under the name of Luisa Ronstadt, was largely responsible for Linda's lifelong interest in the songs of old Mexico. "I had an aunt who was a pretty well known star in the '20s and '30s," Linda said. "She took a show all over the world. She did a lot of Mexican music and performed in regional costumes, in little vignettes, so that they were surrounded by the cultural ambiance they were extracted from."

The year that Linda was born, her Aunt Luisa assembled a book filled with traditional Mexican songs. She entitled her book *Canciones de mi Padre,* and she initiated the project to preserve the songs that she had heard her father singing on warm summer nights in her homeland of Sonora, Mexico.

Not only was Linda's grandfather responsible for exposing his family to Mexican folk songs, but he was also the link to her interest in the music of Gilbert and Sullivan. According to Linda, "My grandfather had an arrangement of *Pirates of Penzance* in 1896 that he wrote. I still have the charts. It was there in my background!"

Her fascination with American jazz and blues tunes can be directly traced to her father, who introduced his children to 78s by Billie Holiday, Peggy Lee, and Ella Fitzgerald. "My dad bought us Ella Fitzgerald records and Billie Holiday records, and he sat at the piano and sang 'What'll I Do,' so I knew those songs from the time I was little," she said. "One of the most influential records my father bought was the Ella Fitzgerald and Louis Armstrong duet album. I was about eight, and I listened all day long. I had this little baby voice, and I'd sing along."

She also recalled, "When I was growing up, my father used to play the records of Lola Beltrán, the great Mexican singer, who has always been the greatest influence on my singing. I've always tried to sing like her, but you can hear it most clearly on my earliest records like 'Different Drum,' in which I made a conscious effort to re-create her vocal tone. Later, in my version of 'Blue Bayou,' I used a falsetto in the end, which is a Mexican vocal trick. Unfortunately, the English language can only accommodate these sounds to a limited extent."

Linda was very impressed with the mariachi bands that she would see on family trips to Mexico. "When I was eight years old," she said, "I would follow the mariachis around town, standing outside the cantinas, because I loved it so much."

It was her older sister Suzi's collection of Hank Williams records that ignited Linda's passion for country and western music. When Linda was six years old, Hank Williams became Suzi's idol, and she bought all of his records. Linda became an addicted Hank Williams fan too. "I used to come home from school, pile up all the Hank Williams singles, and play 'em. All day long in school I'd think about playing those records. It was like thinking 'bout a piece of chocolate cake."

Sharing a bedroom with her sister Suzi, Linda began to acquire a taste for the kinds of music that her sister listened to. She soon started listening to the radio with obsessive devotion.

"I was a real radio kid," she recalled. "I just loved rock and roll. I wanted to be a singer. It was really hot in Tucson in the summer, and we had a cement floor, and I used to lie on the floor because it was cool, with my cheek to the radio. I had grooves on my cheeks. I was about five when I started doing that."

Linda learned at an early age to proceed through life adventurously, but carefully. "I think the greatest sin is carelessness," she claimed. "When I was a child, we lived out in the country in a very dry area and there were scorpions and snakes and brush fires, all kinds of things, and you had to be careful. You didn't stomp on insect's nests, or send dirt clods down the hill, or throw matches around."

When Suzi was twelve, and Linda was six, Suzi played a part in a school production of Gilbert and Sullivan's *H.M.S. Pinafore.* Watching Suzi rehearse, Linda learned all of the songs to that operetta. (Ironically, one of the songs from *H.M.S. Pinafore,* called "Sorry Her Lot," was one which Linda performed on Broadway during the run of *Pirates of Penzance* at the Uris Theater in the 1980s. The producers wanted to have

Linda perform another Gilbert and Sullivan solo in the show, so they inserted "Sorry Her Lot," which happened to fit neatly into the plot of *Pirates.*)

There doesn't seem to be a musical influence from her childhood that Linda has missed re-exploring as an adult. As a teenager she became mesmerized by music. "The only way I got through high school," she admitted, "was by keeping a record player going constantly in my mind." She fell in love with the music of Elvis Presley, and as a tribute to him in the 1970s she recorded her own interpretation of Presley's 1956 hit "Love Me Tender." Talking about the songs of Elvis at the time, she explained, "I knew them by heart. I hadn't heard them for years, but I knew all the little licks."

Linda's entire childhood was permeated with sounds of country, rock, mariachi music, jazz, the classics, and even opera. Her first memory is turning to her parents and saying, "Play me some music." She remembers singing with her mother and father when she was four years old. Her mother was playing the banjo and her father was strumming the guitar and singing when little Linda joined in on the singing. "You aren't singing the melody," her father said to her instructively. "I know," she recalled replying.

"My father always had a rich, melodious, lovely slow vibrato," Linda said. "He was a baritone, I guess, but he could get it way up to tenor notes. Beautiful voice, just so thick, it's like honey. His voice has lots of soul and no time. My dad had the worst time in the universe. It comes from not playing with a band a lot — he has Creole drag time. I can always harmonize with him because I know exactly what kind of sense of time he's got. But boy, it really rubbed off on me."

The first person she ever tried to imitate was her brother, Mike Ronstadt. "I was four or five, and he was the soloist in the choir, and he had a perfectly glorious-sounding voice, the purest, clearest tone I've ever heard. I just idolized my older brother, as most little girls do."

The next time she tried out her vocal powers was with her older brother and her sister Suzi. "We were all sitting around the piano singing, and I was five or six, and my sister was playing the piano," she distinctly remembered. "My sister was playing, and my brother was trying out something, and I went, 'I want to try that' . . . and I started to sing. And she just stopped and looked at my brother and said, 'You got a soprano here.' And it was like I had become *valid* somehow. You know, my *existence* had been affirmed. I was so pleased to know that that was what I was in life: I was a soprano.

"So, I was a soprano for a real long time," she continued, "and then one day, I was fourteen, my sister and brother were singing some folk song that was probably something they learned off of a Peter, Paul

& Mary record. It was called 'The Stockade Blues.' I came walking around the corner, and I just threw in the high harmony. I did it in my chest voice and I surprised myself. When I started out, with my chest voice I could only sing straight, with no vibrato. As I have gotten older, my voice has turned more like my father's. My older brother really had the most musical talent."

When Linda started stretching out musically in the 1980s and re-corded the music of Billie Holiday, Lola Beltrán, Gilbert and Sullivan, and old Mexico, it seemed like a natural move for her. The fact that her fans were used to hearing country and rock and roll from her was merely circumstantial. "People think I've been changing," she said in 1988 when she was launching her *Canciones de mi Padre* concert tour, "but in fact I've been singing all these kinds of music all the time. The thing that was a change for me was rock and roll. I never heard rock and roll until I was eight years old, and I never tried to sing it until I was about sixteen or seventeen, where this other stuff I'd sung forever. It was nor-mal for me. I've always sung that. The other stuff was the branching out. The public has a tendency to think that when they don't see you, you've disappeared. Whatever they don't see you doing — you must not be doing. So, when I went to sing 'Pirates,' they said, 'You can't do that. We've never seen you do that. How do you know how to do that?' But my mother had a big Gilbert and Sullivan [record] collection. I've heard those songs since I was two. My grandfather did an arrangement of 'Pirates of Penzance' . . . It was the same way with the Nelson [Rid-dle] records.

"When my sister said, 'We have a soprano,' I just went, 'I'm a singer, that's what I do,' " she continued. "When I went to first grade, as far as I was concerned, that's what I was. I remember there'd always be a certain time of the day to get up and sing, you'd have to sing some hymn, or the way you sing in churches. Everybody would be real em-barrassed and wouldn't want to do it, but I knew I could. It didn't occur to me that I wasn't very good until I started to do it for a living. I realized that it was hard, and I wasn't real great." Obviously, time and experience made up for the lack of formal training that she had as a child.

"All the time I was growing up, I thought of our family as Mexi-can . . . my father played Mexican music. It's such rich music. It has all the qualities that attracted my mother to him. And they attract me, too. Funny how that works," she said.

"Growing up in Arizona, we'd often run across the border to shop or for lunch," she recalled about her childhood. "I always thought I was Mexican until I went there and everybody called me 'gringo' . . . I felt very Mexican, but also strongly German. Our cultural tradition was all

Mexican, with all the Mexican holidays. My great-grandfather was the first German mining engineer in northern Mexico and later had a cattle ranch, and then northern Mexico was taken over by the United States. So that part of the family has been there a long time. I felt Mexican, but then I also started to place myself in the culture as a German ethnic pool in the middle of this Latin culture."

It's obviously only a matter of time before Linda records an album entirely in German. Kurt Weill songs or bawdy cabaret songs from 1930s Berlin sound like natural choices for Linda's future musical expeditions.

Several of Linda's character traits were formed at an early age. To this day she claims to be reticent about performing on stage: "When I was four, I hated my birthday parties, because I didn't like being the center of attention." But recollections of her upbringing reveal a well-adjusted child: "I knew I had good values and I knew I had a fairly keen judgment of human nature. My parents gave me that; they gave me a standard of what human beings should be."

While attending Catholic school in Tucson, Linda's favorite activity was flirting with the boys. "I was boy-crazy in the first grade — still am!" she exclaimed. "Ever since I was six years old, I've been looking for the perfect boyfriend. But I wanted to be a singer since I was two, and when it came down to it, I would never give up the singing for any old boyfriend.

"Maybe it was because there weren't many boys around," she said. "I really wanted them to like me and I was really concerned that they might not think I was attractive. In high school, I really believed that the boys might not like me unless they were physically attracted to me; that I couldn't keep their attention unless they were on the receiving end of that sexual dynamic and that if I didn't set up that sexual tension, they would walk away from me. And, I was often afraid to let go of that and rely on the nuts and bolts of the friendship. So I think I sometimes overloaded that end of it."

As she grew older, especially during her teenage years, she developed a rebellious attitude toward school. "The nuns hated me," she recalled. "They hated the way I talked about boys. I was too giggly and wore too much lipstick and dressed too sexy. I came on too strong. I still do. I find myself thinking, 'Oh God, red nail polish — I look like a sleaze,' or I really get into it and put on red nail polish and 500 pounds of make-up. I never know how far to go."

Remembering her adolescent pranks, she said, "I am so wicked. We had this young priest in catechism — you had to pass catechism. He had just been ordained, and who knew the problems he was going through? We used to write the answers to the catechism on our legs, up real high. We would slide up our dresses, and he would turn his face away, and we would copy down the answers."

Catholic school evidently left a lasting impression on Linda. She once confessed to *Time* magazine, "My big fantasy is to seduce a priest."

The facts of life were explained to Linda when she was seven. "My cousin Phil told me," she said. "He was a year older than I was. My mom was pregnant with my little brother and my cousin said, 'I know what your parents have been doing.' I said, 'No, my parents don't do that. No they wouldn't!' "

She went to Catholic school through the eighth grade and hated it. "They didn't let me wear Levi's. [The] nuns were ignorant. Nuns are the worst fascists . . .

"Those nuns still make me uptight. I never learned anything in school. Fortunately, my father taught me to read at home, but I still can't add. I had to jump into what I wanted to do right away. I've never had a job other than singing. If I couldn't sing for a living, I'd be stuck."

When she was growing up, Linda's father encouraged all of the children to learn to ride horses and to hunt, in the good old wild west tradition. Linda had a pony as a child. And she remembered, "When I was a little kid, my father used to take my brother hunting all the time, and I wanted to go too, because I wanted his attention, to be part of the gang. I was about four. I thought, I have to walk that way and be able to talk that way, and be real tough, and carry my .22, which was bigger than I was. We used to target practice with rotten eggs, and it was important for me to be able to do that. I couldn't do it very well because I was so young, but it meant so much, because I was a girl. My sister was a good shot. She shot a wild pig once, and I thought that was the greatest thing, because she had succeeded in the man's world on a man's terms. To me that was always the ultimate thing you could do."

Her hunting lessons also taught her valuable career lessons. In the 1970s, when rock and roll was dominated by male rock groups, Linda Ronstadt became the first woman to successfully sell Platinum rock albums in a formerly male-dominated field.

"I lived twenty miles out of town," she remembered about her Arizona childhood. "I learned a lot about animals. I thought town kids were limited. They didn't have horses. They wanted to squish bugs."

When she was fourteen years old, Linda joined her brother Mike and sister Suzi to form their own singing trio. At first they called themselves the Three Ronstadts, and then settled on the name the New Union Ramblers. They sang a repertoire of country and western, bluegrass, Mexican and folk music. "We were the Anita Kerr Singers of Tucson," Linda laughed. "I'm very country derivative."

Linda's sister Suzi recalled of the New Union Ramblers, "Linda had a solo spot. She sang things like 'The Trees They Do Grow High.' She was so cute and little, and she wore a black dress with a string of pearls."

However, what Linda most distinctly remembers is the stage fright that preceded her debut performance with her siblings. "When I was a little girl, I knew that what singers did was get up and perform," she explained. "I'd get real nervous, but I wanted to do it — I wanted to show them that's what I was. The first time I really sang in public as a teenager, there it was. I just all of a sudden was on fire and wanted to do it, and it really showed." It wasn't long before she found herself addicted to performing. Although she still isn't always 100 percent comfortable on a stage, she has learned to deal with her initial pre-performance paranoia.

While she was singing with her brother and sister, the group used a local musician named Bob Kimmel as their bass player. Kimmel loved Linda's voice, and he encouraged her to become a professional singer. According to Linda, she was already immersed in music, and singing was all that she could concentrate on.

Moving from Catholic school to the local public high school, Catalina High, didn't make her education any more enjoyable. Linda didn't get involved in the high school choir or with the productions of the theater department. "I guess they thought I didn't have the discipline," she surmised. She found that she shared very little in common with her classmates. "The big goals with the girls I grew up with were going into a convent or getting married. I never wanted either one. I just wanted to go on the road. I just always wanted to get up on stage and sing."

The year that Linda began high school, Bob Kimmel moved to Los Angeles to seek his fortune in the music business. During the three years before she graduated, Linda corresponded with Kimmel. The idea of packing her bags and heading west to L.A. appealed to her, but after she received her high school diploma, Linda was persuaded to stay in Tucson to attend the University of Arizona.

Linda's high school yearbook portrait is almost unrecognizable. That year she had bleached her hair blonde, and wore it in a heavily hairsprayed "bob." It only accentuated the roundness of her then-chubby face, which was heavily made-up.

She tried hard at conforming, but she would always manage to add a touch of cynicism to everything she had to do that was "establishment" oriented. When she "came out" at a local debutante ball, she wore a beautiful white gown, but underneath she wore black panties as a silent protest against conformity.

"I don't believe in chastity," Linda proclaimed. "Sex is only corrupting if your attitude is that it's bad. I thought that, even when I was a little girl. I had a bad reputation even in junior high school because my skirts were too tight. In high school, I decided to change my reputation, but I failed. I had sex when I was seventeen. I had a friend in high school who had a bad reputation, but she didn't deserve it. Her problem was that one day her water broke in study hall! She just picked up her books and walked out."

About the only fun Linda had in school was the time she spent with her sister and brother as the New Union Ramblers, singing in "funny weird little clubs" and assorted gigs at coffee houses and campus fraternity houses.

At the age of eighteen, in the middle of her first semester at the University of Arizona, Linda came to the conclusion that she was going to go out into the world to see if she could become a successful singer. During the fall of 1964, Bob Kimmel wrote to Linda and asked if she was interested in moving to L.A. to start a singing group with him. In his letter, Kimmel said that he could line up musicians, and all they needed was a female singer. He had immediately thought of her. That was all the encouragement she needed. "I said, 'Sure,' hopped in the car, and drove over. So, that's how it all began," she recalled. With that, she dropped out of college, packed her bags, and headed for California.

Although her older brother and sister enjoyed singing, only Linda had the passion to go out into the world and pursue a singing career. Her sister Suzi raised a family instead of seeking a career. As Linda explained it: "She got married and had a million kids!" Mike ran the family hardware store with their father until recently. Pete ended up becoming the chief of police in Tucson. "He's a cop. He's good at that, too," Linda said. "He always wanted to achieve things like that. He likes to be on the street."

Gilbert Ronstadt raised all of his children to be independent and adventurous, but it was his youngest daughter who proved to be his most daring offspring. Linda had no idea what awaited her in Los Angeles — but she was determined to go there to try her wings.

After the Stone Poneys broke up, Linda found herself thrust into the spotlight as a solo singer.

(Photo: Joseph Sia/Retna Ltd.)

The Stone Poneys

2

Before she left Tucson, Linda scraped together $30, announced to her English teacher she was moving west to become a rock star, and bid her family goodbye. "There was nothing else I could have done," recalled Linda. "My feet just started moving." As she was leaving home, her father imparted a bit of advice to his aspiring rock star daughter: "Never let anyone take your picture with your clothes off."

She would later explain leaving after her single aborted college semester. "I thought that everyone who came to California had a hit record. It's a good thing I didn't know better, or I'd never have come. I'd have stayed in Tucson in terror and been a housewife with four kids."

Fame didn't come quite as quickly to Linda as she had anticipated. In fact, it would take ten years, and the release of the breakthrough *Heart Like a Wheel* album, before she became a bona fide star "star." Arriving in Los Angeles in late 1964, she found her way right into the center of an exciting circle of aspiring musicians who were writing music, exchanging ideas, taking drugs, and preparing for their ascension up the record charts.

Jackson Browne and Bonnie Raitt were among the L.A. natives who hung out in the same circuit. Several out-of-towners, like Neil Young, Joni Mitchell, and Stephen Stills, ended up in the Laurel Canyon area. Don Henley dropped out of North Texas State and headed for

Los Angeles. Likewise, Glenn Frey migrated from Royal Oak, Michigan; and local musician/guru Frank Zappa was holding court at a mansion that used to be owned by silent cowboy movie star Tom Mix.

Meanwhile, down on Sunset Strip, and in surrounding areas, rock clubs were being looked to as discovery spots for hot new musical talent. The Whiskey-A-Go-Go, the Troubadour, the Trip, Ciro's, the Galaxy, Stratford's, Brave New World, Bido Lido's, and the London Fog were all clubs where up-and-coming rockers were busily honing their singing and songwriting style. Everyone was going through one metamorphosis or another, trying to achieve the right sound that would land them the much sought-after commodity: a record deal. Kenny and the Cadets became a huge smash when they began singing surfer tunes and changed their name to the Beach Boys. The Crossfires were a hit after they started calling themselves the Turtles. And members of the Byrds and Buffalo Springfield eventually joined forces and found maximum success when they became known as Crosby, Stills, Nash and Young.

From 1964 to 1969 the music business was exciting, booming, and constantly changing. In Los Angeles especially, musicians and singers were trying to find the right sound, songs, and image that would bring them fame. Out of this same circle of musicians came The Mamas and the Papas, Three Dog Night, Jim Morrison and the Doors, and the Lovin' Spoonful.

When Linda arrived in Los Angeles to join her old friend Bob Kimmel, she discovered that her career would have to go through all sorts of changes before any record deals were made. She wasn't quite certain how everything was going to unfold, but she liked the idea of becoming the member of a singing group, as opposed to becoming a solo headliner. She didn't have the slightest idea that she was going to grow and evolve to become the highest paid female rock star of the 1970s. In fact, at the time she was just looking forward to a creative but modest career, making country/folk music. Reality would eventually exceed her dreams.

"When I came to L.A. in 1964," she recalled, "I kind of looked around and thought that maybe the kind of career Judy Collins had was perfect. She was quietly putting out things that seemed tasteful and sold respectably. That was the kind of career I wanted; a career where you earned a nice living, your records sold well, you had the respect of other musicians and did things in good taste. I never tried to become 'the next big thing.' It seemed that was something to be guarded against at all costs."

The first place that Linda stayed in L.A. was the house where Bob Kimmel was living. When she got to town, he told her that he had met a guitar player named Kenny Edwards. Their original concept was to form a rock group with five musicians, an electric autoharp, and a female singer. Enlisting the services of a drummer and a bass player, Bob, Kenny and Linda found themselves — for a very short period of time — as the three core members of a folk group who called themselves the Kimmel Brothers. Linda and her partners were big fans of the Chambers Brothers, and so chose a similar name. The Kimmel Brothers soon disbanded, and Bob, Kenny and Linda decided to become a folk-singing trio, called the Stone Poneys. This time around their name was chosen for the Charley Patton song, "The Stone Poney Blues."

Fashioning their sound after the tight harmonies of Peter, Paul & Mary, the Stone Poneys began working on a repertoire of blues and folk songs. One afternoon, Linda and her singing partners were in a coin-operated laundry, washing their clothes and singing in between cycles, when their impromptu concert was overheard by a pair of music industry managers.

"There was a place called Olivia's Cafe," Linda remembered, "which was a soul food place in this little neighborhood where everybody hung out. We were in the laundromat across the street, and these guys were in the cafe eating lunch, and they heard us singing while we did our laundry. I've got such a loud mouth that they heard us over the dryers, the traffic, bacon frying and all the rest, and they signed us right up. It was like the movies, and I went, 'Hey this is silly.' And, it turned out to be really silly."

Their new "managers" were convinced that they could get the Stone Poneys a recording contract, so the trio went along with the program. When a meeting was set up with representatives from a record company, it looked like their dream of musical stardom was within their grasp. However, the bubble soon burst when Linda, Bob and Kenny discovered what was planned for them.

Mercury Records was interested in signing them to a recording deal, but the label wanted to change the Stone Poneys' name to the Signets, and record them a la the Beach Boys — singing "surf " music. The idea of singing about searching for the "perfect wave" and "hanging ten" didn't appeal to them at all, and they realized they were definitely off on the wrong foot. Consequently, their association with their two newfound managers ended just as quickly as it began. "Those corny managers we had took away all our amplifiers when we fired them," Ronstadt explained, "so we stuck with what we had, which was acoustic guitars."

Freed from their first set of "managers," the Stone Poneys set about the task of defining their own sound. While they were working out their repertoire of folk/rock songs, Linda and her two partners began to pick up gigs on "showcase" nights at the local clubs. Slowly they built a small following, and their onstage experimentations grew into paid bookings. According to Ronstadt, "When I was singing in bars in Los Angeles in 1965 and I discovered I could make a *living* that way, it was one of the great moments of my life."

The club called the Troubadour, located on Santa Monica Boulevard, was responsible for putting them on the right path, as it had done for many performers in L.A. during this era. In the mid-to-late '60s, the Troubadour was *the* place to hang out if you wanted to be discovered, and for meeting the "who's who" of the music business. "I used to hang out at the Troubadour every single night," Linda said. "I didn't even drink, but I was in the bar every night, and over in the corner was Doug Dillard and Gene Clark, and that's where I met J. D. Souther, and Jackson Browne, and all the Eagles, and the Byrds, and Buffalo Springfield. They were all there, and it was real fun."

By simply being in the right place at the right time, the Stone Poneys landed their first scheduled gig at the Troubadour. On Monday nights the club would offer up-and-coming new talent three-song audition sets in front of a live audience. Sharp-witted managers would fill the place on Monday nights, looking to sign up acts on the spot. It was there that Linda met and formed a business relationship with her first manager. Although she did not sign a contract with him immediately, he was ultimately the man who brought the Stone Poneys to Capitol Records.

As it was throughout her tenure with the Stone Poneys, the only notable thing about the trio was Linda and her distinctive voice. Although her singing style was still in a formative stage, she was both impressive and memorable. Right after their debut Troubadour set, Linda was approached about leaving Bob and Kenny and singing on her own as a solo act.

One of the people in the audience at the Troubadour that night was manager/promoter Herb Cohen. He wasted no time finding Linda after the set and introducing himself. Cohen was fascinated with Ronstadt, and he invited her to join him for a drink after the show. When Bob Kimmel caught up with Linda at the bar next door, Cohen was trying to convince her to drop out of the Stone Poneys and become a headliner. When Bob asked Herb what he thought of the group's potential, Cohen was frank in his observations. As Linda recalled, "I remember Herbie saying to Kimmel, 'I don't know whether I can get you guys a contract, but I can get your girl singer recorded,' and that was sort of the beginning. Trouble in the ranks. And I said, 'No, no, I won't sing without the group.'

"I kept saying in those days, I didn't want to be a single, I wanted to be in a group. My confidence was devastated and redevastated," she said. She especially lacked confidence because she couldn't play the guitar, and was still experimenting with her own vocal capacities. "When I first got to L.A., I could play C, G, and F on the guitar — and there were all those hot guitar players and I just put the guitar away. Literally did not touch the guitar for eight years," she explained.

The Stone Poneys soundly decided to remain a unit, and they were rebooked at the Troubadour for another gig. This time they were hired as the opening act for soul singer Oscar Brown, Jr., and his band. However, the crowd that came to see Brown was decidedly not interested in the folk harmonies of the Stone Poneys. Linda distinctly remembers that Brown "had a band and this amazing chick he married [Jean Pace], and he got a very uptown black audience."

Completely discouraged by the audience's poor reception, the Stone Poneys temporarily disbanded. Linda moved to Venice Beach, and her mother had to send her money to help her pay the rent. Ruthmary Ronstadt later recalled this phase of her daughter's life with awe. "It was the dregs," said Linda's mom. "I went to see her at most of the places she lived in and even *I* had to sleep on the floor, on the couch, anywhere I could."

With the Stone Poneys in a "holding pattern," Linda began to get desperate for money. She called Herb Cohen and told him that she had decided to acquiesce to his plans to land her a solo recording deal. Cohen tried to place Ronstadt in several creative situations, but none of them seemed to pan out. One of Herb's aborted plans involved having Linda record a song with Frank Zappa. When Herb's attempts at finding her work failed, Linda continued to sing from time to time with Kenny Edwards, and eventually the Stone Poneys got back together.

Recalling those days in 1965 and 1966, when the trio was lucky to earn $100 each a month, Bob Kimmel said, "Looking back, I don't know how we managed. I have no idea how Linda coped." But she did, and it wasn't too long before her perseverance paid off.

Watching Linda Ronstadt and the Stone Poneys plod along and polish their act, Herb Cohen decided that he would do what he could to try to land them a record deal as a trio. Cohen introduced them to a record producer named Nick Venet, who was concurrently moving over to Capitol Records to begin work as a staff producer. Venet was impressed with what he heard, and he presented the Stone Poneys to the executives at Capitol.

Like history repeating itself, Capitol Records was impressed with Linda's voice but uncertain about the Stone Poneys. At Ronstadt's urging, Venet convinced Capitol to sign Linda as part of the trio. She recalled, "It was true, I wasn't ready to do anything. I still wasn't ready when I *became* a single!" She was much more confident performing with Bob and Kenny by her side, and so began Linda's association with Capitol Records.

In late 1966, Bob, Linda and Kenny went into the recording studio with Nick Venet and began work on their debut album, *The Stone Poneys* (also known as *Linda Ronstadt and the Stone Poneys* and rereleased in March 1975 as *The Stone Poneys Featuring Linda Ronstadt*). Although their sound was firmly out of the folk music trio mold, Venet did coax Linda into recording three solos among the LP's ten cuts.

Six of the songs on the debut Stone Poneys album were original compositions by Kenny Edwards and Bob Kimmel. One song, entitled "Back Home," was written by Kenny, and the traditional folk song, "Wild About My Lovin'," was adapted by Ronstadt, Kimmel, and Edwards. The three songs that were Linda Ronstadt solos were outside compositions found by Venet. Already he was positioning Linda apart from the group, even on their first album as a trio.

The album opens with the acoustic Kimmel/Edwards composition "Sweet Summer Blue and Gold," which sounds like something directly off of a Peter, Paul & Mary album. On that song, and the successive cut, "If I Were You," Linda's performance is basically a harmony vocal, blended into Bob and Kenny's singing. The harmonies on the one-minute-and-fifty-eight-second "If I Were You" likewise sound like they are emulating the sounds of another popular 1966 group — The Mamas and the Papas, whose debut album *If You Can Believe Your Eyes and Ears* had gone Gold earlier that year.

However, as the needle on the record player reaches the third cut on *The Stone Poneys* album, Fred Neil's "Just a Little Bit of Rain" — Linda's first solo — the sound is totally unique. The recording is rudimentary, the arrangement is sparse, but the distinctive and torchy quality of Ronstadt's voice comes through crystal clear. Although she had yet to discover the power and confident control that she would display on her later recordings, her voice was there — expressive and unmistakably intense.

Her other two solo outings on the album, "Orion" and "2:10 Train," were both compositions by a songwriter named Tom Campbell "Orion" is a much darker song that is similar to Grace Slick's early work with Jefferson Airplane. "2:10 Train," while a folk tune, has a jazzy sound to it that seemed to loosen Linda up a bit, and she belts a note or two, as though she is just trying out her wings.

The three Linda Ronstadt solos on this album seem to be part of an entirely different disc. On all eight of the "trio" songs, the group sounds like they are trying to match the folksy sing-along quality of Peter, Paul & Mary's "Puff the Magic Dragon." However, their attempt at light folk giddiness comes across as forced and uninspired. Linda's "Just a Little Bit of Rain," "Orion," and "2:10 Train" have a passionate intensity to them that all of the other songs are lacking. Although she is unaware of her own voice's strength, there are enough flashes of brilliance and fire to make it obvious why everyone was trying to encourage Linda to become a soloist.

According to Linda at the time, "I really like soft, pretty, simple music. Which is not to say I don't like to sing loud, but the simpler the better, for me anyway. I like uncomplex stuff. I like everything to be very distinct; I don't like to record with ten thousand instruments, and have some of it dialed way down to sort of rumble along in the background. I'd rather just use one instrument, like we did with just the cello, and have every single thing be heard."

Looking back at her first recordings with the Stone Poneys, Linda would later express her frustration over her own inexperience. She never took over any of the control that she could have exerted at the time. Basically, she just did what she was told to do in the recording and hoped for the best: "I had less control, because I didn't know what I was doing. I didn't know how to get what I wanted."

The Stone Poneys album was released on January 30, 1967, and the single "Sweet Summer Blue and Gold"/"All the Beautiful Things" hit the record stores in February. Unfortunately, no one noticed. The year 1967 was a year in which the music business made a dramatic shift away from folk rock music and into the psychedelia that was personified by the Beatles' "Sgt. Pepper's Lonely Hearts Club Band" and the searing soulfulness of songs like Aretha Franklin's "Respect." The Stone Poneys' music sounded more like it fit on the playlist of 1962, when the Kingston Trio and the Limelighters were still the rage.

Needless to say, both the album and the single were tremendous "bombs." Not to be discouraged by the results of their debut recordings, they quickly returned to the studio to record their second album, *Stone Poneys: Evergreen Volume II,* which was also produced by Nikolas Venet.

Released in June of 1967, the second Stone Poneys album seemed destined to suffer the same fate as its predecessor. However, the one single that was released from it became one of the biggest "sleeper" hits of the year. The song, "Different Drum," was released in July of 1967, but it wasn't until early 1968 that it peaked on the *Billboard* magazine singles charts at Number 13. The ironic thing about "Different Drum" was that by the time the single became a hit, the Stone Poneys had already grown discouraged and broken up!

Following the release of *Evergreen Volume II,* the Stone Poneys had been sent out on the road. When they arrived in New York City as the opening act for Paul Butterfield, they were savaged by the critics. Devastated by their disastrous press reception, Kenny Edwards not only quit the band but left the country and headed for India. That was, after all, the "summer of love" when the Beatles (and everyone else who could afford it) were heading for the Himalayas in search of a mystical guru who had the meaning of life. Likewise, Linda and Bob decided that their career as Stone Poneys had run its course, so they went their separate ways.

Meanwhile, the single "Different Drum," written by Mike Nesmith of the Monkees, began to receive airplay. Several radio programmers gave the single a spin on their turntables simply because one of the Monkees had written it. When they heard it, they liked it. By November, "Different Drum" started climbing up the charts. All of a sudden there was a demand for live appearances by the Stone Poneys. Kenny was still in India, so in early 1968, Linda and Bob hit the road with a group of session musicians and embarked on a Stone Poneys concert tour — opening for the Doors.

Nick Venet continued to come up with non-Stone Poney material to show off Linda's voice and set her off from the group's dated sound. The only other Stone Poney sound on "Different Drum" is Kenny Edwards' guitar work.

At the time, Linda explained of the Stone Poneys' future recordings: "We'll probably be going into a lot more delicate things. 'Different Drum' was kind of a freak. It was one song on that album that I didn't think sounded like any of the rest of the album, and it happened to hit. I consider that only one side of what we can do, musically." Unfortunately, the Stone Poneys' days together as a group were numbered.

After Bob and Linda's tour as the opening act for the Doors, Kimmel decided to split as well, leaving Linda to complete the third Stone Poneys' album with Nick Venet. Fortunately, Kenny Edwards returned to America from India in time for the recording of the group's final LP, as a guitar player. Hastily recorded, the album *Linda Ronstadt: Stone Poneys and Friends* was released in April 1968. Two singles were pulled off of the album, "Up To My Neck in Muddy Water" and Mike Nesmith's "Some of Shelly's Blues." Only "Up To My Neck in Muddy Water" made it onto the *Billboard* charts, peaking at a dismal Number 93 in 1968. While *Evergreen, Volume II* had made it to Number 100 on the LP charts, *Linda Ronstadt: Stone Poneys and Friends* failed to make an appearance on the chart.

With that, Linda and Kenny parted company. The Stone Poneys were history. However, as the "lead singer" of the group, Linda found herself obligated to complete the seven-year recording contract that she had signed with Capitol Records. In a way, the three Stone Poneys albums were merely a ploy to get Ronstadt under contract and develop her talents from that point on. And that is exactly what was to happen. Unfortunately, the third Stone Poneys album went seriously over budget in the recording process, and Linda was destined to begin recording her first solo album with her royalty account seriously in the red.

"They [Bob and Kenny] weren't fired," Linda was later to explain of the demise of the Stone Poneys. "What happened was that we were originally signed with the idea that I was going to be forced to become a solo star, which I resisted. All I wanted to do was join another band, because neither Kenny or I thought the music was very strong, and we were right. So Kenny quit the band and went to India, and we had a hit record all of a sudden ["Different Drum"], so that when the band had naturally broken up on the grounds of mutual disgust with each other's inability to play music, we kept on for another year — just because of a giant hit record. It was awful, because I knew the music wasn't good enough, I knew we were faking it, and it was just humiliating. At that point, my musical taste was getting much more sophisticated at a very rapid pace, and my ability wasn't catching up with that sophistication, so I created my own credibility gap, which was real painful."

There were, however, several positive effects that Linda's experiences as one of the Stone Poneys imparted. By harmonizing with her old Tucson friend Bob Kimmel and her newfound friend Kenny Edwards, she was able to feel the same supportive energy that her brother Mike and sister Suzi had given her in the New Union Ramblers. Although basically shy, when accompanied by an emotional "support group" of friends on stage with her she was able to abandon her inhibitions and perform.

This would become a lifelong pattern for Linda. She has always become close friends with her co-workers. Often this has spilled over into her lovelife as well, especially during this era of her singing career.

Several of the people Linda worked with on the first Stone Poneys album became lifetime friends, compatriots, and co-workers. Her partner in the group, Kenny Edwards, worked with her throughout the 1970s and has continued to work with her, right up to the 1987 *Trio* album. Guitarist Bernie Leadon, who played on Linda's first Stone Poney solo, "Just a Little Bit of Rain," played on several of her early 1970s solo albums, until he went on to become one of the original members of the Eagles.

Songwriter Tom Campbell, who composed two of Ronstadt's solos from the debut Stone Poneys' album, became Linda's first live-in boyfriend. This would mark the start of her habit of falling in love with her musicians and her managers.

"That was the beginning of the process of stumbling and groping," recalled Linda in the 1980s. "The years and years and years of trying to evolve something, which is what I do now. I didn't sing like a boy soprano anymore. And I didn't even think about becoming a high soprano. That was just a little dream I put on the shelf."

Not only was she learning about her voice, but she was busy defining her own interests and developing her musical taste. "We were all learning about drugs, philosophy and music. Everything was exciting," she said of her era of self-discovery in the late 1960s.

When the Stone Poneys disbanded in 1968, Linda Ronstadt's course was clearly charted. Although she had resisted the idea of becoming a solo performer, by October of that year she was in the studio, recording her first solo album.

When she began her solo singing career, Linda was so shy on stage that she wanted to be seen as just a member of the band.

(Photo: Joseph Sia/Retna Ltd.)

Flying Solo

3

After three disjointed folk/rock albums as one-third of the Stone Poneys, Linda Ronstadt shifted gears on her first three solo LPs and headed directly into the country and western mode. She had been veering towards a decidedly more "countryfied" sound on several of the selections that were contained on the third Stone Poneys album — especially on Tim Buckley's "Hobo" and Mike Nesmith's "Some of Shelly's Blues."

Saddled with the obligation of assuming the Stone Poneys' Capitol Records contract, Linda shouldered the responsibility and prepared for her first solo recording sessions. She expelled very little mental energy mourning the demise of her former group. In a way, it was a big relief.

"The Stone Poneys tried to combine the roots [of folk and country music] with rock and roll, and we were miserable," she would later recall. "We started off as an acoustic rock band, and played clubs like the Insomniac, and a lot of beer pads. Places like that. We had some good times and some bad times, but we were always breaking up. We were always playing in opposite musical directions."

Everyone who heard the Stone Poneys agreed that the only thing that distinguished them in any way was Linda Ronstadt's singing. Reviewing one of the group's final concerts in 1968, *Billboard* magazine made a prediction that everyone seemed to unanimously agree upon: "Watch out for Linda Ronstadt."

31

Instead of making her more confident, the success of "Different Drum" had intimidated her a bit. The song received a lot of airplay, and all of a sudden everyone knew who she was. "Having a hit record when I was 21 made me real visible to the music community," she recalled, "and I didn't feel I was ready for that examination. I wasn't very good and it made me real embarrassed. I felt people in the business resented me."

Whether she was ready or not, by mid-1968 the scene was set for her to begin her solo career. It would take her three lukewarm albums before she would hit her singing stride, but the period from 1968 to 1972 was crucial in developing her musical taste and learning her real vocal strength. She would later self-critically define her first three solo LPs as "indifferent albums."

To comfortably ease her transition from "group member" to "solo star," Linda chose to surround herself with familiar faces and sounds. Not only did she record compositions by her friends Tom Campbell and Kenny Edwards, but she had her two brothers sing background vocals on her first Capitol album.

Hand Sown . . . Home Grown was recorded in the fall of 1968 and released in March 1969. The album's producer was Chip Douglas, who had found his greatest success at that point as the producer of several of the Monkees' biggest hits. His Monkees productions included the Number One Gold albums *Headquarters* (under the name of Douglas Farthing Hatlelid) and *Pisces, Aquarius, Capricorn & Jones Ltd.* in 1967, and the Top Ten million-selling hits "Pleasant Valley Sunday" and "Daydream Believer." While working with the Monkees, Chip Douglas was able to take the group away from the manufactured giddiness of their two multimillion selling debut LPs and into musical directions that appealed to the four individual Monkees. Working with Mike Nesmith on the songs "You Just May Be the One" and "What Am I Doing Hangin' Round," Douglas recorded Nesmith in a fashion that was "country" enough to appeal to the singer/songwriter, and "rock/pop" enough to still attract Monkees fans who never thought that they would find themselves listening to country music.

How appropriate indeed that Chip Douglas should move from recording the writer of "Different Drum" to the lady whose voice made the song a hit. The music contained on *Hand Sown . . . Home Grown* ran the gamut from excellently emotion-filled ("Bet No One Ever Hurt This Bad") to embarrassingly bad ("The Only Mama That'll Walk the Line"). In an attempt to capture fans of both country and rock and roll, the album unfortunately failed to find an audience on either side of the fence.

Linda's most successful performances on the *Hand Sown . . . Home*

Grown album were her "cover" versions of the Bob Dylan compositions "I'll Be Your Baby Tonight" and "Baby You've Been on My Mind." Kenny Edwards contributed the mid-tempo ballad "The Long Way Around," while Linda's boyfriend Tom Campbell was represented on the album by the lamenting "A Number and a Name." Linda's strongest singing was heard on her version of Randy Newman's "Bet No One Ever Hurt This Bad," which Three Dog Night had recorded on their 1968 debut album, *One*. Linda's interpretation of the song shows off some preclusionary sparks of great things to come from La Ronstadt.

Unfortunately, *Hand Sown . . . Home Grown* was a dismal failure, and never made it onto any of the music charts. It was released in 1969, the year of the Woodstock music festival and the controversy over nudity in *Hair* on Broadway. No one cared about hearing the country twang of Linda Ronstadt bleating folksy songs like "We Need a Lot More of Jesus (and a Lot Less Rock and Roll)." One of the best things that this album contained was Linda's first version of the Springfields' 1962 hit "Silver Threads and Golden Needles." Her brothers Pete and Mike sang background vocals on this particular cut; however, not even the pleasant harmonies of the three Ronstadts could save this album from obscurity.

The same month that the album was released, Linda made her solo performing debut, at the famed Whiskey-A-Go-Go in Los Angeles. She was mortified at first, but she soon got used to the idea of being the focal point of the audience's attention. "It took me four years to get to the point where I could get on stage as a single," she said. "At first I just couldn't open my mouth on stage. I was so shy."

This was the year that Ronstadt established her hillbilly look on stage, by performing barefoot whenever possible. The look was also perpetuated on the cover of the *Hand Sown . . . Home Grown* album. The photographs of twenty-two-year-old Linda depict her as a brown-eyed Appalachian beauty. On the front cover, Linda stands barefoot on a rock in the middle of the woods, wearing a white pantsuit with flowing fringe. On the back cover she sits barefoot on a wooden chair, wrapped in a yellow shawl, in front of a run-down stone cottage surrounded by trees. She looks as if she is dressed to film an episode of "The Beverly Hillbillies."

The cover photos on that album were taken by Ed Caraeff, who shot all of the Three Dog Night album covers as well. Jimmy Greenspoon, the keyboard player for Three Dog Night, recalled being introduced to Ronstadt by Caraeff during this era: "I first met her at a party at [Caraeff's] house. I remember seeing this little countryish looking girl with this nice little print dress on, and no shoes, sitting in the corner. I said, 'Who's that?' Ed said, 'Linda Ronstadt.' Everybody knew who she was based on 'Different Drum,' but she was quite unassuming at this party. Who knew at the time that she was destined to become a huge superstar?"

Talking about her musical taste at the time, Ronstadt explained, "I'm a texture freak. For me, if I can get a lot of different groovy weird textures in a song, then I like it the best, 'cause I have a lot of different textures in my voice. That's the kind of thing I concentrate on, like volume, or softness, or prettiness. I like to see how many different ones I can throw in there."

Since her first solo album failed to gain much attention in either the rock or country arenas, the decision was made for Linda to go all the way to Nashville to make her follow-up disc *totally* country and western. In many ways, this was a good ploy, as it gave Linda a valuable opportunity to work with several of "Music City's" top session musicians and expose herself to new outside influences. Although a couple of the cuts were recorded in Los Angeles, the steel guitar-accented songs that were crafted in Nashville dominate the album.

The resulting LP, recorded in January 1970 and released that March, gave Ronstadt her initial taste of success — including her first solo Top 40 pop hit, her first Grammy Award nomination, and her first major network television exposure. She was finally being seen in the public eye as more than just a "one-hit wonder" and the voice of the Stone Poneys. Although her flirtation with big-time success was brief that year, it was at least a sign that she was on the right track.

Like its predecessor, the second solo Linda Ronstadt album was very spotty. Half of the songs were very good, and the other half were dull mistakes. Among the successes were Linda's version of Patsy Cline's hit "Lovesick Blues," the Shirelles' "Will You Love Me Tomorrow?," and Dale and Grace's 1962 Number One smash "I'm Leavin' It All Up To You." However, the album's high point came on the hit single "Long, Long Time," and Paul Siebel's lamenting ode about a prostitute's suicide, "Louise."

On the album cover's liner notes, Linda's singing style was referred to as a combination of Bob Dylan, Billie Holiday, Jerry Lee Lewis, Edith Piaf, Hank Williams, and Johnny Cash. In a way she did touch on the strongpoints of each of these singers, but she was still feeling her way around in the dark for the most part. The confidence that she exuded during her post-1974 hit-making years had yet to emerge.

According to her, she had her own misgivings about the *Silk Purse* album and her trek to Nashville: "I wasn't keen on the idea. It was very interesting in that there's such an enormous difference between country music in Nashville and country music in California. It's just another situation entirely, and I don't think we had any business playing music together. But I made a lot of good friends there and they're still some of my favorite players, people like Weldon Myrick and Buddy Spicher, but they have a different concept of rhythm section down there, and their taste is so different. They're coming out of a completely different bag — down there, they can make an album in three days, just assembly line stuff, although some of that's starting to change. Some of them are frustrated R&B players, and they want to break out and play R&B, because that's what they really like. And California music is real hybrid, very specialized, and it doesn't have anything to do with Nashville."

Basically, Linda left all of the decisions about the *Silk Purse* album up to producer Elliot F. Mazer and the executives at Capitol Records. However, Linda insisted that Gary White's composition "Long, Long Time" be included on the *Silk Purse* album. She recalled, "That was another song that I fought for, because people heard it and said, 'How syrupy — what are you going to do with that? It's a ballad, it's going to put everyone to sleep.' I was convinced it was a hit, and we went into the studio at ten o'clock in the morning. And that was Nashville — those guys liked that song so much that they got out of bed at nine o'clock on a Saturday and came down to do it, which is really something. But I don't think I sang it very well, although I was into it at the time. Believe me — I was really feeling that song, but what can you do at ten o'clock in the morning?"

However, at Linda's insistence, Capitol not only agreed to let her record the song but released it as the album's only single. In the autumn of 1970, "Long, Long Time" hit Number 25 on the *Billboard* pop chart, and the album *Silk Purse* made it to Number 103 on the LP chart. The real prize came when Linda was nominated for a Grammy Award, for "Long, Long Time" in the category of Best Country Vocal Performance, Female. Although she ended up losing the trophy to Lynn Anderson's song "Rose Garden," at least Linda was seen in a whole new light.

Riding the success of the song "Long, Long Time" on both the pop and country charts, Linda made her network television debut, appearing on "The Johnny Cash Show" and on a Glen Campbell special. Her immediate acceptance in the world of country music brought her an appearance on the Grand Ole Opry that year as well.

One of the most famous aspects of the *Silk Purse* album is the cover photograph of Linda. She is seen wearing only a short pair of cut-off jeans and a flimsy blouse, seated in the middle of a pig sty, next to several porcine pals. The photo concept was a take-off on the comic strip "Lil Abner" character named Moonbeam McSwine — a mountain beauty who spent most of her time with her pigs.

Linda explained, "When I cut *Silk Purse,* I was living in a part of Topanga that reminded people of Dogpatch, and I would remind them of Moonbeam McSwine — the girl in 'Lil Abner.' The one who was always sitting with pigs. She was real foxy-looking, but she smelled terrible, and no guys could get near her."

Before the photo shooting could progress, Linda had to make friends with the pigs before they would pose with her. "I came into their pen with my earrings on and all my make-up," she said. "I sat down, but they kept running from me . . . I tried to feed them some ham sandwiches, but they were highly offended. Finally I sat down with them for a while and got to know them. They were real sweet. They all wanted to come over and cuddle and put their heads in my lap."

Of all of her albums from this era of her career, *Silk Purse* is the one that Linda dislikes the most: "I hate that album! I'm sure [producer] Elliot [F. Mazer] doesn't think it's very good either. I couldn't sing then, I didn't know what I was doing. I was working with Nashville musicians, and I don't really play country music — I play very definitely California music."

After all of the hoopla from *Silk Purse* died down, Capitol released a single from the *Hand Sown . . . Home Grown* album — "The Long Way Around" — backed with a song that doesn't appear on any of her albums, called "(She's a) Very Lovely Woman." The two-sided single made it to Number 70 on the pop charts in early 1971. Meanwhile, Linda decided to take a temporary break away from her career. Traveling to England and France, she reflected about what she was going to do with her life and her career.

With her batteries recharged, she returned to Los Angeles and began hanging out at the Troubadour on a regular basis. She was determined to dive right back into the middle of things, and the Troubadour seemed like the right place to begin. "That's where I'd met Bernie Leadon and where I met Glenn Frey, who was in a group called Longbranch Pennywhistle with my boyfriend at that time, John David Souther," she remembered. "I could never get it together on a domestic level. I was always just living everywhere, crashing here and crashing there. And I wasn't quite sure how I was supposed to be, if I was supposed to be true-blue and faithful to one man, or if I was supposed to be hanging out at the Troubadour every night." For the time being, the Troubadour won out.

She especially remembers how everyone in her circle would look out for each other: "Jackson [Browne] and J. D. [Souther], they pulled each other through some awful times. They encouraged each other about their writings, became each other's fans. And the women, there

were very few of us, and we were really oddballs. We really didn't know
how to act, or what to do, or how we were supposed to be. We didn't
know whether we were supposed to be real earth mamas like Maria
Muldaur, you know, with a baby under her arm and a fiddle in her hand
. . . or what."

One particular night, while watching Jackson Browne at the
Troubadour, Linda picked a fight with a drunk who wouldn't shut up.
"I hauled off and punched him right in the mouth," she said. "I mean,
I really *hit* him. And he went back and into the wall and would've gone
down if the wall wasn't there. And of course that made it worse!"

In 1971 Linda found herself in New York City, where she was
asked to participate in an all-star record album called *Fire Creek*. It was
the brainchild of a promoter who wanted to give several musicians with
top rock groups a chance to "jam" with their contemporaries. Enough
material for a two-record set was recorded, and the session players included members of Canned Heat, the Flying Burrito Brothers, the First
National Band, Three Dog Night, the Byrds, Nitty Gritty Dirt Band,
and Emerson, Lake and Palmer.

Jimmy Greenspoon recalled the recording sessions and participat-
ing on several cuts: "The first session that I did for the *Fire Creek*
album, I was with the guys from Canned Heat, and we did a fifteen-
minute version of the Rolling Stones' 'Symphony For the Devil.' We
did that session in a couple of hours and we partied and hung out. There
were sessions going on all week. I was also invited to play keyboards on
a couple of songs with Linda Ronstadt. It was all of those guys who
played with Gram Parsons at different times — real country stuff. I remember having a lot of fun playing with all of those guys. There was a
steel guitar player named Red Rhodes who used to play with the Byrds.
I remember we all got into the country mode by drinking Jack Daniels
during the sessions."

Ronstadt sang two country/rock songs during the *Fire Creek* sessions: "Living Like a Fool" and a remake of the Bernie Leadon composition "He Darked the Sun." The song "He Dark the Sun" was included
on the *Silk Purse* album (spelled "Dark" not "Darked") and recorded
with a rather flat treatment. In the new version, produced by Bernie
Leadon, Linda's performance had more conviction, and the music had a
twangy country and western sound to it.

"Linda was great to work with," said Greenspoon. "We did the
tracks, and she did the vocals. Everyone got along really well, and we
had a great time. She was a sweet and wonderful person with a great
voice, and I could tell that she was genuinely into her music."

After several delays, the *Fire Creek* album was finally released and
disappeared into instant obscurity. Like the second two Stone Poneys'

albums, *Fire Creek* has gone on to become a real collector's item. In 1977 Capitol Records released a "limited edition" twelve-inch single, pressed on transparent yellow vinyl, and billed it as "Linda Ronstadt and Friends." The "A" side is "Living Like a Fool," and the "B" side is "He Darked the Sun." Like the *Fire Creek* album, the "Linda Ronstadt and Friends" record is nearly impossible to find.

Since her *Silk Purse* album had been recorded with Nashville studio musicians, what Linda needed most in 1971 was her own band. She began assembling one, composed of her friends from the Troubadour. She had already met Randy Meisner, Glenn Frey, and Bernie Leadon there, and on another night at the club she was introduced to the man who was the missing puzzle piece to her band-less predicament: Don Henley.

According to Linda, "Don Henley came to town with a band from Texas called Shiloh, and one night I was walking through the performing part of the club on my way to the bathroom when I heard Shiloh playing 'Silver Threads and Golden Needles,' and using the exact guitar break off my album *Hand Sown*. Right after that, we needed a band, so I hired Don and Glenn."

How could she have known at the time, when she hired Don Henley, Glenn Frey, Randy Meisner, and Bernie Leadon, that she had just assembled the original configuration of the Eagles?

While Linda was busy trying to find a new musical direction, Elliot Mazer had begun working on a new project. He was in the recording studio working with Neil Young on a new album entitled *Harvest*. Seven of the ten cuts on the album were co-produced by Elliot and Neil, two songs were produced in London by Jack Nitzsche, and Henry Lewy and Neil produced the live cut "The Needle and the Damage Done." Linda had known Neil for years, having met him and the rest of Buffalo Springfield at — where else? — the Troubadour.

While they were working on *Harvest,* Neil and Elliot invited Linda Ronstadt and James Taylor to come into the studio and sing background vocals on two of the most memorable cuts on the album: "Heart of Gold" and "Old Man." Linda's voice can most distinctly be heard at the end of "Heart of Gold," which happened to be the first single off of the album. When "Heart of Gold" was released in early 1972, it became a huge Number One hit, selling over a million copies and being certified Gold. Likewise, the album *Harvest* hit the Number One mark and also went Gold.

Through her singing on Neil's *Harvest* album, Linda got her first taste of what it was like to perform on a Number One hit album and single. Now she had to put her own solo career in order.

This period was one of the lowest ebbs of self-confidence for Linda.

"I was so intimidated by the quality of everybody's musicianship that instead of trying to be better, I chickened out and wouldn't work," she said of the year-and-a-half break she took from solo recording, following the release of *Silk Purse.* Working with Neil Young, getting to know Jackson Browne and Maria Muldaur and the members of her new band made her feel much better. They were basically all in the same boat, just starting out with their music, and trying to find their way amid the changing sound of the early 1970s.

One of the most important things that happened on the music scene at this particular time was the unprecedented success of Carole King and her phenomenal *Tapestry* album. The Grammy-winning, multimillion success of Carole's recordings in 1971 and 1972 opened up several new doors to a host of female singers, including Joni Mitchell, Carly Simon, Bonnie Raitt, and Mary Travers (who was pursuing a solo career at the time, apart from Peter, Paul & Mary). The albums that these women released in 1971 and 1972 comprised equal parts of folk, country, and rock and roll.

Until this point, for a woman to be successful on a rock and roll level she had to be a screaming maniac like Janis Joplin, a blues soul sister like Aretha Franklin, or a sweet ballad singer like Karen Carpenter. When Carole King made the sudden transition from 1960s pop songwriter to 1970s hit-maker, she did so without compromising her music. It was time for female singers to break free from the Connie Francis and Diana Ross image of a successful female pop star. And in this new atmosphere of creativity, Linda began to record her third solo album — with the Eagles as her back-up band.

"Before, we lived under the shadow of Tina Turner, feeling we had to do hot blues licks — or be considered a little butch," she said. Carole King changed the image of the female troubadour and set the scene for the recording of Ronstadt's third solo album.

Although her 1972 *Linda Ronstadt* album didn't sell as well as *Silk Purse,* and was the last of her three self-labeled "indifferent" albums, her singing was much stronger and more assured sounding. There were, however, complications. One of the major conflicts was the fact that she turned over the producer's reins to her new lover, John Boylan.

"I was so unsure of myself," she recalled of this era. "I was afraid to tell the musicians what to play or to assert myself in the management situation. I have a tendency to let other people shape me. If I'm going with someone and he gets at all critical of my music, the bottom falls out for me."

Recording of the *Linda Ronstadt* album commenced in August 1971, with three "live" recordings. Backed by her new band, Linda was captured "in concert" on the songs "Rescue Me," "Birds," and "I Fall

To Pieces," singing to an enthusiastic audience at — naturally — the Troubadour. The rest of the album was completed in September in Hollywood, and at the Muscle Shoals studio in Alabama.

The material contained on the *Linda Ronstadt* album was much more to her own personal liking, although she failed to score any major hits. The one single release off of the album was Jackson Browne's uptempo "Rock Me on the Water," which spent three weeks on the *Billboard* pop chart, climbing to Number 85 in March 1972. The "live" cuts from the Troubadour were the most satisfying selections off of the album, which also included "cover" versions of Johnny Cash's "I Still Miss Someone" and Woody Guthrie's "Ramblin' Round." While the album only made it to Number 163 on the LP chart, it did add to Ronstadt's cult following.

The *Linda Ronstadt* album impressed several people. Not only did it give Linda a solid foundation and a more focused musical direction, but everyone was in love with the music that accompanied her. Asylum Records was so impressed with Glenn, Don, Randy, and Bernie that they were offered their own recording contract. *Voila!* Enter: the Eagles.

In 1972 Linda found herself with her best album to date, and suddenly she had lost the band that created the music. Recalling the sudden split, Don Henley said, "John [Boylan] and Linda gave us our blessing. I respect Linda Ronstadt. She's got a good heart. She's never been selfish enough to hold anybody back." With that, the Eagles recorded their first album, *Eagles,* which went Gold and yielded their first Top Ten hit single, "Witchy Woman."

However, Asylum Records' president David Geffen was not only impressed with the band that he heard on the *Linda Ronstadt* album; he was also taken by the sound of the lead singer, and he offered her an immediate recording contract as well. Although she had signed a seven-year, seven-album contract with Capitol Records, she began negotiating a new recording deal with Asylum. It seemed all of her friends were ending up at Asylum Records, including Jackson Browne, who had just scored his first Gold album (*Jackson Browne,* 1972) and his first Top Ten hit with "Doctor My Eyes." Lured by Asylum's hit-making capabilities — as demonstrated by the Eagles and Jackson Browne — Linda realized that she was at the wrong label, and she quickly signed a contract with Asylum. She felt that Capitol Records had been ineffective at marketing her, and she was happy to end her relationship with the executives at that company.

When "Witchy Woman" and "Doctor My Eyes" became big hits for the Eagles and Jackson Browne, respectively, Linda felt encouraged about the direction in which she was headed. "It was beginning to be apparent that country music and rock and roll could be synthesized," she would later point out. "People didn't realize that the Everly Brothers and Elvis Presley had been making zillions out of the synthesis for years."

The strongest cut on the *Linda Ronstadt* album, a remake of the Patsy Cline hit "I Fall To Pieces," illustrates this same synthesis of styles as well. While recognized as a country music legend, Patsy Cline's music was as much pop and blues as it was country and western. Linda was obviously affected by Patsy's disregard for the constraints that musical labels place on a singer. Patsy's songs succeeded because they were emotion-filled and expertly sung, not because someone could stick them into any one particular musical category. Linda had to arrive at that same level of self-confidence before she was to break through. This album represented the beginning of her solo strength.

Although she wasn't quite out of the woods yet, in 1972 the path was being cleared for Linda to achieve her incredible leap to the top of the charts. It wasn't long before everyone was fighting for her attention. Over the next two years, she would be torn between two boyfriends, John Boylan and John David Souther, and two record companies, Capitol and Asylum. After the two simultaneous games of tug-of-war were over, Ronstadt was going to find herself in an exciting new atmosphere — at the top of the record charts.

Linda Ronstadt embodied the 1970s synthesis of country and western and rock and roll music. In 1975 the album Heart Like a Wheel *made her an overnight superstar.*

(Photo: Jim Shea/Mark Bego Archives)

42

Heart Like a Wheel

4

Before she started straightening out her career and her personal affairs, things would get complicated for Linda. She had interwoven her business life with her lovelife — in an outrageously tangled fashion — and the period of time from 1972 to 1974 was quite a confusing blur for her.

While she was at the height of her affair with John Boylan, she not only made him the producer of her albums but also appointed him as her manager. That alone would have been fine, except for the fact that she already had a manager she was paying: Herb Cohen. She had signed with Cohen as her manager while she was part of the Stone Poneys, and he in turn negotiated her record contract with Capitol.

As she began recording songs for her first album for Asylum Records, with Boylan as producer, her personal relationship with him was ending and her affair with singer/songwriter John David Souther was just heating up. Although Boylan was still actively her manager, and in the studio with her, she asked current beau Souther to take over producing her album. It was beginning to become a regular soap opera in the recording studio, one that would take its toll on Ronstadt emotionally.

"That is always a bad idea," she commented in retrospect about mixing business with pleasure. "First there is business, then business and sex, then the business goes sour, and then there is no more sex!"

On the subject of Boylan, Linda was later to explain, "He started out to be my boyfriend, then he was managing me and was my producer. Then he wasn't my boyfriend, but he was still managing me and producing me. Then he wasn't producing me, but he was still managing me, and then he wasn't managing me anymore. All those troubles stem from the fact that in our personal relationship, we couldn't resolve things."

She remembers how complicated the recording of her *Don't Cry Now* album was. "We argued a lot," she said about Boylan, "we competed enormously in the studio. I just didn't trust him. I didn't trust anyone then, and I was always afraid that something was going to get pulled over me. I was punch-drunk from producers."

The next phase of her on-again/off-again relationship with Boylan was that after co-producing one of the songs for the *Don't Cry Now* album with John David Souther, he was also out of the picture as Linda's manager. When that binding tie was severed, Linda claims that she felt lost. Since her only obligation to Herb Cohen was financial, his tenure as her manager was over when she turned her back on Capitol. So, she had gone from having two managers to having none. After Boylan was out of her life, though, she would still consult him about her every moment: "I'd wake up and call him and ask, 'Gee, what should I do today? What socks should I put on?' "

While she was in the middle of recording her new album, she left Los Angeles for a three-and-a-half-month concert tour, opening for Neil Young. At the time, Neil Young was a major league superstar. He had built a following of millions of fans, who had followed him through his years with Buffalo Springfield; Crosby, Stills, Nash and Young; and his recent solo success.

Linda learned very quickly how difficult it can be as the opening act for someone very famous. "The lights would dim," she said, "and they'd expect to see Neil Young — and there I'd be. All the girls in the audience would immediately think, 'Arghh! A girl on tour with Neil!' And, I'd have to overcome their resentment every single night."

According to several sources, Linda relied heavily on drugs to relieve her frustration on the road. Meanwhile, she had the pressure hanging over her that her album wasn't getting any closer to completion. "I didn't know what I wanted then," she remembered. "Really, I was depressed, and we kept interrupting the recording to go on tour, sort of one hustle after another."

When she did return to the recording studio, she wasn't at all happy with the results that she and John David Souther were coming up with. "We were like kids in the studio, just inept, and we took a lot of time. But I learned a lot and it was worth it, almost, because it was such hard work. After that experience, I knew so much more when I went into the studio."

Linda decided that what she needed the most was an objective manager who could pull this particular album project together — and one who could make some sense out of the complicated mess she seemed to be in.

"In the early '70s I was in a rut," she explained. "I didn't know how to get out of it. I was on this plateau that seemed endless. I was so numb. I could hardly see or feel. In fact, it all feels now like a murky dream." According to her, when she came out of her murky dream, "It was thanks to my relationship with Peter Asher."

While manager shopping, Linda said she wanted someone from Nashville, because she "wanted to explore the country area some more." However, several of her friends recommended Peter Asher, who was then managing James Taylor and his sister, Kate Taylor. When she approached him about handling her, Asher declined, feeling that there would be competition between Kate and Linda, and a strain on the amount of time he could spend on both their careers. Suddenly, Kate decided to retire from show business.

"I became friends with Peter," Linda said. "We hung out a lot. But he was managing Kate Taylor at the time and he felt that if he took on another girl singer in the same market, it wouldn't be fair to either one of us. Then I ran into Kate, and she said she was going to stay home then, so why didn't I call Peter?" And so she did. The rest is history: Peter Asher's management decisions made all the difference in the world.

According to Linda, "When Peter Asher and I started working together, that's when it got right. Peter's a professional, he knows what he's doing, and we were just sort of muddling around until he came into the picture, when all of a sudden things were organized, they had a focus, and they were planned properly.

"Peter was the first person willing to work with me as an equal, even though his abilities were far superior to mine. I thought I couldn't understand machines, you know, and it turns out that the joke's on me. I finally realized, 'Gee, I can learn about digital delay . . .' All of a sudden, making records became so much more fun. I used to get so depressed when I was in the studio, that I would slither under the console and go to sleep with the monitors blaring, just to escape."

Asher's first piece of business after he became Linda's manager was to pull together her *Don't Cry Now* album. He surveyed the material that was already in the can and co-produced two additional cuts with John David Souther. Finally, under Peter's direction, after over a year of starting and stopping, Linda's first Asylum album was completed —

at a final cost of $150,000. The album had gone way over budget, and she was going to have to sell a ton of them if she was ever going to see a profit.

Two days after completing her album, she left town on a concert tour with a new band she had just finished assembling. Instead of bowing to the pressure that she was under, she simply composed herself, packed, and began her tour. "That's when I realized it was up to me; I'd have to pull it together, get up on stage and take command. And I did," she recalled.

The *Don't Cry Now* album was released in September 1973, and although it did not become the sales success that it could have, it was the first important album of Linda's career. The crisp quality of the music and the up-front brilliance of Ronstadt's voice marked a vast improvement over the sound of her 1967–1971 releases on Capitol. On her first six albums, it sounded as if she had been recorded from across the room. On *Don't Cry Now,* her singing became the focal point, instead of coming across as just another instrument that was lost in the mix.

While the material was a bit inconsistent, the album contained Linda's first two signature songs: "Desperado" and "Love Has No Pride." The emotion that Linda evoked on this album was almost nonexistent on her previous recordings. Although she was only twenty-seven years old when this album was released, her voice had finally hit its peak, and she put a lifetime of passionate energy into each performance.

The patchwork quilt configuration of different producers and combinations of producers on the *Don't Cry Now* album makes one wonder how this disc was ever completed. Two songs, "Colorado" and "Love Has No Pride," were produced by John Boylan. "Everybody Loves a Winner" and the remake of "Silver Threads and Golden Needles" were co-produced by John Boylan and John David Souther. Four cuts were produced by Souther alone, including his compositions "Don't Cry Now," "I Can Almost See It," and "The Fast One," in addition to the Don Henley and Glenn Frey composition of "Desperado." When Peter Asher was brought into the project, he reportedly had to re-record several of the tracks, and ended up with co-production credit with John David Souther on Randy Newman's "Sail Away" and Neil Young's "I Believe in You."

Linda said the quality that was found on her first Asylum album was directly due to Asher's salvaging the project: "Peter has a very rounded musical background, like I do. He listens to everything. His taste is eclectic. But there is a thread of taste and quality that runs through everything he does and because of the consistency of the quality, I was able to really trust him. And because I trust him, he is a good sounding board for all the things I want to do."

When it was released, the *Don't Cry Now* album made it to Number 45 on the LP charts, and eventually was certified Gold (after *Heart Like a Wheel* became a huge success). Two singles were released from *Don't Cry Now.* In early 1974, "Love Has No Pride" peaked at Number 51 on the pop singles chart, and that spring "Silver Threads and Golden Needles" made it to Number 67. Although these releases didn't burn up the charts, Linda Ronstadt was seen in a new light, and the album established a strong legion of fans for her.

Based on the success of the LP *Don't Cry Now,* and the attention that her 1973–1974 touring schedule was garnering, Capitol Records decided to do what they could to cash in on the hot new interest in Ronstadt. In January 1974 they released a compilation album entitled *Different Drum,* which contained five Stone Poneys' songs and five selections from her first three solo albums. Based on the success of *Don't Cry Now,* the *Different Drum* LP hit Number 92 on the LP chart in *Billboard,* which was higher than any of Linda's other Capitol albums, with or without the Stone Poneys.

In June 1974, Linda Ronstadt began recording the album that was going to make her into an international singing superstar: *Heart Like a Wheel.* It was her first Number One album, and her first million-selling, across-the-board success. It was also her first album to be entirely produced by Peter Asher. Her association with Peter, which continues to this day, is directly responsible for her transformation into a 1970s rock and roll legend and a 1980s top song stylist.

Although he is best known on the music scene as one-half of the 1960s singing duo Peter and Gordon, Peter Asher's show business career actually dates back to his childhood in England. He and his sister Jane were both child stars and appeared in several films and theatrical productions.

"When I was eight or so," Peter said, "both my sister and I evidently looked cute. At any rate, somebody said, 'They oughta be in movies,' and he got us an agent. As it turned out, Jane and I never worked together. I did a few films, some stage acting, and lots of radio acting."

The most notable film that he appeared in was *Outpost In Malaya* in 1952, which starred Claudette Colbert and Jack Hawkins (original British title: *Planter's Wife*). Meanwhile, his sister Jane played the ingenue in the Walt Disney film *The Prince and the Pauper,* and she was the youngest actress to play the part of Wendy in the West End production of *Peter Pan.*

Peter and Jane came from an affluent British family, and they were encouraged in their artistic endeavors from an early age. Their grandfather was the attorney for the real Lawrence of Arabia. Their father,

Dr. Richard Asher, was a noted psychiatrist at the Central Middlesex Hospital, and he was also an expert on blood-related diseases. Their mother, Margaret, was a professional musician who taught the oboe at the London School of Music. She once gave oboe lessons to record producer George Martin, who produced all of the Beatles' recordings.

Peter's acting career was cut short when he was fourteen years old and "school interfered." He became more interested in music, learning to play the piano, oboe, and the double bass. However, he recalled, "I never played anything well."

At the age of fifteen, Peter picked up the guitar and performed with a local skiffle band ("skiffle" was a British forerunner to rock and roll). After graduating from Cambridge, he developed a strong interest in American rock and roll, especially Elvis Presley, Buddy Holly, and the Everly Brothers.

In 1962 Asher and a friend named Gordon Waller formed an act that emulated the harmonies of the Everly Brothers. They called themselves Peter and Gordon. For two years, they performed in and around London in small clubs. One night at the Pickwick Club, Peter and Gordon met a recording manager from EMI, and the next thing they knew, they were signing a recording contract.

Although the Beatles didn't hit it big in America until 1964, in 1963 they were already huge stars in England. They were local celebrities, with Number One records and plenty of television appearances. Jane Asher was a frequent guest on one television show, "Juke Box Jury," and she was "teen correspondent" on the BBC radio show called "Radio Times." In the spring of 1963, Jane was covering a pop concert at Albert Hall that was attended by the Beatles. From that point on, Jane and Paul McCartney began dating, and they were a steady item for the next five years.

During the years that he dated Jane, Paul McCartney got to know Jane's entire family and became especially good friends with Peter. When Peter and Gordon landed their recording contract, Paul provided the duo with a song that he and John Lennon had written, called "World Without Love." The song went on to become a huge Number One hit in England and America.

From 1964 to 1967, Peter and Gordon placed several hit singles on the charts, on both sides of the Atlantic, including "I Go To Pieces," "To Know You Is To Love You," "True Love Ways," and "Knight In Rusty Armour." In 1966, when the Beatles were the undisputed superstars of the decade, Paul McCartney decided that he wanted to see if one of his songs could make it on the music charts on his merit as a songwriter, and not his name. He gave Peter and Gordon a song he had written called "Woman." The songwriting credit carried the fictional name Bernard Webb. When the Peter and Gordon single version of "Woman" made it into the American Top 20, McCartney admitted that the song was one of his.

Peter and Gordon's last big hit was the song "Lady Godiva," which made it to Number Six in America and Number 16 in the United Kingdom. That was in 1966, which turned out to be the duo's last full year together. In 1967, they released two singles, "Sunday For Tea" and "The Jokers," and then called it quits due to management problems and Gordon's desire for a solo career.

Disenchanted with his career as a recording star, Peter decided that he was more interested in exploring record producing. His first productions were three singles that he recorded with Paul Jones, who used to be the lead singer for Manfred Mann. One of the songs that Asher cut with Jones was a version of the Bee Gees' "And the Sun Will Shine," on which Paul McCartney played the drums and Jeff Beck and Paul Samwell-Smith of the Yardbirds were heard on guitar and bass.

When the Beatles became so rich that they had to invest their money to avoid massive taxes, they formed their own record company, Apple Records, in 1968. McCartney offered Peter a job with Apple as the head of the A&R (artists and repertoire) department. He was in charge of signing and overseeing new talent at the label.

During this same period of time, an American group called the Flying Machine had come to London and had subsequently broken up. The lead singer and songwriter of the group was an unknown kid named James Taylor. The Flying Machine's guitar player was a musician named Danny "Kootch" Kortchmar, who had been the guitarist behind Peter and Gordon before they broke up. Kootch gave Taylor the phone number of Asher at Apple. Taylor called, and two days after he had begun working for the record label, Peter Asher signed James Taylor to a solo recording contract.

The resulting Apple album, *James Taylor* (Apple Records, 1968), was unfortunately a complete "bomb" when it was first released. After the album failed to hit the charts, both Asher and Taylor became discouraged and left Apple Records. Asher was ready to leave Apple for other reasons. The Beatles knew nothing about running a record label. Since all four of them were equal partners, they would all give conflicting orders to their workers, and a vast quantity of time, money, and energy was ultimately wasted.

Peter landed himself a job in America, working for MGM Records. However, he was not happy with the job, and he soon quit to begin running his own management company. It wasn't long after Peter had moved to Los Angeles that he resumed working with James Taylor.

His first order of business was to negotiate a recording contract for Taylor at Warner Brothers Records. He then proceeded to produce the monumental James Taylor album *Sweet Baby James* (1970) and the two biggest hits of his career: "Fire and Rain" and "You've Got a Friend." With Asher's guidance, James Taylor became the top rock troubadour of the early '70s. Although Peter hasn't been the producer of all of Taylor's subsequent recordings, he has been directly responsible for steering him in the right direction management-wise.

From 1970 to 1973, Peter Asher was involved in several other projects as well, while simultaneously managing James Taylor. Through James, Peter began working with his sister Kate Taylor, and together with Nat Weiss he co-managed Cat Stevens for a short time. Peter made a qualitative decision to keep the roster of artists that he worked with small and exclusive. When Kate Taylor decided to take a break from recording in 1973, it was perfect timing for Linda Ronstadt to turn her career over to Peter.

"Peter was the first person willing to work with me as an equal, even though his abilities were far superior to mine. I didn't have to fight for my ideas," recalls Ronstadt of her initial experiences with Asher as her manager and producer. "His enthusiasm for it is real contagious, so he explains stuff to me. As I start to understand how things will work, it makes it easier for me to communicate what I'm trying to say . . . I guess he really just encourages me."

The real test to the effectiveness of the teaming of Ronstadt and Asher came in June of 1974, when they began recording the *Heart Like a Wheel* album. The first crucial decision that had to be made concerned the choice of material for the album. Linda's taste leaned toward the country and western mode, which was a whole new ballgame for Peter, whose experience was with pop ballads.

According to Asher, "I was never a country fan. I've certainly become more of a fan since knowing Linda. Before, I really did think that country music was all cowboy boots and yodeling. It's more musical than I gave it credit."

With regard to selecting songs, Linda explained: "What Peter does is to act as both editor and contributor. I might come up with five ideas and four of them will be turkeys, and Peter will know instinctively which is gonna be the most appropriate one and how to latch on to some of these developing ideas in their embryonic stage and allow them to bloom. It's so difficult to describe exactly what a producer does. I mean, a producer can do absolutely nothing, or he can do everything, like Burt Bacharach used to do, and tell everybody exactly what to sing and what to play. But he can do the other thing, which is just float around, as Peter does, and get into every facet of the record so that it's always a team effort. He's also able to deal with everybody's delicate temperaments — and I'm telling you, there are some delicate temperaments going on in there. And it's handled by everybody being fair. Peter's real out front with people. The hardest thing to do is when you ask somebody to come and do something and it's not working, and rather than grease them by keeping them doing it over and over again, trying to pretend that you're gonna use it, he's real good at saying very clearly, 'This doesn't work because of this reason.' He keeps a very journalistic tone so nobody has to feel personally rejected if an idea is rejected."

Although the *Don't Cry Now* album had set Linda in the right direction artistically and saleswise, it was the 1974 *Heart Like a Wheel* album that marked the big breakthrough in her career. This time around, the songs were hand-selected by Ronstadt and Peter Asher, and their choices proved to be right on target. The album became the blueprint for the winning formula that she used successfully throughout the rest of the decade: a little country and western, a little rock and roll, and a lot of borrowed tunes from the past, updated and crackling with energy and excitement.

The two most popular songs on the album, "You're No Good" and "When Will I Be Loved," had both been chart hits in the 1960s for other people. "You're No Good" had been a pop hit for Betty Everett in 1963, and "When Will I Be Loved" was a Top Ten hit for Peter Asher's idols, the Everly Brothers, in 1960. Three more of the selections had also been taken from pop charts of years gone by. "It Doesn't Matter Anymore" was a Number 13 hit for Buddy Holly in 1959, "Dark End of the Street" hit Number 77 when James Carr recorded it in 1967, and the Hank Williams classic "I Can't Help It (If I'm Still In Love With You)" had made the pop charts five different times, from 1958 to 1969, when recorded chronologically by Margaret Whiting (1958), Adam Wade (1960), Johnny Tillotson (1962), B. J. Thomas (1967), and Al Martino (1969).

The album was completed with compositions provided by several of Linda's musician friends. James Taylor was represented by his song "You Can Close Your Eyes," John David Souther wrote "Faithless Love," Anna McGarrigle composed "Heart Like a Wheel," and "Willing" was provided by Lowell George of the rock group Little Feat.

While the *Heart Like a Wheel* album featured the same mixture of country and rock and roll that the *Don't Cry Now* album possessed, it represented a progression in both musical areas. "You're No Good" was totally rock and roll, while songs like "Willing," "When Will I Be Loved," and "I Can't Help It (If I'm Still In Love With You)" sounded as if they were straight out of Nashville. A third distinctive category of songs was also represented on this LP, namely the blues. As personified by "Faithless Love," "Heart Like a Wheel" and "Dark End of the Street," Linda proved that she excelled at singing songs about the pain of love. Some of the most effective songs in her career have been about heartache and disappointment, and these particular songs are among her finest forays into the mood indigo.

While this was the first of Linda's albums produced entirely by Peter Asher, it also marked her initial recording experience with several of the key personalities in her career. Singer/songwriter/guitar player Andrew Gold, who was part of the band that she formed after the Eagles went their own way in 1973, has remained an important friend. He has appeared on most of her contemporary pop and rock albums, right up to *Cry Like a Rainstorm, Howl Like the Wind* in 1989. Emmylou Harris, who sang harmony vocals on "I Can't Help It (If I'm Still In Love With You)," and recording engineer George Massenburg were later to become her co-star and her producer, respectively, on the 1987 *Trio* album. Likewise, musicians David Lindley, Jimmy Fadden of the Nitty Gritty Dirt Band, and Russell Kunkel all began their working relationship with Ronstadt on this album.

Andrew Gold was to become a key figure on Linda's next three albums — from *Heart Like a Wheel* in 1974 to *Hasten Down the Wind* in 1976. It was through her old Stone Poney friend Kenny Edwards that she became acquainted with Gold, and in 1974 both Gold and Edwards became the backbone of her new band. On his first three albums with Ronstadt, Andrew did a little bit of everything, from arranging to songwriting, and he played the guitar, piano, clavinet, drums, ukulele, and even the tambourine.

"I joined a group with Kenny Edwards, right before we both joined Linda's band," recalls Gold of his former group, the Rangers. "That was about 1972 or so. We went about two years and then broke up. Some of the tunes from my first album [*Andrew Gold,* 1975] are from that period. The arrangements are sort of verbatim copies of the Rangers. In fact, there's one track that *is* the Rangers, which was Kenny and I and Peter Bernstein, who had been producing the Wendy Waldman album, and a gentleman by the name of Gene Garfin. That one track on the album, 'Resting In Your Arms,' is actually a track of that band."

Andrew played guitar on Maria Muldaur's 1973 debut album and, according to him, Linda heard his work with the Rangers and was impressed. Coincidentally, her band had just quit to become the Eagles, just as the Rangers disbanded. "When that broke up I went and joined Linda's band," Gold said. "I had met her a couple of times just sort of briefly through Kenny . . . She had seen me here and there . . . Kenny then re-joined her band about a month after I joined her."

While the *Heart Like a Wheel* album was still in the planning stages, Ronstadt began assembling an impressive list of friends to assist her. Not only did she have Peter Asher as her producer, but she also had a hot new band to back her up, consisting of John David Souther, Andrew Gold, and Kenny Edwards. And she enlisted her friends Wendy Waldman, Maria Muldaur, and Emmylou Harris to sing background and harmony vocals on the album.

With this album, Linda wanted to strike a harmonious balance between pop and country sounds. A handful of other female singers at the time were actively recording and singing a synthesis of folk, rock and roll, and country and western music. Her friend Maria Muldaur had just scored a huge hit earlier that year with the song "Midnight at the Oasis," and Bonnie Raitt had been pioneering the movement since the release of her self-titled debut album in 1971. Linda felt that Emmylou Harris was especially effective at singing country tunes with a pop flair.

"When I first heard Emmy sing," recalled Ronstadt, "I wanted everybody to hear her. I love Emmy. She's the most inspired singer to me, bar none. I would rather sing with Emmy than with anybody else. She can make me feel the music and the ideas of a song like nobody. I can't imagine Emmy not being successful, because that might mean that I can't sing with her so much. I mean, it's in my best interests for Emmy to be successful and for people to hear her, because she brings up the general standards of the music."

Linda especially remembers the first time she met Emmylou Harris: "I was in Houston on tour with Neil Young [in 1973], and we had a night off, and Emmy was playing with Gram Parsons. I kept hearing about her and that she was the only one doing what I was doing. At that point, we were struggling to get record companies to listen to us sing Hank Williams. I saw Emmy and I died. Here was someone doing what I was doing, only, in my opinion, better. But hearing her finally outweighed the pain of being outdone, and I just thought, 'Well, here is the level, and I'd better get up there; I'd better fight for it.' I sat down with Emmy and sang and I learned a hell of a lot about singing from her, and I still do."

When Gram Parsons suddenly died of a drug overdose in September 1973, Emmylou Harris didn't know what she was going to do with herself. It was Ronstadt who came to the rescue. According to Harris, "Linda has been an incredible friend to me. My world fell apart when Gram died. I didn't know what I was doing. Linda had me come out to California so people could hear me. She told the record company people they had to sign me [as a solo artist]. That kind of support from your peers, especially someone like Linda — I can't tell you how much that means. It really helped my confidence; and people in the business took notice."

The night after their first meeting, Ronstadt and Harris got together again at Liberty Hall in Houston. "They came over again after they'd finished their show — [Ronstadt] and Neil and his whole band — and they all ended up sitting in," Emmylou recalled. "Then later on, Linda and I and Gram's wife sat up all night long and sang and talked. We just became sisters, Linda and I. Our friendship was established that night forever — even if we'd never seen each other again."

Linda recalls at first being apprehensive about meeting Emmylou. She was afraid that Harris would be so good at singing country/pop, that Ronstadt herself would have to cash in her chips and find another genre to sing. "Everyone was telling me for two years that there was this girl who was doing everything that I was doing, and they were raving about her. I felt threatened by it. I was scared; I was afraid to meet her, I thought, 'Oh, no, what if she's better than I am?' And, I met her, and she was! I feel that she is the best country/rock person!" exclaimed Linda. "I was stunned, because I had been doing this for a long time, and I knew exactly how her talents compared to mine. And I also loved her immediately when I met her, because she's honest and she's nice. There was no way I couldn't like her."

Thanks to Linda's intervention, Emmylou soon signed a recording contract with Warner Brothers Records and began work on her solo career. Instead of being rivals, Linda and Emmylou have become recurring singing partners, beginning with the song "I Can't Help It (If I'm Still In Love With You)."

During this period, Linda came to rely on her friends in the record business, especially the other female singers who were trying to establish their own identities in the music world. Remembering this period of her life, before the release of the *Heart Like a Wheel* album, Linda claimed that, "When you're a musician, you're going to gravitate to other musicians, and because they're like you are, they don't want to be held down, and everybody has to have a certain degree of freedom. So, we have to depend on each other. In the old days [early 1970s] we couldn't afford psychiatrists. Maria Muldaur, Bonnie Raitt, Wendy Waldman and I kept each other from having nervous breakdowns for years. And my attitude towards anyone who is new on the horizon is that if they're good, and it's honest, then it has to be helped; those people have to be brought in. My feeling about girls that are better than I am is that we need 'em, because they'll make the music better, and I can learn from them. There's always somebody who's better than you."

One of the early signals that Linda Ronstadt was about to break through to major league success came in 1974, when Capitol Records and Asylum Records began fighting over her. Although she had spent her contracted seven years at Capitol Records, both solo and with the

Stone Poneys, she owed them a total of seven albums. After she signed with Asylum and released *Don't Cry Now* on that label, Capitol threatened to sue her if she didn't release *Heart Like a Wheel* on their label. She had no choice but to comply.

According to Andrew Gold, everyone who was involved with that album sensed that they had a hit on their hands. "We started recording that record," he explained, "and I realized it was coming out real well, and suddenly I found myself in a position of playing all of these instruments and stuff, and I knew it was going to be a Gold record . . . It's still my favorite, because the songs were particularly good. She had most of those songs before we even went in to the studio . . . The whole experience of recording on that album was fun. We recorded the strings in England — in London — it was fun . . ."

Gold's premonition was to prove accurate. The *Heart Like a Wheel* album was going to more than live up to everyone's expectations — it was going to surpass them. The album was released by Capitol Records in November 1974, and by January 1975 it was already certified Gold and on its way to Platinum. True to the musical styles that the album contained, her first two singles were huge Number One singles, scoring on both the pop and the country charts. "You're No Good" became a Number One pop hit and a Number Two country and western hit; "When Will I Be Loved" became a Number One country and western hit and a Number Two pop hit. All of a sudden, Linda Ronstadt had the best of both worlds, and in one fell swoop she became an overnight superstar on both the country and the rock charts. No one was more surprised than Linda herself.

"I was going along, making country/rock albums, experimenting," she said. "I felt I was somewhat of a pioneer in that area. I felt like I was throwing some new ideas onto the pile. My records were selling O.K. I thought I had arrived. That was before *Heart Like a Wheel*. I had no idea I was destined to be more.

"When I left Tucson, I thought it would be a big deal to have your name on the marquee of a club. That was the pinnacle of success. I never dreamed I'd have a Number One record. After *Heart Like a Wheel* happened, I finally got out of debt. I remember that I really wanted a washing machine, because I was tired of carrying stuff to the laudromat from my $150 apartment. I thought if I could just have a washing machine, I'd be set. When it arrived, the washing machine was a very tangible example of having money, of being affluent."

After ten years of working as a professional singer, Linda suddenly found herself a very visible and recognizable singing star. In early 1975 she was an "overnight sensation," and her first instinct was to bring all of her own personal insecurities right to the surface. Instantly, she was hounded for press interviews, she couldn't go to the local grocery store without being hounded for her autograph, and she felt undeserving of all the attention.

"The most miserable tour of my life was in 1975," she explained, "after *Heart Like a Wheel*. It was as if all your dreams of success came true, and you still felt like the same old schlep you always felt like. You really freak. I was still feeling very unworthy.

"When *Heart Like a Wheel* went to Number One, I just walked around apologizing every single day. I could see that my supposed friends resented me. I went around going, 'I'm not that good of a singer . . .' And I got so self-conscious that when I went on-stage, I couldn't sing at all. It almost made me go crazy . . . I mean I needed a lot of help."

Two years later she was able to look back on this era of self-doubting and state, "Now I realize that it's 'not my fault.' I worked hard and I earned it and it's up to me whether I enjoy it or not. I choose to enjoy it, and I'm really having a great time now. I've got a lot of politician friends, for instance. I tour in their world and they tour in mine. But that's not all. I'm learning faster and more now than I've ever learned. There's information coming into my brain like cannons. I feel like I have to run away sometimes so I can have the chance to store it in my memory banks so I can go out and get some more."

However, before she arrived at that newfound sense of self-fulfillment, she sought professional help to sort out her emotions. "I found a psychiatrist who really put me on the right track," Ronstadt said. "He got me through all those little obstacles. If it wasn't for him, I probably would have quit . . . I didn't want to live and I didn't want to sing again. But I feel stronger now than I've ever felt. This is not my fantasy of what I want to be, but it is the reality and it's a lot more comfortable to live with."

While she was going through this career catharsis, she found that many of her closest friends couldn't relate to Linda's self-imposed fear of succeeding. With her success came new pressures. "When I first started doing this," she claimed, "there weren't really any other woman singers [in rock and roll] except for Maria Muldaur and Grace Slick. But Maria was the only one I really knew, and neither of us could afford to go to psychiatrists then. Nobody had gone ahead of us and broken any of the ground on the kind of emotional problems that you experience being a woman in this particular place."

When *Heart Like a Wheel* hit the Number One slot on the *Billboard* album chart and proceeded to sell a million copies, Linda could suddenly afford a lot of things that she'd only dreamed of before. Not only could she afford a washing machine and a psychiatrist, but also a big

split-level house in Malibu (for which she paid nearly $200,000). All of
a sudden she found herself living the glamorous "Life in the Fast Lane"
that her friends the Eagles were to glorify in their 1976 song of the
same name.

Linda's lovelife was changing as well. In 1974 she was living with
a young comedian named Albert Brooks. He would later find fame as
an Academy Award-nominated actor in the 1987 hit film *Broadcast
News,* but at the time both Brooks and Ronstadt were still struggling
performers on the fringes of success. After Linda hit it big with *Heart
Like a Wheel,* her relationship with Brooks ended. When she moved to
Malibu, she decided to try living alone for a change.

"I'm learning to live by myself, and I love it," she said at the time.
"I lived alone for two months once, in an apartment, but I've always
either been on the road or shacked up with one guy or another, or living
in some kind of hell. I've gone a long time now without falling in love
and without having that neurotic tendency to define my existence."

Finding herself in uncharted waters, Linda felt quite vulnerable,
and she took a break from always having a boyfriend. Her view of her
position in the music business was changing just as fast as the changes
in her personal life. "Anybody can hurt my feelings, it's not very hard
to do," she confessed, while briefly living the solo life. "But they don't
get a second chance. I am not a professional victim, and there's plenty
of those in this business, because they see vulnerability as something attractive. If I see that someone or something is going to hurt me, I'll get
the fuck out of its way. It's too easy to get destroyed. But, yeah, I
worry. I try to walk that fine line between being strong and trying to
avoid becoming callous. As soon as you're callous, you not only shut out
all the pain, but all the good stuff too. You either close the door or you
open it. I keep the door open with the screen door slammed . . . and a
strong dog at the door. That's the policy of my heart."

Instead of longing to be someone's "girlfriend," Linda found that
her needs were changing. She wanted to find someone to have a relationship with, someone who was an equal. She proclaimed in *People*
magazine, "I'm so disorganized, what I really need is a good wife!"

One of her devices for retaining her sanity during this period was
to think of herself as "one of the boys" when she was with her band, in
the studio or on the road. "I know when I'm on the road for a long
time, I adopt male attitudes, real rock and roll attitudes. I come back
home talking like a trucker. I'm not as nice to people," she said.

Linda found a need to strike a balance between her own femininity
and her ability to relate to men as an equal. "I had a woman cousin at
Yale, one of the first women to graduate," she explained, "and they
studied these women very carefully and found that they developed all

these masculine mannerisms . . . in other words, they completely succumbed to the peer-group pressure in order to get recognition and acceptance. They all began to walk like a man. They began to cop butch
attitudes, you know, and that's what's happened in this male-dominated business. I felt it happening to me, and I decided to strike that
from my personality. I like being a girl.

"The first thing I had to do after *Heart Like a Wheel* went Platinum
was stop feeling guilty about my success, stop walking around apologizing to every single person I knew," she found, after being enlight-
ened by her psychiatrist and after tapping her own inner-strength. She
arrived at a new plateau of confidence in the process.

Several months after having been catapulted to the top of the record charts, she proclaimed, "I'm a stronger person now. People don't
blow me out of the water the way they used to. I do think a lot of people
have just come along and fucking taken swipes at me. I think men have
generally treated me badly, and that the idea of a war between the sexes
is very real in our culture. In the media, women are built up with sex as
a weapon, and men are threatened by it as much as they are drawn to it,
and they retaliate as hard as they can. I'm not saying I've got a corner
on the market, and I don't say I haven't been mean back, but I don't
think it's all in my head, either. A lot of women fall into that trap.
They love to act like a victim — they love it. They think some Prince
Charming is going to come along and rescue them, and all that happens
is somebody looks down and says, 'Why can't you stand on your own
two feet?' They might help you up once or twice, but after a while
they get sick of it, and you have to do it by yourself."

However, when she was on tour, she found that for the time being
her new manager Peter Asher played the perfect Prince Charming
whenever she felt like a damsel in distress. "Out on the road," she explained, "if I'm having a bad time, he has to keep the political dynamics of the relationship between me and the band; the band between each
other; the band and the crew; me and the crew; the tour manager and
the band; the tour manager and the crew and the truck drivers. Its stag-
gering when I think about the actual amount of workload he has to handle. Its like being the president. When we're performing someplace, he
has to deal with all the people that want to get to me. He's real good at
dealing with those people by keeping them from moving in on me like
a herd of barracudas until there's no flesh left on my bones."

In addition to her *Heart Like a Wheel* album, Linda was also singing country and western music on the Nitty Gritty Dirt Band's 1975
Dream album. She sang lead vocals with the group on their version of
the Hank Williams classic, "Hey Good Lookin'." This became a career-
long occurrence for Ronstadt, making guest appearances on her friends'
albums and inviting them to play on her recordings.

While the *Heart Like a Wheel* album was making Linda Ronstadt's name a household word, she was busying herself with recording her sixth solo album, *Prisoner in Disguise*. Finally free from her contractual obligations to Capitol Records, this album resumed her ongoing relationship with Asylum Records. The sessions for *Prisoner in Disguise* took place in Los Angeles from February to June of 1975, with Peter Asher producing and Val Garay as her recording engineer.

The same winning formula that had been employed the year before on *Heart Like a Wheel* was again tried. And the effect was an even more solid success. From this point on, it seemed that every one of Linda's albums was an even bigger success than its predecessor had been.

More than half of the songs on the *Prisoner* album were written by the composers who had contributed to *Heart*. Neil Young was represented by "Love is a Rose," James Taylor wrote "Hey Mister, That's Me Up on the Jukebox," "You Tell Me That I'm Falling Down" was composed by Anna McGarrigle, John David Souther wrote "Silver Blue" and the title cut, and Lowell George gave her one of his tunes, "Roll Um Easy."

Two of the most successful songs on the *Prisoner in Disguise* album were borrowed from Motown, and they went on to provide Linda with her next pair of Top 40 hits. Her version of Martha and the Vandellas' classic "Heat Wave" peaked at Number Five on the pop chart, and her first Smokey Robinson and the Miracles cover tune, "Tracks of My Tears," hit Number 24 in early 1976.

"Heat Wave," which was one of the most successful singles in Linda's entire career, almost didn't get recorded. "I've turned down so many hits, you wouldn't believe it," she explained, "especially in the days when I really needed them too. 'I Don't Know How To Love Him' was one; 'Help Me Make It Through the Night' was another. I even felt that way about 'Heat Wave.' I loved it when Martha Reeves sang it. I threw it into my show when we were playing bars, because it was something fun that people could get drunk and rowdy to. I never had any intention of making a record out of it, but David Geffen said, 'You've got to record that, it's a hit,' and at that point, I realized that if I went ahead and did it, it would be good for me to have a hit. It would just make more sense for me in the long run, because then I could do more music that I wanted to do. The more secure my position was, the more I would be able to influence the music with my own taste. I did 'Heat Wave,' and I'm still sorry, because I hate to sing it. I don't think I sing it well, I don't think the record was good, and I cringe when it comes on the radio. I'm not doing it in the show anymore, and people are going to be bitching at me."

Just as she had done on the previous album, Maria Muldaur sang the harmony vocal behind Linda on an Anna McGarrigle song. Anna, who had written the title track to *Heart Like a Wheel,* was represented by "You Tell Me That I'm Falling Down" on the *Prisoner in Disguise* album. Anna and her sister Kate McGarrigle, and their country/bluegrass tinged songs, were among Linda's favorites.

"I love the McGarrigles," proclaimed Ronstadt, "I'm their biggest fan. I think they're brilliant. I don't know whether they're ever going to be commercial; I don't care. It's the most honest music there is. They're not copping an attitude, they're not trying to intimidate anybody. They're just making very pure and beautifully crafted stuff. They're just very innocent — and by innocent, I mean no guilt. The rarest and finest quality in music is innocence."

"Heart Like a Wheel" and "You Tell Me That I'm Falling Down" were Linda's choices when it came to selecting material for both of these million-selling albums. She met resistance from Peter Asher and from the people around her. "I had gotten vetoed on things, but eventually," she explained, "if I come to a producer with a song and he thinks it's the corniest thing he ever heard, and I ask my manager and he thinks it's corny too, then usually I'm reluctant to record it. For me, that song ["Heart Like a Wheel"] was very special; it was not just a song. I just thought it was a revelation in some way or another, and one of the most beautiful things I'd ever heard in my life. It was very precious to me, and I wanted to protect it. I thought maybe it would be one of those things that I would love and the rest of the world wouldn't be able to understand. And really, to this day, people will come up and say, 'Gee, that's the corniest thing I ever heard.' "

One of the most effective songs on the *Prisoner* album was J. B. Coats' composition, the lamenting ballad of "The Sweetest Gift." The song is a bittersweet tale of a mother visiting her son in prison, just before she dies, leaving only her memory behind. On the song, David Grisman plays the mandolin, David Lindley plays the fiddle, and Emmylou Harris sings the harmony vocal. As maudlin as the subject matter is, Linda's interpretation of it is devastatingly powerful.

It was during the sessions for this album that Linda and Emmylou found that they shared something in common — namely, their choice of their own personal favorite female singer. During a break in the recording of "The Sweetest Gift," the subject came up, and they both agreed that Dolly Parton was their all-time favorite. When Emmylou was recording her first album for Reprise Records, she included on it her version of Dolly's "Coat of Many Colors." Likewise, when Linda was choosing songs for *Prisoner in Disguise,* she included Parton's "I Will Always Love You" on the album. This marked the beginning of the mutual admiration triumvirate of Dolly, Linda, and Emmylou.

Prisoner in Disguise was an instantaneous smash. It was released in September 1975, and within one month it had already been certified Gold and was on its way to Platinum. In their review of the album, *Time* magazine claimed that, "A year ago, Ronstadt's amazing *Heart Like a Wheel* album helped make her top woman singer in the Top 40's, or pretty close to it. Ronstadt sings about loss and desperation; her big, beautiful soprano radiates vulnerability. She comes naturally to heartbreakers like Dolly Parton's country classic 'I Will Always Love You' or the old Smokey Robinson hit 'Tracks of My Tears.' "

All of a sudden, in 1975, Linda Ronstadt had made the transformation from country/rock singer with a cult following to America's top pop singing star. Oddly enough, Ronstadt continued to be her own harshest critic. "I hate the sound of my voice," she exclaimed at the time. "I never listen to my records. I like to sing, but I don't like to hear myself. Most people are like that. There are probably a few people who like the sound of their own voice — probably Joni Mitchell might like the sound of her own voice, it's such a beautiful-sounding instrument. She must know it's good. I don't mean that it's vanity. I just think it would be foolish not to hear that her voice sounds incredibly pleasing. My voice sounds very nasal and harsh, and a little constricted. That bothers me a lot. I have horrible sinus trouble, and that's the first thing I hear. Maybe that's the thing that people like. Diana Ross has a real nasal voice and people like that. But I hate it in me. If I could do what Bonnie Raitt could do, I'd be out bragging on myself day and night. Because she sings effortlessly, she never makes a mistake, she plays great guitar and she's very funny. I know she has an inferiority complex too. I want to shake her sometimes. Someone else who is like that is Phoebe Snow. Phoebe Snow puts herself down all the time because she thinks she's not beautiful. I think she's beautiful. To me, someone who is intelligent and fine and sensitive and talented makes me like them, and whatever I like defines what I think is beautiful."

One of the things that bothered Linda at the time was her tendency to giggle whenever she talked to an audience between songs, amid her concerts: "It's awful, it makes people think I'm flighty or stupid. I don't think I'm either one. What I am is nervous."

That year, when photographs of her were suddenly featured all over the pages of magazines, she was constantly referred to as "sexy" or "beautiful." Linda also found this lavished praise hard to take seriously. "I'm not a beautiful girl," she would argue. "I don't have good skin or good hair or a fashion model figure. I'm a food junkie, and I have the metabolism of a slug."

In 1975 Andrew Gold became the second recording artist to branch out of the Ronstadt camp and land his own album contract. Like the Eagles before him, Gold was offered a record deal by Asylum Records. While working on Linda's *Prisoner in Disguise* album as an arranger and jack-of-all-trades musician, he recorded his own self-titled debut album.

Andrew grew up in a very musical household. His father, Ernest Gold, was the composer of film scores (including that for *Exodus*) and his mother was Marni Nixon, who provided the singing voice for several film actresses (including Audrey Hepburn's singing voice in *My Fair Lady*). Linda gave him plenty of encouragement, and she sang background vocals on his first two albums. When it came time to embark on the *Prisoner in Disguise* concert tour that fall, Linda was the headliner, and Andrew was her opening act. Gold would perform his set, and then after the intermission he would play in her backup band. It was similar to the successful formula that Bette Midler had employed in 1973, having her musical director, Barry Manilow, play his own set on the bill with her two-act concert show, as well as playing with her.

Although she had been working out her instant stardom insecurities with her psychiatrist, Linda still dreaded the *Prisoner in Disguise* concert tour. "I threw up on the way to the airport," she said, "and for the first two weeks of the tour. I had taken six months off [from touring] because I'd become a physical and emotional wreck, and now I thought I had an ulcer. I just didn't think I was good enough. Finally, I just went, 'O.K., I can go home and forget about it and get sued by every agent and promoter in the world and be completely unprofessional,' or I can say, 'Look, it can't get great in a month, but I'm going to do a little better every night.' By the end of the tour, a month later, I was looking forward to every night.

"Believe me," she continued, "things are not hunky-dory. They haven't invented a word for that loneliness that everybody goes through on the road. The world is tearing by you, real fast, and all these people are looking at you like you're people in star's suits. People see me in my 'girl singer' suit and think I'm famous and act like fools . . . it's very dehumanizing."

She finds that her relationship with her band members really helps to make touring a rewarding experience — or not. "I think it's helping each other out that makes it bearable. The only way to deal with it is to have that real close camaraderie and to keep recycling it and teasing and keeping the humor level up all the time. You have to do it in an aggressive manner, though, or else it turns ugly. It was like group therapy, only worth more."

The tour had many high points. During the show that she did in Santa Monica, she returned to the stage for her encore accompanied in song by her friends Bonnie Raitt and Maria Muldaur. *People* magazine called the trio of Ronstadt/Raitt/Muldaur "the dream team of '75." This was the first of Linda's successful outings as part of an all-star, all-girl trio.

While she had dreaded the beginning of that particular concert tour, she wound up being depressed that it came to an end. "When we came back to end the tour in L.A., I had my first feelings of a let-down," she revealed. "Suddenly, all these people weren't down the hall and you can't all sit around and drink coffee. We were so lonely that we turned to each other, then they all went home to their old ladies, and I came home to the dog, you know."

With the success that Linda had experienced in 1975, she suddenly found herself on a new plane of creativity. She began to get over her guilt complex about her newfound fame, and started to exchange ideas with several people in the music business. One of the most important people that she met was Dolly Parton. It was while Emmylou Harris was recording her second Reprise album, *Elite Hotel*. She invited Linda to sing on the songs "Amarillo" and "Till I Gain Control Again." While she was in the recording studio with Emmylou, Dolly Parton dropped into one of the sessions.

"I've never met anybody so free of neurosis as that person!" Linda exclaimed after she'd spent some time with Dolly. "I was devastated by her honesty and her charm and sweetness. I'm sort of this Northern thinker, and she's just kind of a Southern magnolia blossom that floats on the breeze. But she's no dummy. She taught me that you don't have to sacrifice your femininity in order to have equal status. The only thing that gives you equal status with other musicians is your musicianship. Period. It doesn't matter how butch you act, how much dope you can take or how many nights you can stay up in a row."

Dolly had recalled meeting Linda briefly, years ago, when Ronstadt had performed at the Grand Ole Opry in Nashville: "Linda was just beginning to become popular . . . She was there with Randy Scruggs and some people, and she came over and someone introduced us. She said that she was a big fan of mine. Then I came to Los Angeles and she and Emmy were friends already. When they met, I guess they'd discussed me. So, when I got to L.A., Emmy invited me to her house and she invited Linda, too."

As 1976 began, Linda Ronstadt was riding high on the success of her latest single, "Tracks of My Tears." On February 28 she was presented with her first Grammy Award, for the song "I Can't Help It (If I'm Still In Love With You)," which was named the Best Country Vocal Performance, Female.

According to Peter Asher, that was the year that Linda began to get over the initial shock of becoming a superstar and started to explore her new power in a creative sense. "For the first time, Linda feels more in control of her career," he stated in 1976, "she knows when she has a month off, when she has to do an album. She can see a pattern, a kind of reality to things. It's more like working for a living, as opposed to going through all the craziness. Before, she always felt that events were just rushing her along . . . in the direction that was really up to the wind."

The success of the *Prisoner in Disguise* album had proven that Ronstadt's arrival on the scene wasn't just a one-shot fluke. Now she was looking forward to recording her next album. Instead of feeling that she was just a victim of circumstance, timing, and record company politics, she was at last free to concentrate on her music from a position of creative control and a well-earned sense of self-confidence. She was about to embark on the most successful phase of her career as a rock star.

In 1976 Linda's revealing braless shots from the Hasten Down the Wind *photo session instantly labeled her as the rock world's number-one "sex symbol."*

(Photo: Ethan A. Russell/Mark Bego Archives)

Ronstadt: Rock Star

5

From 1976 to 1978, Linda Ronstadt proceeded to rack up accolades, awards, and Gold and Platinum albums at an astounding rate. With her 1976 albums *Hasten Down the Wind* and her first *Greatest Hits* package, both certified as million-sellers within weeks of their release, she was beginning to break sales records right and left. That same year she became the first female performer to have four consecutive albums go Platinum. Not even Barbra Streisand, Aretha Franklin, or Diana Ross could claim that feat. (Eventually Streisand racked up four Platinum LPs in a row, but Ronstadt continually surpassed her, ultimately producing seven consecutive million-sellers.)

The beginning of the year was spent in the recording studio, working on the *Hasten Down the Wind* album. The last six months of 1976 she spent on the road, amid an extensive concert tour of the United States and Europe. She had been voted the top female vocalist of the year by several magazines, including *Rolling Stone, Circus,* and *Playboy,* so she was just beginning to enjoy a renewed sense of self-confidence — as far as her music was concerned.

One of the most publicized aspects of Ronstadt's appeal during this time was her overtly sexy image. On stage she did not hesitate to perform in short cut-off jeans and a halter top. When she appeared on the cover of the December 2, 1976, issue of *Rolling Stone,* she was wearing only a red slip, with one of the shoulder straps falling down her arm. In the interior of the magazine, photographer Annie Leibovitz shot Linda facedown on a rumpled bed, in a red teddy, with her well-shaped rear end most prominent in the shot.

Likewise, when Ethan A. Russell photographed Linda for the cover of her *Hasten Down the Wind* album, she was shown braless in a flimsy, unlined white cotton dress with the outline of her nipples distinctly defined through the transluscent cloth. All of a sudden she had created a sexy image for herself, and the press began to ask her probing questions about her sex life and her views on sex in general.

"I love sex as much as I love music, and I think it's as hard to do," said Linda at the time. "I don't know how good a sex symbol I am, but I do think I'm good at being sexy. The sexual aspect of my personality has been played up a lot, and I can't say it hasn't been part of my success. But it's unfair in a way, because I don't think I look as good as my image. Sometimes I feel guilty about it, sometimes I feel embarrassed about it, sometimes I feel I have to compete with it. But that's part of the fun, too — that's part of the charade.

"When you look at someone like Jean Harlow real close, she really did have an exquisitely formed face and beautiful hair and beautiful skin and a real gorgeous figure, and those are things I just don't have. But I don't think they're essential to being attractive. Sometimes they're more of a handicap than a help. I think vitality is what is attractive to people. That's why there are a lot of pretty girls that are kind of boring to look at. If I get a hot romance, my sexuality is likely to work whether I curl my hair and put make-up on or not. When it's successful and I'm at my shining best, I like to think of it as sassiness that incorporates sexuality and strength. It's aggressive without being intimidating. As long as there's strength in my attitude, I like it."

With regard to the red lingerie shots from *Rolling Stone*, Linda explained that, "Annie saw that picture as an exposé of my personality. She was right. But I wouldn't choose to show a picture like that to anybody who didn't know me personally, because only friends could get the other sides of me in balance; only they could get the full dose. That's why that kind of picture would be called 'intimate.' It defines the word. That picture implied that when I said girls didn't have to be butch to be equal to the guys, that I meant they had to go to the other extreme and look real dishy all the time. The point is to be yourself, to be a female person."

According to her, the revealing photo on the cover of the *Hasten Down the Wind* album was strictly an accident. "It's funny," she said, "I didn't have a concept for this album cover, and neither did anyone else. I wanted a picture of me in mid-air, falling. I wanted to look like I was floating. We tried to shoot it in a swimming pool; I tried jumping off a ladder. But it didn't work — I *looked* like I was jumping off a ladder. So we were out on the beach, and the photographer wanted to use this day-for-night technique with the strobe light. I didn't even know my tits were showing through; I didn't want any nipples in that picture . . . We didn't notice it was happening until we saw it in the picture. We wondered whether we should retouch it, and I said, 'Aw, fuck it.' I never looked that good a day in my life anyway.

"So we weren't trying for a sexy cover, but it's the frosting on the cake. If people like to look at it, let 'em look at it. It's a little bit weird for me, because I feel like I end up competing with myself. I go to the market in my overalls and people go, 'Yecch! She looks like sin.' But most people don't get to meet me, and if they like to have something nice to look at on their album cover: groovy!

". . . there's such a strong emphasis placed on physical beauty, especially in California. I've always been very resentful of that. My mother was very unvain; I was probably the vainest one in the family. She was always on my case, trying to drag me away from the mirror. I was always worried that my sister was much prettier than I was; I didn't think I was pretty enough. My mother would say it was stupid, that form follows function — if something is functional, it's beautiful. When I got over here [Los Angeles] I was just overwhelmed by how many people were so gorgeous, and I wasn't . . . It would be stupid for me to say that I don't think men find me attractive. But basically I'm not like one of your classic beauties. I don't have classic bone structure, I don't have nice hair — I don't have a real good figure, I hate clothes, I'm not a good dresser, I have bad skin. It doesn't really matter, I suppose, and when I find myself with men for whom that does matter, I think they're shallow. And if I have a zit and that means that they're not going to like me, there is something wrong with them, that I wouldn't like them anyway. It is kind of heartbreaking sometimes, when you just feel you want to have that extra edge, that if you were sound asleep with your mouth open snoring, you'd still look gorgeous."

Regardless of what she thought of her own degree of sex appeal, the majority of male rock and roll fans in the 1970s found Linda Ronstadt to be the ideal idol. The cover photo of her attracted as many record buyers as the music contained on it. What Linda wasn't taking into consideration was the fact that although she saw minor flaws in herself, it didn't matter. Who cared if she had an occasional zit? What did make an impression was the composite image that she presented. At the time, she was the perfect embodiment of a female rock star. She looked as sexy in a pair of jeans and a halter top as any of the reigning songstresses who spent a fortune making themselves up for hours, wearing designer gowns and enlisting the help of high-fashion stylists.

That was a large part of Linda's appeal at the time. She exuded natural beauty. She wasn't pristine like Karen Carpenter, tough like Helen Reddy, or over-glamorized like Diana Ross. She projected a strong sense of identity and an attractiveness that didn't appear to be manufactured or put on. She was more street smart than the majority of country singers at the time, yet she appeared far more vulnerable than most of the rock and roll women on the charts. Whatever she was doing during this era was just perfect, as far as the way she looked and the honest feeling that her music carried.

In March 1976, just after taking her first Grammy Award, Linda, Peter Asher, and her band checked into the Sound Factory recording studio in Los Angeles and began to work on her *Hasten Down the Wind* album. The sessions lasted until June, and simultaneously, Peter, Andrew Gold, Linda, and the rest of the band were working on Andrew's second solo album, *What's Wrong With This Picture?*

"Linda was doing *Hasten Down the Wind*," recalled Gold. "We'd go in and record Linda's album, and then take a dinner break and with the same players from her LP, we'd work on my record . . . it was a simultaneous thing . . . the same people and the same music, everybody hanging out together, almost like living together, all of us, for a time. Whatever happened criss-crossed."

At this point in time, Linda and her troupe were at the height of their intuitive interaction with one another. They all played off of each other exceedingly well, and they were enjoying the recording process. According to Ronstadt, having Peter Asher at the helm was the perfect sounding board for creating great music. "Everybody always knows exactly what's expected of them, and they try to do it the best they can. If they get off the track, he's real precise about guiding you back . . . He's precise about saying exactly what it is when you're missing the mark, so nobody's ever wandering around in a state of confusion. The sessions are really well organized and well run, and I find it's like that notion — from the most discipline comes the most freedom. It just seems that when you provide a real strong framework like that, then everybody has the confidence to do their best."

There is a more unified tone to the songs on the *Hasten Down the Wind* album. Unlike *Heart Like a Wheel*, which had distinctively contrasting rock and country songs, here both rock and roll and country and western elements blended together throughout. In addition to the recurring cast of characters from Linda's past three albums, including Don Henley and Wendy Waldman, she was joined for the first time by musicians Waddy Wachtel and Dan Dugmore.

Again, the eclectic choice of material came from various sources: something from this friend, something from that friend, and an old favorite or two thrown in for fun. One of the key people that Linda and company had become friendly with was a singer/songwriter named Karla Bonoff. She provided Linda with three songs for this album: "Lose Again," "Someone To Lay Down Beside Me," and "If He's Ever Near." She happened to be writing the kind of songs that Linda was looking for at the time, and Linda even invited Bonoff to sing background vocals on two of them with Wendy Waldman. To reciprocate, the following year, when Kenny Edwards was producing Bonoff's self-titled debut album for Columbia Records, Linda sang background vocals for Karla on the song "Home." The Bonoff album also contained the majority of Ronstadt's crew: Andrew Gold, John David Souther, Glenn Frey, Waddy Wachtel, and Dan Dugmore.

The title cut, "Hasten Down the Wind" was provided by another up-and-coming singer/songwriter named Warren Zevon, who was also part of this same musically incestuous group of California musicians. Jackson Browne produced his 1976 self-titled debut album on Asylum Records, and co-produced (with Waddy Wachtel) Zevon's 1978 LP, *Excitable Boy*. Linda sang background vocals on the title track to *Excitable Boy* and continued to record Warren Zevon compositions on her next two albums as well.

Linda had first met Warren Zevon backstage after one of her concerts in Los Angeles. Her first impression of him was that he was a virtual madman. "He looked like a psychopath," she said. "Just like Richard Speck. I thought he was a maniac and bound to do something weird. I was positive he was completely deranged. He scratched his head and kept opening his mouth, but no sound would come out. My manager Peter Asher knew it was a misunderstanding and wanted to intervene, but I wouldn't stop quacking. I felt like such a fool. I was positive he'd think I was completely demented and he'd never take anything I said seriously. Then I couldn't apologize enough. That was even worse. Then, when I got to know him — he was such a shy, sensitive person."

Zevon's flair was indeed for bizarre story/songs about drug addicts ("Carmelita"), murderers ("Excitable Boy"), gunslingers ("Frank and Jesse James"), and sadomasochists ("Poor Poor Pitiful Me"). However, Ronstadt found his songs emotionally imaginative, and she found him to be a fascinating addition to her California circle of musical comrades.

From the Buddy Holly catalog came the 1957 song "That'll Be the Day," which Linda rocked out on, complete with Kenny Edwards and Andrew Gold providing her with doo-wopping background vocals. One of the most effective performances on the album was Ronstadt's interpretation of "Crazy," the Willie Nelson composition that Patsy Cline made into a Top Ten pop hit in 1961. John and Johanna Hall's "Give

One Heart" was presented as a bouncy reggae excursion, and Tracy Nelson's "Down So Low" quaked with an intense gospel/blues delivery.

For the first and only time in her career, Linda tried her hand at songwriting. Together with Kenny Edwards and her father, Gilbert Ronstadt, she wrote the ballad "Lo Siento Mi Vida," which was sung mostly in Spanish. Another ballad, the lamenting "Try Me Again," was written by Linda and Andrew Gold.

Originally, she had shied away from putting her emotions down on paper, rationalizing, "I'd hate to add to the ever-increasing pile of bad songs." Or she'd insist, "Writing is a totally foreign process: I'm an interpreter."

However, with the encouragement of Andrew and Kenny, she relented. "I'm not a writer and never will be," Linda explained when *Hasten Down the Wind* was released, "but there's no harm in trying to come up with something and throwing it on the wall to see if it sticks."

The song "Try Me Again" is about driving past the home of a former lover and begging the person to give love another try. It is widely suspected that the song was written with John David Souther in mind. Although they had long broken up as lovers, Linda still referred to him as "my one love." However, she would not publicly identify the object of her affections in the song. "It's too revealing of my feelings," she would later insist. "It's embarrassing to tell everybody, I felt that bad. It makes my face red."

After being that revealing on "Try Me Again," and having everyone hound her to identify the lover in the song, Linda decided to hang up her fountain pen and continue to rely on singing other people's songs instead. "Like I've said before, I don't really consider myself a songwriter," she insisted. "I was really amazed I wrote that song. That's not really something that I do. Some people sit down every day and they write, but I don't do that. I have a few ideas cooking, but my goal in life is not to be a songwriter. The fact that I wrote a song was like an added bonus in my life. But something pretty intense has to happen and it's got to be something I can write about in pretty specific terms. That whole combination of events has to happen in order for me to write a song. I just don't have that kind of craftsmanship that a writer would have to construct things out of everyday experiences, in a way that makes it real interesting. I mean Paul Simon is the most gifted at that. He can write songs outside of his own experience so eloquently."

Describing her song-finding process, Linda revealed, "Mostly, I get them from my friends. And from those situations late at night when a bunch of people have gotten together and gone through a lot of social ritual and the defenses are down and you get real bored. The best cure for boredom is music, and that's when the ideas start coming and your fingers start to ache, and you start harmonizing, and then someone says, 'I just wrote a tune,' and you take the plunge. I keep getting all these funny demos from housewives and I keep praying one of those songs is going to be brilliant. It never is."

The *Hasten Down the Wind* album was released at the beginning of August 1976, was certified Gold on August 30, and was certified Platinum on October 28. Ultimately, the album yielded three pop hits ("That'll Be the Day," "Someone To Lay Down Beside Me," and "Lose Again"), made it into the Top Ten, won a Grammy Award for Linda in the Best Female Pop Performance category, and was heralded as one of the ten Best Albums of 1976 in *Time* magazine.

To capitalize on Linda's success on the charts, Asylum Records released Ronstadt's *Greatest Hits* album in December 1976, just in time for Christmas. Again, it went directly into the Top Ten. It was certified both Gold and Platinum on January 9, 1977. The *Greatest Hits* album reprised all of Linda's biggest pop hits, from "Different Drum" with the Stone Poneys to "Tracks of My Tears." The album also included "Desperado," which was never a single but had become something of a trademark song for Linda. In October 1989, Linda's *Greatest Hits* album was certified Quadruple Platinum for sales of over four million copies — making it her all-time biggest seller.

In April 1977, Capitol Records put together a two-record set entitled *A Retrospective.* The double album contained twenty-two of the most popular Ronstadt performances from her three Stone Poneys albums and from her four solo albums for the company. Several of the cuts were from the *Heart Like a Wheel* album. The previous year, Capitol had re-released the first Stone Poneys album, also meant to capitalize on the success that Linda was experiencing at Asylum Records with Peter Asher.

For Linda Ronstadt, 1977 was a big year. She was all over the music charts and was one of the hottest magazine cover girls of the year. Her pretty face graced the covers of *Time, Rolling Stone, People, Circus,* and many other publications.

In January of that year she was in Washington, D.C., for the inauguration of Jimmy Carter. She performed at the new president's inaugural concert. "I was so nervous," she later revealed. "My God, I was awful!" Amid all of the inaugural festivities, Nancy Kissinger played hostess at a State Department tea party. Linda and several of the other entertainers who were going to perform at the concert were invited to the tea party, including Shirley MacLaine and opera singer Clamma Dale. Linda wasn't about to play dress-up, regardless of who was on the guest list. True to form, she arrived in her blue jeans.

In early 1977, Andrew Gold scored a Top Ten hit single from his

What's Wrong With This Picture? album. The song, entitled "Lonely Boy," featured Linda singing background vocals. He figured that it was as good a time as any to head out on his own and really define his existence apart from Ronstadt's band.

"Originally I took Linda's job as sort of a temporary job," he explained in February 1977. "Of course it's completely helped me expand musically as well as just getting known. I do enjoy recording with her a lot, and I do enjoy touring with her too. I've been with her about four years now. I'm going to have to do a lot less, and I don't think I'll be touring with her anymore, and I'll be doing a lot less with her on record, because I can't do both things at once. But she's expected that from when we first joined. She naturally assumes that if she gets somebody that she considers a pretty good player, that if he's good enough, he'll probably have something to do. It won't be a shock.

"I want to stop putting my guitar licks on her records," he continued, "not because I dislike putting them on her records, but I want to keep a focus. This way, if you want to hear an Andrew Gold guitar solo, you can buy this record or that record. Well, how about buying Andrew Gold records!?" By the time Linda went back into the recording studio, in May 1977, Andrew was off on his own.

Speaking about his last concert tour with Linda, Gold explained, "We went to Europe, and then we came back and did a bunch of dates including Nassau Coliseum on Long Island: that place is awful. It just sounds weird. It's too big, and it just sounds like an airplane hangar. Then we stopped for a month, and then we went back out on the road. We've just sort of been out for the last two months. After this tour I'm going to take two months and do zero, except for writing songs."

When "Lonely Boy" was released, Andrew went out on a tour of his own, playing in small clubs. It was a refreshing change of pace after playing in gigantic stadiums with Linda. "I haven't played clubs for like five years or something. It's neat, because everybody's right there. In a [large Ronstadt] concert you come out — there's this huge mass of people, a big crowd, a faceless crowd, and then you go backstage, and you never see the audience. Everybody gets whisked off to the hotel, and you don't get any sense of time or the city. Here, you're sitting there, and the people are sitting right there, and I can see them," he said.

Meanwhile, back in Los Angeles, Ronstadt also took a rest, hanging out at home with her musician friends. Explaining her social life at the time, she claimed, "At eight, the eight o'clock musicians arrive and hang out till twelve. Then the twelve o'clock musicians arrive and hang out till four. And then the four o'clock musicians come and hang out till seven."

She left L.A. for an extended stay in New York City, where she ended up doing some heavy-duty partying and playing with her friends. While in Manhattan, she accumulated several new ideas for her next album, *Simple Dreams*.

"I came home with six months off and I was going to stay home, but I went to New York and just hung out," she explained. "When I was in New York playing, I really worked harder at playing and having fun than I did when I was working. I would come back from New York just exhausted, but it was fun. And from that I got so much input. I got this whole album together, all the ideas for the concept of the album and the tour, and what the whole focus of it was. Also, I met these New York musicians there . . . so even when I was in New York playing, I brought home enormous amounts of stuff to put back into my work from that. I don't know what I'd do with six months really 'off.' I can't sit around and do nothing, it drives me crazy. I really have a hard time with an unstructured existence."

The recording sessions for Linda's *Simple Dreams* album began on May 23, 1977. Before they could start the sessions, Linda and Peter had to find a way to fill in the gap that had been left when Andrew Gold departed. Peter Asher explained of the transition, "We were trying for a 'band album,' and we knew we had to replace Andrew Gold, because he was going off to work on his own, and drummer Michael Botts was really not available much now, because Bread was suddenly successful. In those two cases, it was Linda's idea to use Don Grolnick [keyboards] and Rick Marotta [drums]. I already had worked with them."

Ronstadt found that by making Waddy Wachtel a permanent part of her band, the sound of her recordings changed. "Waddy is a little bit more rock and roll where Andrew is more rock. And Andrew's style was beginning to mature so rapidly and turn into Andrew Gold. It wasn't like Andrew quit or was fired, he just wanted to make Andrew Gold records. When we replaced him with Waddy things got a little more aggressive. We were looking for a guy that could play real well, and we got the attitude to boot. Kenny [Edwards] knew him. Kenny was responsible for getting Waddy and Dan Dugmore into the band. Dan just comes up with these amazing things. He came up with the iba introduction on a song called 'Blowin' Away.' The iba is some strange instrument, the Stonehenge of the steel guitar," she said.

With her new band, Linda was beginning to look forward to getting into the studio to record. "The most important thing to do is something that's satisfying and something you do well, and that you enjoy doing. If you're doing that it doesn't matter," she explained, claiming that she enjoyed working with Peter Asher and her band. "Because of the teamwork aspect," she elaborated, "communication with a

Linda Ronstadt in her famous Cub Scout outfit.
(Photo: Nancy Barr/Retna Ltd.)

bunch of people I really know. I can understand what they're going to do on the records and Peter and Val [Garay], the engineer, and I have got this team thing down with the band, where it's amazing. And I love it when one person says, 'Well, I have this idea,' and then somebody else goes, 'Oh, yeah, and this and this and this.' That's just like sitting around with a bunch of people that are great to talk to and you start an idea, and the rest of the people begin to illuminate the idea until it gets into this sort of full-blown wonderfulness.

"Making albums is physically tough on me," Ronstadt insisted. "I always wind up looking like I got run over by a cement truck. I get up in the morning, put on my track shoes and shorts and I go down there. We try to keep banker's hours, banker's hours being regular hours. My feeling is that if you're in there for more than seven hours, you've really gone stale. Sometimes you get something that's plain old mechanical work and you've just got to finish it up, and sometimes you just think you hit a hot streak and you come back the next day and you sound like old, tired, weird people."

Linda directly attributes her love of recording to her interaction with Peter Asher as producer: "I can't imagine working with someone else. There are things that he has to tolerate about me — my insecurities, I'm disorganized, I'm late or whatever. Sometimes it's hard for me when he gets shy, times he has his own insecurity to overcome. We've worked past those things. We have developed tolerance in the sterling sense of the word for each other's faults, and sometimes we get angry at each other, but we pass over it. It's like a marriage."

She said he loves his role in creating her albums. "He's never gonna run any little nasty games down on you. I never have the feeling that he's trying to flesh out his frail identity by everybody else's, and I think a lot of producers do. They try to live vicariously and they try to live out their fantasies of what they would be as artists through their artists. Peter is a producer. The funniest thing he talks about is making deals with himself. He says, 'In my producer's hat, I would make this deal, but in my manager's hat, I couldn't give myself that many points [recording terms for record royalty percentage].' He always comes out being overly generous to me in terms of going out of his way to not have a conflict of interests there."

The album that Linda Ronstadt recorded from May to July of 1977 would become the most successful album of her career, ultimately selling over three and a half million copies in less than a year — in America alone. It also spent five consecutive weeks at Number One on the album charts, and produced the biggest-selling single of her career: "Blue Bayou."

The selection of her band members and the choice of material was never so important as it was on this particular album. On *Simple Dreams,* who made the selections — Linda, or Peter Asher? "I pick the tunes and I often pick a general setting to them," explained Ronstadt. "Peter figures out the best ways to implement that. I also chose the band. I chose them all for their particular style and ability, and I just let them play. And then Peter and I both act as editors when it comes to making arrangements. Choosing the players is like doing the arrangements in a sense, 'cause you know what they're going to play."

According to Asher, they both have some input with regard to song choices, and in certain instances, he comes up with the tunes. "We both do, and we both sort of have a power of veto," he says. "I mean, if it's a song that I really hate, we don't do it and then she's real convinced. On this album she wanted to do 'Blue Bayou.' 'It's So Easy' was entirely my idea. She wasn't terribly keen on this 'cause it's such a dumb song, but I just really *heard* this particular arrangement of it. I would say the majority of the song choices are hers, but I exert influence over which ones end up being chosen."

"I'm more secure musically now than I was," added Linda at the time, "but I never wanted to become the boss lady. As I see it, it is always a team situation involving me, Peter and the band. I never want to feel like the boss. Peter doesn't want to feel like the boss. We jointly make the final decision about everything. Neither of us wants to do the whole job. We're too lazy. If we disagree on something, I really re-examine it and if I still think I'm right, I go ahead. I remember 'Blue Bayou' — Peter was afraid it wouldn't be a hit. He said we should shop around for some insurance. I said, 'O.K., get the insurance.' But I knew it was a hit and it was the biggest single I've ever had. Sometimes he is real wild about stuff, and I say, 'Oh, no. That will never go.' There are those times when I am just plain sure, when I have that incredible right feeling; and when I have that feeling about a song and I put it on a record, it usually doesn't miss. But sometimes it works the opposite way.

"I don't ever sing anything that isn't personal," she insisted. "I can only sing about my own emotions, and I always wear my emotions pretty close to the surface. I don't know how to live any other way. My image is focused because I've not on many occasions stepped too far out of character. I don't do things that aren't authentically me. Anything I feel is not authentic gives me a headache. Even if I stumble, it's still authentically me stumbling.

"Lots of times I've felt I haven't gotten enough credit for the arrangements; lots of times I feel I haven't taken enough responsibility. What I did on this album was pick the musicians, pick the tunes, pick the style of the arrangements and then just let everybody do their job, and it all worked. I think *Simple Dreams* is a great statement about California music."

When the *Simple Dreams* album was released in August 1977, neither Ronstadt nor Asher were certain which of the songs contained on it were going to end up being the singles. According to Asher, "Really, the choice of singles is sort of not in anyone's hands. It's kind of in the lap of the gods. We can put an album out and tell them that one thing is a single, but they all start playing another one, *that's* the single. If the major radio stations make it a single, they'll put it on their charts; they'll play it, they'll push it up their charts — it might as well be out. In other words, a thing can be a single without ever being released as a single. We put 'Blue Bayou' out as a single, and then we were pretty much forced to put 'It's So Easy' out. A number of radio stations, particularly on the West Coast — KHJ in Los Angeles — went on it determinedly and wouldn't take it off because it was a hit. They played it, they got phone calls, and I knew I didn't want to pull 'Blue Bayou,' because I was convinced it was a hit, so that's why we decided to put both out at once."

"Blue Bayou" was released in September 1977, and "It's So Easy" was released as a single less than a month later. Both songs became Top Ten hits, with "Blue Bayou" hitting Number Three on the pop chart, and "It's So Easy" peaking at Number Five. "Blue Bayou" ended up selling over a million copies as a single, becoming Linda's first Gold single. It was such a popular song that she also recorded and released a Spanish-language version of the old Roy Orbison hit, which translated to "Lago Azul."

Linda, who doesn't speak conversational Spanish, asked her father (Gilbert Ronstadt) to interpret Orbison's lyrics into Spanish for her. In taking the translation down over the telephone, Linda made a few grammatical mistakes. When the Spanish version of "Blue Bayou" was released, it too became a huge hit, but it wasn't long before she heard from Hispanic record buyers who were less than amused over the translation job. "We got an *irate* letter from Spain," says Linda, "and the guy said because the tense and gender changes throughout the song were wrong, I sounded like a hermaphrodite in a time machine!"

In addition to recording Roy Orbison's "Blue Bayou" and Buddy Holly's "It's So Easy" on her *Simple Dreams* album, Linda also chose two songs from her band members. John David Souther's "Simple Man, Simple Dream" provided the album's title, and Robert "Waddy" Wachtel penned "Maybe I'm Right." Linda also chose to revive two traditional country/bluegrass tunes: "I Never Will Marry" and "Old Paint."

"I Never Will Marry" was especially effective, and it was quite a milestone, as Linda invited Dolly Parton to sing the harmony vocal with her on the song. According to Linda, it was Dolly's "angelic" voice that made the song so artistically successful: "There are people who act like catalysts for me. They make me do things I can't do on my own. When I sing with Emmy, she can make my voice go into a corner I can't reach by myself. And as for Dolly, when I sang 'I Never Will Marry' in the studio, it just didn't have any magic. But all of a sudden, when Dolly started singing with me, wow!

"Sometimes I need an interpreter," she continued speaking about her influences. "Waddy taught me how to sing 'Tumbling Dice.' He really understands the Rolling Stones better than anyone except Keith Richards. And if you want to know about the Beatles, you go to Andrew Gold. If you want to know about Roy Orbison, you ask J. D. Souther. If you want to know bout Neil Young, you ask Dan Dugmore. And if you want to know who to ask, you ask me. I'm the expert on who to ask. There are some people who work well all by themselves. Some of those Swedish fiddlers who sit in front of the mountains and just emote this passion are wonderful. But I live in a complex society and there are a lot of people around and I just need somebody to come in and put the other parts of the puzzle together for me."

Two of the songs on the album, "Carmelita" and "Poor Poor Pitiful Me," were Warren Zevon compositions that appeared on his debut album. "Carmelita" is about the desperate plea of a heroin addict, and "Poor Poor Pitiful Me" ends up with a verse about picking up a girl who wants to be beaten up. Linda loved Zevon's unique story songs, but she was at first afraid of tackling such strong material. She ended up recording "Carmelita" the way it was originally written, but on "Poor Poor Pitiful Me" she convinced Zevon to write her a new verse — to remove the S&M sequence.

"I'd always wanted to record 'Carmelita' and 'Poor Poor Pitiful Me,' " Ronstadt explained, "but I felt the lyrics were too strong. Now I sorta feel like I've grown into the lyrics. I don't know why, but they're not too strong anymore. It's like not liking hot chili when you're a kid and all of a sudden you can't find the chili hot enough."

Referring to "Poor Poor Pitiful Me," Linda said, "I've never been into sado-masochism. I've never gotten *that* far out ever. To me that song seemed like the purest expression of male vanity. Step on you, be insensitive, be unkind and give you a hard time, saying, 'Can't ya take it, can't ya take it!?' Then if you tease men in the slightest bit, they'll just walk off with their feelings hurt, stomp off in a corner and pout. I mean that's the way men are. I swear. I thought the verse turned around to a female point of view was just *perfect*. The gender change worked perfectly."

One of the lines in the song "Carmelita" refers to scoring heroin at the Pioneer Chicken stand on Alvarado Street in Los Angeles. The Pioneer Chicken stand became an "in" joke with Linda and her comrades. She explained, "To me, that song is just a narrative. I don't even think of it in terms of drugs. To me it's L.A. nostalgia, just a classic L.A. song. Ya know that L.A. boys club? Jackson Browne, J. D. Souther and Glenn Frey — the ones who stomp around in their cowboy boots — I call them 'the Pioneer Chicken Stand Brigade.' "

Ronstadt said that the original idea of recording "Blue Bayou" came from John David Souther and Glenn Frey. The song came up during one of the all-night songfests that Linda and her friends had one evening. She recalled, "J. D. and Glenn simultaneously suggested 'Blue Bayou' to me sorta like Tweedle Dee and Tweedle Dum. We sat up all night talking like mice at incredible speeds, playing and singing half the songs we knew, all of us singing in different keys. I've got a tape of it, and it's the fastest tape I've ever heard. It sounds like R2D2."

In 1976, like the Eagles and Andrew Gold before him, John David Souther had been offered his own solo recording career on Asylum Records. It was beginning to seem that Linda Ronstadt was being looked to as Asylum's prime talent scout. Naturally, Ronstadt, Andrew Gold, Kenny Edwards, and the whole gang took part in Souther's debut LP, *Black Rose*. The album was produced by Peter Asher, and Linda sang on the song "If You Have Crying Eyes." Not only did the Souther album contain his own versions of the songs that Linda had made famous — "Faithless Love" from *Heart Like a Wheel* and "Silver Blue" form *Prisoner in Disguise* — but it also featured a new composition that she fell in love with, called "Simple Man, Simple Dream."

"I feel very close to that song," she was to explain. "I really love that line 'Maybe I'll kill you, maybe I'll be true,' because these days you never know what will happen if you get involved with somebody. I mean, a relationship could be the worst thing that's ever happened, ya know? It could be the worst thing that happened to their career. Or my career. It's so weird, since we all live in fishbowls, it's so difficult to have successful relationships."

When the recording sessions for "Simple Man" began, Linda confessed that she felt something was missing — not having Andrew Gold's input. "I missed Andrew a lot," she proclaimed. "He came down to the studio a lot and stood around like a piece of furniture just so we wouldn't feel weird. We were so used to having Andrew's face around even though he wasn't playing."

Finally, when Linda was recording the song "Poor Poor Pitiful Me," Gold joined in and sang background vocals. However, his participation remained a well-guarded secret, masked by an inside joke between Ronstadt and her Pioneer Chicken Stand Brigade. On the record liner notes, Gold is billed only under the pseudonym "Larry Hagler."

Linda laughed about their Larry Hagler joke. "Years ago when we were in Lubbock, Texas, there was this guy standing outside the hotel who wanted to see me. I was getting on the bus because we had to go, and for some reason he threw his college ID on the bus. It turned up in *my* pocket. His name was Larry Hagler, and his name became the tour slogan. Everything was 'Larry Hagler.' We'd go into a restaurant and page him. If anyone mentioned Larry Hagler, we'd all crack up and die laughing. I carried this ID around in my pocket for a year of this strange person I'd never met. Larry Hagler where are you?"

One of the most out-of-character songs on the *Simple Dreams* album was the Rolling Stones' 1972 Top Ten hit "Tumbling Dice." Linda explained in 1977, "The band used to play that all last summer at sound check. I really loved it too, but nobody knew the words. Then Mick [Jagger] came backstage when I was at the Universal Amphitheater and he said, 'You do too many ballads, you should do more rock and roll songs.' I, of course, told him he should do more ballads, because I think he's a great ballad singer. Of course he's a great rock and roll singer too, but I'm especially fond of his ballad singing. So we started to tease each other, with me telling him to do more ballads and him telling me to do more rock and roll, then I thought, 'Well, nobody's right . . . rock and roll as a concept.' You know, hardly anybody really writes rock and roll anymore. The greatest rock and roll writers were in the '50s and '60s except for him . . . So, I made him write down the words to the song, and I learned it and we started doing it."

In addition to the Top Ten single success that Linda had with "Blue Bayou" and "It's So Easy," both "Poor Poor Pitiful Me" *and* "Tumbling Dice" went on to become big Top 40 hits when they were released as singles in early 1978. With the *Simple Dreams* album, Linda cemented her claim to the title of "the most successful female singer of the 1970s." Country, rock and roll, blues, and even bluegrass standards were all in her expressive command.

Linda was very excited about the results of the *Simple Dreams* album. She had stretched herself into a couple of new directions, and she wasn't certain how her fans would respond to her singing aggressive rock and roll on "Tumbling Dice," and about heroin addiction on "Carmelita."

"With this new album, people will either think I have a sense of humor, or that I'm real sick," she said at the time. "I was definitely laughing a lot on this album. After all, I *do* have a sense of humor. That's why the feeling on this album is different. It's completely different. *Hasten Down the Wind* was so DOWN. I was very depressed then.

But this new album is kinda like: 'Oh yeah! OH YEAH! What else are ya gonna hit me with!?' This new album is a real two-fisted record!"

The reviews for the *Simple Dreams* album were absolutely glowing. She had clearly come a long way since she had sat down in the middle of a pigsty and warbled about having the "Lovesick Blues." *People* magazine claimed, "The First Lady of country/rock has delivered a sweet and simple work — her finest, most focused to date. Ronstadt's voice is a consistent and precisely tuned instrument of vast range and feeling." And *Rolling Stone* called her "rock's supreme torch singer," citing that "the thing about Linda Ronstadt is that she keeps getting better, and we keep expecting more and more of her . . . What Ronstadt's blossoming skills suggest is a kind of latter-day Billie Holiday, a woman whose singing constitutes an almost other-worldly triumph over the worst kind of chronic pain."

Country Music magazine proclaimed that "Linda Ronstadt is easily the most successful female rock and roll AND country star at this time," and Britain's *Melody Maker* glowed that "No other female singer has as natural a feel for country/rock." Even *The New York Times* referred to her as "the most popular woman singer in the world."

Immediately after the album was completed, it was back on the road, for the 1977 concert tour. There were initially a few bugs to work out in the show. Not only was there new material off of the *Simple Dreams* album to translate to the stage, but she hadn't toured before with her new band.

"Obviously the new band is an adjustment," she said at the time. "And it *is* a real band. Rick [Marotta] has my favorite groove of any drummer. He plays way back behind the beat and I have the bad habit of rushing like a fire engine. So when I sing with Rick I have to concentrate on not rushing three songs ahead. If I sang at my normal speed, I'd leave them all behind in a cloud of dust. I feel I'm having to come up to their level in some way or the other, and it's very difficult. God, when I listen to the tapes of the first concert . . .

"It's more rock and roll," she continued, "but it's just the best band I've ever had. The level of musicianship is so high. This band is really exceptional. I was worried at first because Dan Grolnick loves jazz, you know, and he can play so much more stuff than the stuff he plays in my music. And I worried a lot that he would feel frustrated. But in fact, in his own words, what a great musician always searches for is musical agreement. And if there's musical agreement going on on the stage, then a musician will get off. And when I realized that those guys are getting off on the music, well, it wasn't up to me to entertain the band *and* the audience. So I stopped worrying, because the audience seemed to like it.

"I have three of the old guys, but then I have these two New York guys," she explained about her new band for the *Simple Dreams* tour. "And so it was a little bit like New York and L.A. lifestyles adjusting to each other. The band's gotten incredibly close, everybody's real tight now. Instead of being polite and just getting along, amazing friendships have developed from it."

Linda admitted that she became very close to all of the members of the band during that tour. "Well, this time it just happened faster and a lot more intensely," she said. "And the other thing is, I was worrying too much. You know, I just take it personally if I feel that someone isn't completely happy all the time. Regardless of whether it has anything to do with the tour or whether it's something outside of the tour. I'm always sort of terrified that people aren't happy in the tour."

That autumn, Linda was invited to sing "The Star-Spangled Banner" at the first game of the World Series. According to her, "Peter came to me and said, 'Listen, all the Dodgers got together and they voted.' And then he looked at me, and he says, 'You know what's coming . . .' And I thought, *'They want me to throw out the first ball!'* He said, 'They want you to sing the National Anthem!' And I just went: 'Oh God!' 'cause it's just the worst song in the world! It's a *turkey*. Who even knows the words?"

To show their appreciation for Ronstadt entertaining their offer, the Dodgers sent her a blue warm-up jacket that she really liked. She was originally going to turn the request down, but she thought it over. "Finally I just couldn't say, 'No,' because I love the jacket," she claimed. "I was so nervous. If they'd asked me to *pitch,* I would have been less nervous. And everybody was going, 'Oh, it'll be great, it'll be great!' Well, Peter didn't do any of that stuff. He was just saying, realistically, exactly what was gonna happen. He said, 'O.K., you're gonna have to go stand in center field and it's gonna be like this and like that.' He was thinking about what the problems could possibly be. 'There's gonna be this horrible echo, and watch out for the organ, and watch out for this . . .' Then he said the funniest thing. He said, 'Ha, ha, you're gonna have to stand in center field and sing that all by yourself.' He said, 'I wouldn't do that for all the money in the world, and you're doing it for free!' It cracked me up."

In September 1977, playing Universal Amphitheater in Los Angeles, Linda bounded onto the stage wearing one of her most famous outfits — a little boy's Cub Scout uniform. Photographers had a field day shooting Ronstadt in the child's outfit that was short enough to show off the length of her shapely legs.

Reviewing that particular September 20 concert, *Rolling Stone* magazine noted that, "Linda Ronstadt onstage in a Cub Scout outfit —

with a properly knotted regulation kerchief — has got to be the epitome of coyness. But that coyness was underscored on this evening, as it is on her records, by a stark vulnerability, a need to engage her audience more than entertain it . . . she gave the audience what they wanted — a country/rock signature or two — and in turn, they gave her what she needed — reinforcement. That exchange, which occurred repeatedly throughout the show, was almost of a sexual quality at times, in the sense of a mutual release of sorts and in the sense that Linda employs the powers of flirtation and suggestion very knowingly."

Discussing her scant onstage outfits, Linda explained, "Well, I wore shorts one night halfway by accident. The night before I'd worn a dress that made me feel real polite and stupid, and by communication failure, the girl who's helping me with my clothes brought the same dress the next night. I thought to myself that I couldn't get back in that dress, so I wore shorts. The shorts were too big, though, so the next day we all went and bought all these different things everyone thought I should wear. I sing better according to what I wear. First of all, all these summer gigs are real hot, because they're in outdoor pavilions. It's been real muggy and hot, and you can't wear anything that's going to be hot to start with. And there's just something about sports clothes that lend themselves to movement, to feeling a little bit freer with your body. They also look real good. Dresses for some reason . . . well, some are good. Sometimes I like dresses, but they're difficult and awkward and all. It's sort of like when you would go to the prom and do the bop in your formal, you know. You would feel stupid. I had all these great dresses made and they're beautiful and I love wearing them standing there singing a ballad, but you can't do 'Tumbling Dice' in some silly sort of dress!"

Although Linda was having fun dressing up in short shorts and skimpy halter tops, not everyone was amused by her fashion sense. In fact, when designer Mr. Blackwell announced his annual list of "Worst Dressed Women" in 1978, Ronstadt made Number Two on the tally, right after Farrah Fawcett-Majors. According to Blackwell, Linda Ronstadt "looks as though she bought her entire wardrobe during a five minute bus stop."

The Associated Press story that carried the list went further: "Running a close second on Blackwell's list . . . was rock singer Linda Ronstadt, whose penchant for wearing Cub Scout uniforms and short shorts was cited as 'bad taste.' " Blackwell claimed that Linda's singing pal Dolly Parton looked like "Scarlett O'Hara dressed like Scarlett O'Hara dressed like Mae West in 'My Little Chickadee.' "

The Blackwell list was announced on Tuesday, January 10, 1978, and only six days later, Linda, Dolly, and their friend Emmylou Harris were together at Parton's Nashville house, no doubt having a good laugh over their inclusion on the list of "fashion victims." The reason for the meeting: the first attempt at the famous Ronstadt/Parton/Harris *Trio* album.

They had been discussing the possibility of getting together to record as a trio, and they all decided to take the plunge and see what they could come up with. On January 18, the three found themselves back in Los Angeles, at Enactron Truck Studio in Los Angeles, for a marathon string of recording sessions. According to Dolly Parton, "It was like a week-long slumber party." The marathon sessions were produced by Emmylou's husband, producer Brian Ahern.

"It was really the brainchild of Brian Ahern," says Emmylou. "I was going to record a Christmas song, 'Light of the Stable,' and we got the idea to have Linda *and* Dolly sing on it . . . We got together in a studio in California and made a demo of the song. It sounded great, so we did a few other songs. That's when we got the idea for a complete trio album. Ask Linda and me who our favorite singer is, and we would both say, 'Dolly Parton!' "

However, before a note was sung, each performer's record label was invited to a "top secret" meeting and asked to get in on the bidding to decide which record company was going to have the honor of releasing the resulting album. Parton was on RCA Records, Harris was on Warner Brothers, and Ronstadt was under contract to Asylum. Ultimately, Asylum won out in the bidding war, and the label's president, Joe Smith, struck a deal to handle the LP.

"In those first sessions we did 'Mister Sandman,' 'When Cowgirls Get Blue,' 'Evangeline,' 'My Blue Tears,' and a few other things. We tried to do it in ten days. It was difficult, but I'm amazed at how much we did get done," said Emmylou.

"It was a ludicrous situation," recalled Linda. "We were trying to make an album in ten days. We three grownups should have known better than to put ourselves in a pressure cooker that way. We just wanted to do it so badly and thought that was our only chance. The potential for hideous and bitchy behavior and accusations was enormous. At the very beginning, we made a solemn pact that at any time our friendship was hurt, we would end the project. Friendship first. And, when I think of the kinds of things that could have happened, it blows my hair. The thing is that Dolly — God, there is not one trace of malice in her — has such a keen understanding of what motivates people that there was never a trace of bitchiness. Basically, what I learned was that I wanted to be on the team with Dolly and Emmy. Singing with them is a precious experience. It was like musical nirvana. I learned a lot about music and about morality, and Dolly was responsible for that."

Linda has always proclaimed that Dolly Parton (left) is her favorite female singer. In 1977 Dolly joined Linda on Ronstadt's Simple Dreams *album.*

(Photo: Chris Walter/Retna Ltd.)

Linda, Dolly, and Emmylou found the whole experience of singing with each other to be sheer delight. But the project ended up bogged down in record company politics, scheduling problems, and too many businessmen, managers, and record company demands pulling all three singers in different directions.

"We had problems," said Dolly, "because we were all three on different labels. Everybody thought it was such a spectacular idea. Everybody was pushing and shoving us, trying to get it done for business reasons. And we thought, 'Well, we want to do it and do something great, and if it sells, wonderful, and if it don't, then . . .'

"They were really thinking only money, and we were thinking creativity . . . We thought, 'The hell with this. This isn't worth the wear and tear everybody's putting us through, because we were not having any problems with each other.' So, we just sat down and had a powwow, and we decided there were just too many people pulling us too many directions, and we weren't gettin' what we really wanted. Everybody had a different opinion on what we should be recording. They'd say, 'We gotta cut some pop songs, because we have Linda Ronstadt here and we could make a fortune.' "

By the early part of February, several rough tracks were completed, and Brian Ahern was working on mixing the handful of songs that were completed. Emmylou's own Hot Band played the majority of the instruments, with Nashville session musicians David Briggs and Larrie London flown in to complete some of the tracks. Linda's own band members worked on some of the overdubs, but the whole project ended up indefinitely put on hold.

"It was just hard to get everyone back together again," said Emmylou. "So, eventually those tracks came out — mostly on my records. We always thought we would have time to get together and do it again." Unfortunately, it wasn't until 1986 that they would make their second attempt at becoming an all-star singing group.

Linda spoke of the problems that the original *Trio* album encountered: "We're going to make it, it's just going to take a long time. It's not easy for three different record companies to come to an agreement. Say we made a record, and Dolly's record company thought that it was something that she shouldn't have out just then. Say she had an album out then and it would be competing with her own album. It's also difficult trying to find a style to record us in when we have three completely different styles."

Referring to Emmylou and Dolly, Linda said, "They called me up when I was on the road and said, 'Hey, let's do this,' 'cause we've talked about it for so long and wanted to do it for so long. And I just went, 'Oh, sure, we'll do it, we'll just go out and sing and we'll make this record and it'll come out and everybody will say, "Isn't that nice," and that'll be the end of it.' I told Peter [Asher] about it, and Peter just sort of went, 'Ohhh.' He didn't stand in my way — he never does if I want to do something — but he knew that it was going to be a hell of a headache, and it was.

"We recorded some stuff," she said, referring to the handful of completed tracks, "but let me tell you, we did it in ten days. Now, I've never made a record in less than three and a half months, and I don't think Dolly has, and I don't think Emmy has either. But we got scared because Emmy had to go on the road, and Dolly had to start writing her album, and I only had a certain amount of time off, and we wanted to do it so badly. I remember Dolly just making these decisions. She said: 'We're just going to have to try.' And Emmy's got kids — Dolly was such an inspiration to her, because she's so well-organized. I remember Emmy saying, 'Well, I'm just going to do it for Dolly, because it shows me that I'll just have to get things organized, I'll simply have to do it.' "

Ronstadt spoke of the impossibility of recording in ten days: "We thought that somehow we would just break all the rules and we would do it, and we didn't. We got a couple of things that are just lovely. One particular thing just turned out gorgeous, just the three of us with an acoustic guitar, and God, it just killed us when we heard it. I learned so much singing with them."

Two years later, the songs that Ahern had recorded with Harris, Ronstadt, and Parton began to trickle out onto the marketplace. Emmylou's Christmas album, *Light of the Stable,* was released in 1980, containing the title cut that she had recorded with Linda and Dolly. The following year, the trio's "Evangeline" and "Mister Sandman" were released on Harris' *Evangeline* album. "Mister Sandman" ended up becoming a Top Forty pop hit for Harris, and the *Evangeline* album was certified Gold. In 1982 the trio's version of Dolly Parton's "My Blue Tears" was released on Linda's *Get Closer* album.

The year 1978 contained a couple of other unfinished projects for Linda Ronstadt. Not only did the proposed album with Dolly and Emmylou and the much talked-about trio concert dates not see the light of day, but Ronstadt signed a contract with CBS television to produce and star in a TV special that never came about. It was to contain documentary footage about women in show business, and how she was competing in the rock and roll world — which was essentially a man's game, especially in the 1970s. Linda never did tape the network television special; she was too busy with her ultra-hot recording career.

Although the proposed television special did not transpire, Linda did manage to make her motion picture debut in 1978, in the comedy film about rock and roll radio, *FM*. The film was one of the inspirations for the TV series "WKRP in Cincinnati," which debuted on CBS-TV that autumn. The plot of the film centered around a fictitious Los Angeles FM radio station, QSKY, and the conflicts between the employees and the greedy corporate owners of the station. When the parent company decided to add pro-military advertising to the hip, liberal, rock and roll station, the disc jockeys banded together to oppose the action.

Linda Ronstadt and Jimmy Buffet made special appearances as themselves in the film, performing at concerts which were simulcast on QSKY. In addition to performing live versions of "Tumbling Dice," "Poor Poor Pitiful Me," and "Love Me Tender," Linda was seen in a brief sequence, greeting "Jeff Dugan" (played by Michael Brandon) backstage after the concert.

Her appearance in the film is most significant for preserving concert performances of three of the most successful songs from her rock and roll era. Although Linda's singing was top-notch, she also demonstrated her discomfort with addressing the audience between songs. She came across as painfully stiff whenever she had to speak in the movie. When the film was released in the spring of 1978, she flatly refused to promote the movie in any way, or to grant interviews to publicize her role in it.

The film itself was moderately successful, but the soundtrack album was a huge hit. In addition to containing great live versions of Ronstadt's "Tumbling Dice" and "Poor Poor Pitiful Me," the two-record set soundtrack album also featured several of the hottest recording rock and roll artists of the era, including the Doobie Brothers, Boston, Tom Petty and the Heartbreakers, James Taylor, the Eagles, Queen, Dan Fogelberg, Billy Joel, Boz Scaggs, Bob Seger, Steve Miller, and Foreigner. Steely Dan performed the title song, placing the single version of "FM" in the Top Forty. The album became a huge Top Ten hit during the summer of 1978, selling a million copies. It was one of the first big Platinum rock and roll soundtrack albums, and the exposure that it brought to Linda only further validated her position in the record business as the number-one female singer in the business. Linda was the only woman to be featured on the *FM* soundtrack, which illustrates her unique ability to rock and roll with the best of her male counterparts, and to excel like no other female artist of the entire decade.

Reviewing the film *FM*, *People* magazine found that "It's not much of a plot, but what the movie lacks there, it makes up for in fast pacing and wall-to-wall soundtrack." However, they especially praised Linda Ronstadt, by claiming that she "proves as exciting on camera as she is on record."

In June and July of that year, Linda sang background vocals on an album made by her friend, Nicolette Larson. Larson had landed a recording deal on Warner Brothers Records, and she recorded her debut album, *Nicolette*. Ronstadt is heard on three of the cuts: "Mexican Divorce," "Give a Little," and "Come Early Mornin'." The first single off of the album hit Number 15 on the LP chart and was certified Gold. Ronstadt loved to add her "Midas touch" to her friend's records.

While *FM* was playing in theaters across the country, Linda, Peter Asher, and her band were at the Sound Factory studios in Los Angeles, working on her final album of the 1970s, *Living in the U.S.A.* Utilizing the same eclectic formula of *Simple Dreams,* this album was totally devoid of country and western songs. Instead, Linda concentrated on rock classics like Chuck Berry's "Back in the U.S.A.," Doris Troy's "Just One Look," and Elvis Presley's "Love Me Tender." From the Motown catalogue she chose Smokey Robinson's sexy "Ooh Baby Baby," from Warren Zevon's debut album she borrowed "Mohammed's Radio," and J. D. Souther provided the somber and romantic "White Rhythm Blues." Two of the most diverse cuts on the album were Oscar Hammerstein's "When I Grow Too Old To Dream" and Elvis Costello's new wave ballad "Alison."

Riding high on the peak of her popularity, Linda hit Number One on the album charts with the Double Platinum *Living in the U.S.A.* On the singles charts she scored with "Back in the U.S.A." and "Just One Look," but it was "Ooh Baby Baby" that provided the LP's one Top Ten smash.

According to Linda, the recording work that she had done in January with Dolly Parton and Emmylou Harris had forced her to hit notes that she didn't know she could reach vocally. She felt that singing with them had improved her overall performance on the *Living in the U.S.A.* album. "There were times when I would have to match Emmy's vibrato and Dolly's intonation in order to blend, finding out that I could make noises with my throat that I did not normally make. I was able to apply it on this album and really got my voice up another notch."

Discussing her song choices on the *Living in the U.S.A.* album, Linda claimed, "I pick them because something will happen in my life and I want to describe that situation, and it sets off a tape recorder in my head of a song. Peter [Asher] heard this Elvis Costello record and said, 'This is a hit song for somebody.' I really loved the song, but I didn't see any way that I could do it. Then I met a girl like Alison, who became a real good friend to me. So I change it around a little bit in the gender — I made it like I heard the girl had run off with some guy. And I was hoping that she would stay away from my particular property. Whereas with him, it's kind of a vague love song. I reduce it to friendship, but that described this girl. I had a reason to sing it, so then I *had* to do 'Alison.' "

Explaining the recording process for this particular album, she said, "Some of the things we get on the first take. There's a Little Feat tune on the album called 'All That You Dream,' we'd worked all afternoon on. Things kept breaking and we got a track and we just knew we could play it better, and so we left it there and we'd worked the arrangement out all very carefully, and the next morning, while they were running it down — before Peter and I even got there — they cut a track. I came in and listened to it and I went, 'That's it. That's it. It's great!' I put a vocal on it and that was the one we used. And then there were some of them like 'Back in the U.S.A.' where we just walked in and did it on the first take, you know, we just played it once and it was fine.

"We try to think of it in terms of pacing," Ronstadt said, discussing the selections included on her albums. "We always try not to do oldies, and we always wind up doing them, because there is always a song I want to do. 'Ooh Baby Baby' came about because I just wanted to do a song with saxophone player David Sanborn so badly. I went to this stupid Hollywood party, and I heard that song and I went into a dream. I loved the song so much that I was just transported by it."

"Back in the U.S.A." was another song that Linda became reacquainted with by chance. "That came about because I was driving around in the car with Glenn Frey. Glenn Frey is the best single source of material for singers. He's got stacks and stacks of cassettes he's made of all these different things. We were driving and I looked at him and went, 'Remember when we used to sit around the Troubadour bar and go, "Oh it's so horrible and I can't get a record deal." ' We were so broke and so miserable and we'd feel sorry for ourselves and we were so precious about it. Then all of a sudden I looked at him and I went, 'Boy, life's really tough. We're going off to ski and all this money in our pockets, we're going to have a good time and we've got great music on the tape player.' 'Back in the U.S.A.' came on right then and I just went, 'God, that would be a great song to sing. I think I'll do that one.' "

At the time, Linda observed, "To me there's a real resurgence of patriotism in this country. We all went through trying to criticize it in the '60s, but then everybody went, 'Well, we're going to go looking around the rest of the world. It must be better over here and it must be better over there.' But everybody's coming here, so I guess it must be best here. I like that line about 'Anything you want we got it right here in the U.S.A.' or 'Looking hard for a drive-in, searching for a corner cafe where hamburgers sizzle on the open grill night and day and the jukebox jumping with records back in the U.S.A.!' I mean Chuck Berry really knew how to write folk poetry!"

Another song included on the album that ranked among Linda's favorites was Warren Zevon's "Mohammed's Radio."

"I think that's an amazingly well-written song," she said. "I went through that once with a friend metaphor by metaphor, and I really see it. I always think things are about myself, they have to be about me. When I was little, the radio was like a drug for me. It was my complete escape and my whole life. [Zevon] uses the metaphor of Mohammed's radio like . . . it's omnipresent and it's powerful, almost godlike. He used Mohammed instead of Jesus or Buddha. He just happened to pick Mohammed, I guess . . . The first verse deals with the problems of living and then, 'Don't it make you want to rock and roll.' When it comes right down to it, I'd rather just turn on the radio and crank it up loud and just get off on the music. And the last verse says, 'Oh, everybody is desperate trying to make ends meet, work all day, still can't pay the price of gasoline and meat.' And there's one line you just have to yell: 'Alas, their lives are incomplete.' It's like a double twist. It's curious to me that they're incomplete. I feel compassionate, but at the same time I feel like, 'Boy those dumb slobs. Isn't that terrible?' And then the last verse, 'You've been up all night just listening for his drum, hoping that the righteous might just come.' And I remember when I was little, I'd just wait all night long until the moment when something wonderful comes on the radio that's just better than anything else. And you're inspired all over again."

Reflecting the latest fad to sweep the country in the late '70s, Linda wore a pair of roller skates, short shorts, and a satin baseball jacket on the cover of *Living in the U.S.A.* On the inside of the LP's "gate fold" cover, Ronstadt is seen reaching for a bag of potato chips at an outdoor diner, while Peter Asher and the band sit at little tables littered with plastic cups and catsup containers. The artwork suggested the breezy, goodtime feeling that most of the music on the album contained.

When the LP was released, in September 1978, it was immediately certified Gold and Platinum. Asylum shipped an initial order of 2.1 million copies to the stores, and it sold like hotcakes. By the first of November, it was the Number One album in the country.

While Linda's fans snapped up the album instantly, some of the reviews were mixed. She had reached that point in her vast popularity where people start taking pot shots at anything with a winning formula. According to *The Los Angeles Times* review, "Given the ingredients, *Living in the U.S.A.* shouldn't work. But the album does. It's her most inviting collection of tunes since *Prisoner in Disguise* in 1975. The themes aren't as deeply personal as last year's *Simple Dreams* collection, but the arrangements are crisper, the vocals more enchanting, and the overall tone more accessible . . . The new album's blend of rock, pop, country, folk and R&B strains encompasses America's most appealing pop music forms, which helps explain Ronstadt's wide-ranging popularity."

People magazine pointed out that, "Linda has indeed emerged as the undisputed Empress of Pacific Coast Street Life, and the range of her eclectic pipes justifies her reign . . . Any singer who can provide a rock 'n' roll rush with the Chuck Berry classic 'Back in the U.S.A.' and sweep right into the tender 1934 Romberg/Hammerstein lullaby When I Grow Too Old To Dream,' is showing versatility."

Stereo Review exclaimed, "*Living in the U.S.A.* is not only one heck of a good record, but a really heartening sign that Linda Ronstadt is toughening up her act. Growing, even . . . its best moments are as tough and uncompromising as they are surprising, and that's what rock is *supposed* to be about . . . Get up there on that pedestal, Linda!"

Creem shouted, "Ronstadt Revs Up Another Hit!" But *Rolling Stone* declared, "Nobody's perfect . . . Linda Ronstadt strains herself." The latter review claimed that she lost the feeling of the music, by complaining, "Linda Ronstadt's concentration is so single-minded that she often misses entirely the wit and irony of her material . . . Pulling up roots is fine and dandy, but producer Peter Asher lays no new ones down, so *Living in the U.S.A.* jerks from cut to cut." Yet, the review did admit that, " 'Alison' is an understated masterpiece that ranks with Linda Ronstadt's very finest work."

Regardless of any of the reviews, Linda's *Living in the U.S.A.* album was among the four best-selling discs of her career (along with her *Greatest Hits, Simple Dreams,* and *What's New*). This was to be her last consecutive new studio album to follow the formula that had been employed since *Prisoner in Disguise.* She now had six consecutive Platinum albums, and she was going to spend some time exploring new musical vistas before she returned to the recording studio.

As early as 1977, Linda was already talking about stretching out into different musical vistas. "I'm not going to do rock and roll forever," she claimed. "I want some grace and dignity in my old age. If I continue singing I'll probably settle into the notion of a chanteuse, a cabaret singer, doing something timeless."

"Linda is really enjoying herself right now," Peter Asher said after the release of *Living in the U.S.A.* But he was looking into other arenas for his superstar client. At that point he was already thinking of Broadway and discussing the possibility of producing a "rock musical" starring Ronstadt. "Linda seems interested," he explained, "but it's all vague at this point."

In the summer of 1978, the Rolling Stones released their Platinum album *Some Girls* and embarked on an American concert tour. Since Linda and Mick Jagger had become friends, she hadn't seen the Rolling Stones perform live, so she was looking forward to catching them when they played in the Los Angeles area. According to her, "I went to an Anaheim concert, but I couldn't see any of it 'cause everyone stood up. I never got to see the show, and I was real disappointed, so I flew to Tucson just to go. It was a wonderful show. I loved it and I got so many great ideas."

In the middle of the concert at Tucson's Community Center, Jagger announced to the audience, "Now we're going to have a hometown girl sing with us and give her a chance." With that, Linda Ronstadt bounded out onto the stage to join Mick and the Rolling Stones in a duet version of "Tumbling Dice." The crowd went crazy to see Jagger and Ronstadt performing together.

"I loved it!" exclaimed Ronstadt after her duet with Mick. "I didn't have a trace of stage fright. I'm scared to death all the way through my own shows. But it was too much fun to get scared. He's so silly on-stage, he knocks you over. I mean you have to be on your toes or you wind up falling on your face. He's amazing. Mick just scolds all the time, you better do right: he's usually right when he scolds."

Naturally, the press jumped on the subject of Ronstadt and Jagger, and there were all sorts of rumors about them having an affair. In actuality, ever since the success of *Heart Like a Wheel,* and all of the initial publicity that Linda received, the mere mention of her name was usually followed by either an update on her lovelife, or by her views on sex, dating, and/or marriage.

During this time period, she was not only linked with Mick Jagger, but she also dated comedian Steve Martin, and the son of the president of the United States, Chip Carter. However, her most frequent boyfriend was the equally as visible governor of California, Jerry Brown.

Linda would usually disclaim all of the rumors about her lovelife and refused to discuss the particulars of her personal affairs. "Look, if I did all the things that the newspapers said I did, I would have to be cloned. There are simply not enough hours in the day," she claimed. "I worry about the press discouraging candor. It is encouraging people to be secretive about their lives. Just to sell copy, the press distorts and flat-out makes up things. I'm more quiet out of self-protection."

After recording *Hasten Down the Wind,* Linda broke up with Albert Brooks and lived alone in her Malibu house for nearly a year, becoming adjusted to the newfound fame. "Nine months and still not a man in sight," she reported to *People* magazine in 1976.

*Two crazes swept America in 1978: roller skating and Linda Ronstadt's
Multi-Platinum album,* Living in the U.S.A. *She earned an estimated
$12 million that year.*

(Photo: Jim Shea/Mark Bego Archives)

According to Ronstadt, "At first I didn't get married because I was busy getting my career going. Then it was because I hadn't seen enough of the world. I thought I might meet the Man in England, for example. I treated it like shopping for shoes. Now I realize I didn't get married because I just didn't want to. My mobility was more important. As the years have passed, I've come to feel that maybe I never will get married."

To fight off the feeling of day-to-day loneliness, Linda asked a songwriter friend of hers named Adam Mitchell to move into her Malibu house with his six-year-old daughter, Kirsten. She said at the time, "It's completely platonic. That's why it's so comfortable. We can talk about his girlfriends and my boyfriends as close friends."

She gained a reputation as rock and roll's most eligible woman, claiming in 1977 that, "This is a date year, just like high school. I have lots of boyfriends, but it's mostly rush and thrill." She spent the majority of the year enjoying her independence. According to her, she "cruised around and looked at all kinds of lives. I met astronauts, TV people, doctors, politicians. I discovered there was something more to life than the music business, and different kinds of men than musicians. I used to think they were the only men I could get involved with. They aren't exactly the most trustworthy lot."

Although she claimed, "I'm now ready for the advanced emotions, for the more profound feeling beyond the blush of romance — a strong committed relationship," she remained free to play the field. Spending so much time on the road during her concert tours was a big obstacle that she had to confront.

"There are still problems, in terms of the loneliness you have to deal with," she explained. "When we're out on the road, some hot-looking chick will come into the room and they [her band members] can get that charge. I mean, they can go home with a different chick every night. Men do that. I don't. What if I went to bed with every cute boy who came into my dressing room, for God's sake? What would that say about me? . . . I think men are more naturally inclined to promiscuity than women. I don't know if it's biological or what, but men are able to depersonalize sex a lot more than women, and still remain nice persons. The guys I know on the road are holy terrors, but I love them."

One has to keep in mind that these were the promiscuous 1970s — the decade before anyone had ever heard of AIDS. Sex was so free and easy, and lasting relationships were the rarity. Even so, Linda claimed, "I don't like to go to bed with strangers. I like to know what kinds of books they read. I wouldn't be interested in someone who had a groupie mentality."

She was the first to admit that she was more interested in dating men who were also celebrities. They were the type of people who also understood the game of fame, and the pressures of being in the public eye all of the time. "It would be very odd if it turned out that I had had a long relationship with a dentist. I mean, I meet famous people. I tend to have relationships with people I admire, who tend to be successful. I mean, who are you going to get a crush on? Somebody you don't admire? Why would you want to go out with a loser? What would you talk about? How I lost my job last week? But I have lots of friends who are successful and not famous. It's just that when I go out with someone else who is famous, it gets written about — it makes better reading."

What is it that excites her? "I have to get chased a whole lot. I need a lot of convincing, especially if he's famous. I don't want it to seem that I'm standing in line. I have to be convinced he is more interested in me than any of the other women interested in him. I have to know that I'm the exceptional one. I go out with a guy either for a night or for a year. I rarely have boyfriends for less than a year. Some just move over to friendships."

She admitted that she likes to know the score, from the very start of any of her relationships. "You have to explain what the nature of the relationship is, going in," she claimed at the time. "Are we going steady? If you don't promise something that you don't have any intention of delivering, you can move on and not leave bitterness behind. I never felt obligated to be physically faithful to anybody or to be in any way emotionally entwined with just one man. I have never made that promise. I have never had a ring around my neck or an engagement ring or a wedding ring on my finger. If I did make that promise, I suppose I would be mad if I didn't honor it. So I enjoy, and let the other person enjoy, and some of that's sexual."

And how does "love" enter into the picture? According to Ronstadt, "Being in love is the best way to excite the feelings of sexuality. But you can't fall in love with everybody you are hugely, physically attracted to. I think you fall in love once, maybe twice. If you are dumb enough to screw it up the first time or unfortunate enough to lose it and if you're lucky enough to find it again, that's great. Love is a special circumstance. When you fall in love, a whole different set of principles apply. I think shallow relationships are boring. Who wants endless streams of shallow relationships? My relationships are very intense. Whether or not they last five years is totally beside the point. And I don't think my lifestyle is conducive to those kinds of relationships. I don't consider any of my relationships a failure. I think they have all been rather successful. But, boy are they intense!"

When Linda was linked to President Carter's son Chip, the *Na-*

tional Enquirer ran a story that claimed, "Chip Carter is making a fool of himself over singer Linda Ronstadt." In the story it was revealed that she couldn't care less. Chip was estranged from his wife Caron and his two-year-old son. In the story, Linda's mother was quoted as saying, "She can't help it if Chip has a giant crush on her, she doesn't see him that much." Her sister claimed in the same article, "It didn't make any difference to her . . . They happened to be in the same town a couple of times, and perhaps he became interested in her." Insisted gossip columnist Liz Smith, "Chip shows no sign of abating his mad, devastating wipe-out crush on Linda. It is worrying the Carters no end."

However, Linda's most famous and most publicized liaison was with the governor of California, Jerry Brown. Their relationship began with a chance meeting in 1975 at Lucy's El Adobe Restaurant. Although she was leery about lending her name to political candidates, Linda, the Eagles, and Jackson Browne were joined by Brown on stage after a concert in Landover, Maryland, and posed for photos backstage afterward. Linda and Jackson had just finished raising $33,000 at a benefit concert in San Jose to fund Jerry Brown's bid at a California senatorial seat. It wasn't long before the media began to buzz about the rock star and the governor.

Throughout the year, Linda was tight-lipped about her relationship with Brown. The press began to seek them out. When Jerry made it clear that he was interested in entering the 1976 presidential race, there was a lot of speculation about the never-married Brown and the never-married Ronstadt suddenly exchanging vows and ending up in the White House.

They made a controversial couple, to say the least. Jerry's father, Edmund G. ("Pat") Brown, Sr., was the governor of California from 1959 to 1966. He left office when Ronald Reagan defeated him in that election. At first Jerry (who is actually Edmund Gerald Brown, Jr.) showed no interest in following in his father's footsteps. After graduating from high school, he decided upon a life in the priesthood. He spent three and a half years at the Jesuits' Sacred Heart Novitiate. However, he felt that he had "gotten everything possible out of that experience," and moved on to other philosophies. He studied Zen Buddhism, attended Berkeley, and graduated with a degree in Latin and Greek. Later he attended Yale Law School.

During 1976, apart from her social relationship with Brown, Linda at first shied away from actively getting involved with the political arena. "I feel it can be dangerous for me as an artist to get involved with issues, and particularly with candidates," Linda claimed. "But at some point, I feel like I can't *not* take a stand. I think of pre-Hitler Germany, when it was fashionable for the Berliners not to get involved with politics, and meantime, this horrible man took power. But it is difficult for me as a public person. I don't want people to take my word for something because they like my music. That's a danger in itself. I am real aware of my ability to influence impressionable people, and I am reluctant to wield that power. If I am saying things about nuclear power, I want people to go out and learn about it. I don't want them to say 'No nukes!' because Jackson [Browne] and Linda say it. I don't want people to think about issues when they hear my music. I really want them to hook their dreams onto what I am singing. When I'm out in public, I want to be *singing!*"

After the 1976 presidential campaigns were over, and Brown failed to capture enough support to become the Democratic candidate, a lot of the pressure was off of his relationship with Ronstadt. However, when Brown declined living in the $1.3 million governor's mansion that Ronald Reagan had constructed and began using Linda's Malibu beach house as a home base, the speculation heated up again.

Since Brown had previously dated actresses Natalie Wood, Liv Ullmann, and Candice Bergen, there were those who believed that he was just using Ronstadt for further political publicity. Ronstadt claimed that their relationship was quite sincere, and slowly she began showing her support for his campaign aspirations. Brown had his eye on the White House and the 1980 presidential elections, and Linda decided that she had to do her bit to assist him.

"I swore up and down I wouldn't do a benefit for Jerry," Linda was later to explain, after hosting a $1,000 per couple fund-raising dinner at her home, and a San Diego benefit concert for him. "The artistic reason is the selfish reason, but also, I always thought that if I did a concert for Jerry, it would be perceived by the public as him trying to use me. They would say, 'I told you all along: The basis of their relationship is that she can do concerts for him and make him a lot of money.' But there is no way for me to stay neutral. If I won't support him, and I know him best, it looks like an attack. I would like him to be able to speak his ideas. I think they are really important and good and, for the most part, he's right. It's so hard for me, not only as a public figure but also as someone who believes in him, cares about him, is close to him and is on his side. I want to be on his side."

When she hosted another fund-raising concert, this time at the Aladdin Hotel in Las Vegas, he was in the audience and she sang the song "My Boyfriend's Back" to him. In 1979 Brown was talking about running for president again, and Linda was again torn. What if he actually did end up in the White House . . . what would her role be in the picture?

Linda's mother, Ruthmary Ronstadt, said at the time, "Linda has told me that no one in their right mind would want to be in the White House. I don't think there is any way Linda would like him to take on that horrendous job."

"A lot of us were naive in the beginning about doing benefits," said Linda. Speaking about other rockers who stood behind other candidates, she explained, "We tended just to take people's word for things. I don't now. I read newspapers, periodicals. I'm not saying I'm an expert, but I am a hell of a lot better informed than before and better informed than the average person. I think my opinion is informed enough to put out there."

After much thought on the subject, she finally decided that she had to take a stand. "I'm going to take a lot of heat for it, but I'm ready," she said, when things were gearing up for the 1980 elections. "I just don't feel that any of the alternatives are as good as Jerry, and that's what it comes down to. Look at it this way: the Eagles and I, in a way, represent the anti-nuclear concern. Westinghouse is heavily invested in nuclear power. A candidate like Ronald Reagan can go to Westinghouse and ask for lots of money and despite the $1,000 limit, Westinghouse can commandeer huge sums of money. Plus, it can hire lawyers and take out huge ads in the newspapers and continue to brainwash the American public about the safety of nuclear power, which I think is a lie. Jerry Brown can't go to Westinghouse. He can only go to the individuals. He has no corporate financing for his ideology. A candidate like Jerry Brown can't go to Arco for money for solar power, because it's not in the company's interest. I believe it's in the public interest to have a candidate who is interested in furthering technology like solar power and protecting us from things like nuclear power."

Speaking at the time about other celebrities who became heavily involved in politics, Linda proclaimed, "Artists like Jane Fonda, Joan Baez, Vanessa Redgrave, I say, 'More power to them!' They are sticking out their necks. I don't particularly want to stick out *my* neck. But, I don't see how I can *not* take a stand. It's dangerous territory for me, that's for sure. But if Frank Sinatra is going to do a benefit for Reagan, then I guess I have to do a benefit for Jerry."

Linda Ronstadt had lived a wild rock and roll existence since she had moved to California in the 1960s. Several sources talked about Ronstadt's experimentations with recreational drugs, and she even admitted to having indulged in such mood-altering activities. However, when Jerry Brown came closer to entering the 1980 presidential campaign, Linda did what she could to erase any evidence of her past wild life. She claimed in *Playboy* magazine, "I've never taken drugs, not even an aspirin." However, other magazines did what they could to present the other side of the story. In 1979 *The Star* headlined a feature about

Ronstadt with: "Rock Star Linda's Trip From Misery and Drugs to White House Doorstep." This did not help Jerry's campaign.

Entertainment reporter Marcy MacDonald recalled attending a Fourth of July party at the Malibu home of entrepreneur Max Palevsky and running into Linda and Jerry. MacDonald's date at the party was publisher-turned-politician Hamilton Fish, who introduced her to Ronstadt and Brown. According to her, Linda and the governor had apparently just had an argument, and Jerry left the party in a huff. Minutes later, MacDonald ran into Ronstadt in the ladies room. "Ronstadt was upset — smoking and pacing," she said. "Warren Beatty suddenly popped in, introduced himself, and dragged Linda out of the 'loo' and into the limelight. Rejoining the party, I was re-introduced to Linda and Warren by my date. We then proceeded to the 'A' table to join [agent] Sue Mengers and Jack Nicholson. Dinner was announced, and we all went to graze at the buffet table. After everybody returned to the table with full plates, Warren noticed that Linda hadn't budged. 'Linda, want me to get you something to eat?' he asked. In an obviously foul mood, Linda replied, 'Just drugs and coffee.' Both were abundant, but neither was exactly what Linda wanted, so after a couple of tolerant moments, she departed, taking off down Pacific Coast Highway in the direction of the little Governor."

The height of the media coverage of Ronstadt and Brown came in 1979, when she joined him on a trip to Africa. Although they tried to keep the event a secret, the press followed the famous pair into the wilds of "the dark continent." Wherever they went — Kenya, Nairobi, Tanzania, and Monrovia — the press was right there with them.

The "secret" trip turned out to be the media event of the season. The April 30, 1979, issue of *People* magazine made the event into a huge cover story entitled "Ronstadt & The Guv — What Next?" The sub-headline on the cover read, "His safari with the rock singer could ground his White House ambitions."

Linda was getting wary of the media's coverage of her every movement, and the African fiasco was the height of her disgust with the press. "I asked if I could go," she recalled of the infamous trip. "I had been on the road for a real long time and when I got home, the trip had already been planned and I wanted to go. Africa is a real interesting place, and someplace I wouldn't go alone, because it's too strange to me. I never dreamed it would be O.K. At first I didn't even get an answer. Then I said, 'Oh, come on, take me.' He said 'Yes.' I didn't tell anyone, not even my mother. Then my publicist, Paul Wasserman, called and he said he kept hearing from newsmen that I was going to Africa and that he just wanted to warn me that the press was going to be on my tail. I said, 'O.K., forget it.' That was the afternoon before we were supposed to go."

However, she decided that she was not going to be intimidated by anyone. "I thought, 'Why am I surrendering to these people? I am being threatened out of a good time.' Then I thought, 'I can go and not have anything to do with the press. I am not going in an official capacity, and I am not working. I am just going as a sight-seer and all I have to do is stay out of the way. If anybody asks me a question, I just don't have to answer. If anybody wants to take my picture, I'll just turn the other way. It's nobody's business what I am doing.' Also, I was convinced that once we got there, we could ditch the reporters."

Not only did the press find out that Linda was going to accompany Jerry Brown on a trip to Africa, but they also found out what flight they were going to be on and booked tickets on it. "I didn't expect the press to commandeer the entire First Class section of the plane!" she exclaimed. "We went 'Coach,' and the press was furious with us. They saw this as a clear-cut case of our being uncooperative. They kept coming back, trying to interview us. I wasn't talking. The stewardess kept trying to prevent them from taking our picture while we slept. God! If anybody took my picture on a plane, no matter who I was, I would consider that they had no right to do that. There was an actual struggle in the aisle between two photographers for a certain spot and someone clunked this nine-year-old kid on the head with a camera. The pilot had to come back and tell them to stay in their seats. The press were fools. It was an outrage that they would act like what we were doing was hostile to them. They accused us of a publicity stunt. It was the press who needed a publicity stunt, not us.

"It got worse," she continued. "We had this very loose schedule and went to countries and cities we hadn't planned to go to. Then the press came up to us and said they would like us to go on a safari; that would make a good story and good pictures. We had *no plans* to go on a safari! One day we were in the desert, looking at a United Nations desertification project, and a baby camel walked by and it was just the cutest thing and I wanted desperately to pet it. I barely got one finger on it, when all the cameras went popping and the camel ran away. The pictures went back to the States saying, 'Ronstadt on safari in Kenya.' I was no more on safari than I was on a rock and roll tour!"

In another incident, a photographer jumped into Linda's car, scaring her half to death. "The press constantly threatened us. They pounded on my hotel door and said, 'If you don't cooperate, we're going to give you a really hard time; we are going to follow you until we get the pictures we want.' One day I was walking with a friend from my hotel to the car and a photographer jumped into the car. Now, if I were going from a concert hall to my car, and a fan jumped into the car, I would be scared. I would think that person was trying to hurt me. My friend pushed this photographer out of the car, and was scratched all the way down his arm. I should have felt totally within my rights, if someone jumped on me and clawed my arm, to turn around and relieve that person of his front teeth. But, see, if you do anything like that, the photographers scream at you and tell you that you're preventing them from doing their job."

Whether or not the press coverage of Linda and Jerry's African trip cost him his bid at running for president is hard to say. It certainly didn't help his chances in the political race in 1980. Regardless of her political aspirations for him, Ronstadt was relieved that she and Jerry weren't pushed toward the White House. With regard to her possibly ending up as the First Lady of the nation, Linda laughed, "It's a funny thought. But if I thought about it seriously, I would probably die laughing. I like my job — and the pay is a lot better."

As the 1970s came to a close, Linda had made an indelible mark on the music scene. She was not only the highest-paid female rock star of the decade, but she suddenly found herself in a strong and unique position in the business. She had latched onto a formula for creating Multi-Platinum albums, and she had capitalized on it with the maximum degree of success. The music scene was beginning to change in 1979, and the '80s were obviously going to usher in several changes.

Ronstadt was ready to start the new decade with a new look and a new attitude. In November 1979, she was dating Brett Hudson, of the group the Hudson Brothers, and she cut off her long hair. According to Linda, "Kenny Edwards said he hadn't heard any music that made him want to change his hair style, and I thought, 'Well, if I cut my hair, it might inspire me.' "

Arriving at the Roxy on Sunset Boulevard to catch the B-52s, on the arm of Hudson, Ronstadt debuted her short-cropped "punk" look. To her it signified a break with the past, a time to move on. She was tired of being predictable, and she was already plotting to reveal several surprises that she had carefully hidden up her sleeves.

In 1979 Linda cut her hair short and adopted a punk look for her new wave rock album, Mad Love.

(Photo: Richard Dunkley/Mark Bego Archives)

From New Wave To Broadway   6

T
he face of the American music scene was changing in 1979. It was a "boom" year for the record business, with two diametrically opposing musical trends dominating the airwaves. The two factions were the slick beat-dominated "disco," and the stripped-down guitar and drums sound of "new wave" or "punk" rock.

Disco had eclipsed rhythm and blues and was a natural path for singers like Diana Ross ("The Boss"); Ashford and Simpson ("Found a Cure"); the Bee Gees ("Tragedy"); Rod Stewart ("Do Ya Think I'm Sexy?"); Barbra Streisand ("The Main Event"); Cher ("Take Me Home"); and Earth, Wind and Fire and the Emotions ("Boogie Wonderland"). It had also gone on to create its own set of new superstars, like Village People, Donna Summer, Gloria Gaynor, Chic, and the Ritchie Family.

As a backlash to the dance beat of disco, and the electric guitar and synthesizer sound of rock mega-groups like Electric Light Orchestra and Journey, a new faction had emerged. In an attempt to put the "rock" back into rock and roll, in New York, London and Los Angeles new wave and punk bands were headlining small rock clubs and landing themselves recording deals and a cult of followers. From the L.A. club scene came the Knack, from London came Elvis Costello and the Attractions, and from a seedy little dive called CBGB's in the Bowery of New York City came Blondie.

In addition to CBGB's in New York City, Linda Ronstadt's old haunt, the Troubadour, became *the* west coast new wave showcase club for the hottest unsigned punk rock acts. The Troubadour had been the premier club in Hollywood during the late '60s and early '70s, when Ronstadt discovered the individual members of the Eagles there. It had hit a slump in the mid-'70s, but in 1979 it began to spring back. According to Doug Weston, the owner of the club, it was again being looked to as the "charm school for rising rock and rollers." Said Weston at the time, "It is possible that there are 1,000 or more musicians playing original music in unsigned bands and making a living off their club gigs."

A hot batch of new albums was being released by the cream of the new wave crop in '79, including *Get the Knack* by the Knack, *Armed Forces* by Elvis Costello and the Attractions, Blondie's *Eat to the Beat, Outlandos d'Amour* by the Police, and self-titled albums by the B-52s and the Clash. Several other groups were snapped up by record companies looking for "the next big thing." The Motels, Devo, Code Blue, Jules and the Polar Bears, the Bottles, and Storm were all quickly signed to recording deals, in hopes that they would produce hits, and that the so-called "new wave" of rock and roll would continue to gain momentum.

In addition, that autumn a new female singer arrived on the scene, releasing her debut album, *In the Heat of the Night,* and her first hit single, "Heartbreaker." Her name was Pat Benatar, and she was discovered singing — among other songs — a reggae version of "Stairway To Heaven" in a tiny club in New York City called Tramps. She proved right from the start that she could sing blistering rock and roll right alongside the tough boys of the punk world.

Making a most unique move, Blondie, and their sexy lead singer Debbie Harry, became the first of the new wave groups to take the best of both worlds. They mixed a punk attitude and a disco beat to produce the huge million-selling smash "Heart of Glass." Harry and Benatar represented the new breed of female rock singers who were destined to enter the 1980s with their hit-making machinery working in "overdrive."

In 1979 Linda Ronstadt took time off from the recording studio, and she began to check out what was going on in the out-of-the-way rock clubs in Los Angeles. Hearing what Debbie Harry, Pat Benatar, and Martha Davis of the Motels were up to, Linda decided that she was not going to be outdone. It was in mid-1979 that she came to the conclusion that she was going to "chuck" the steel guitars and the self-pitying ballads, and she was going to ride into the next decade on the hard-edged new wave of rock and roll.

Before she turned her back on the country/rock sound that she had pioneered in the '70s, Ronstadt made a final pair of performances in that genre. First she recorded a duet on the title cut of the Nitty Gritty Dirt Band's 1979 album *An American Dream*. The song was released as a single, and went on to become a country and pop hit for the group. Then mid-year, Linda and Emmylou Harris joined Dolly Parton on stage during one of Parton's Los Angeles concert dates. After that, Linda shifted gears and dropped out of the contemporary country and western scene.

While Asylum Records pulled hit singles from Linda's *Living in the U.S.A.* album, Ronstadt took a sabbatical from recording. The *Living in the U.S.A.* LP had been completed on July 3, 1978, and she didn't return to the studio until October 24, 1979. She said she needed the time off to recharge her batteries: "I was coasting on material that had evolved from a previous season. For a while there, the music was like a noise bludgeoning my eardrums, so I did a lot of traveling. I went to Europe with my mother. I cut my hair. I went to Africa with my boyfriend. And, I didn't go to any of those places for musical reasons."

At first, she didn't have any interest in the music scene at all. She occupied herself with "a lot of reading, riding, playing with my dogs. But then I started getting really panicky. I thought there was something terribly wrong with me, because I didn't have any new ideas for the album. I got real desperate," she remembered.

"I visited some of my musician friends. I sat down with Wendy Waldman and we wrote a song. I saw Kenny Edwards, and we stayed up all night singing. I went and saw Emmylou Harris. Then I went to every club in town and saw a lot of new stuff and went to concerts and saw people like Bette Midler. She is an awesome talent I think we've taken for granted. All the juices started flowing again. I realized that a lot of the problems with lack of inspiration — my own and others' — were because of our own cynicism. You know, the idea of ushering in a new fashion in the music business, like they do in clothes, just isn't a natural way for art to function. A lot of new stuff and talent is being taken for granted out there. I just hadn't been looking hard enough. So I really needed to have that rest. I got a chance to put myself in perspective with the rest of the world. I found out that music isn't the center of the universe. But, finally, it became boring to be away from the music.

"It is a strange time for all of us in the music business," she said at the time. "The music is oddly lacking in different kinds of sensibilities. In the '60s, there was such a variety; the delicate, romantic approach of Donovan, Motown, the Rolling Stones, the Beatles, all the country stuff. I like it when it's all messed up like that. Right now there is a whole lot of disco and it's just not the kind of music that inspires you, or that gives you a personality to get involved with. The '70s was a polished-up version of a lot of the things coming out of the '50s and the '60s. I think we refined them past their prime; like race horses that have been overbred — they run fast but their bones break.

"What interests me is that for the first time, American pop music doesn't seem to make a bow to black music — except reggae, which is Third World music. Pop music has always been largely based on American black music: jazz, blues, gospel. And for a while, it was very much the thing for white musicians to be able to play with heavy black affectations; for instance, putting the rhythm emphasis way back behind the beat. If you could do that and keep the groove, that was a real hip thing to do, and now it is the opposite. The grooves are very rushed and fast and the emphasis seems to be very much on top of the beat. And the moves I see are very white. I saw the B-52s and their moves. Well, they look like someone in a Holiday Inn disco, sort of Ohio housewife dancing — very white."

Linda's experimentations in new areas had been precluded on her 1978 *Living in the U.S.A.* album, when she recorded Elvis Costello's "Alison." When it came time to pick new material for her 1980 *Mad Love* album, she decided that new wave — and particularly Costello tunes — suited the way that she felt at the time.

"I'm more excited about this album than about any other one I've done. It was like turning a corner, but everything felt so natural," she explained about *Mad Love* and the new sound that she had shopped around for. "There is almost no overdubbing. This album doesn't follow what seems to be my prescribed pattern: a J. D. Souther song, a Lowell George song, a couple of oldies, kick in the ass, and put it out there. In this album, almost all of the songs are new. It's much more rock and roll, more raw, more basic."

When she went into Record One studios, in Los Angeles in October 1979, Ronstadt brought with her a new band comprising several of her musician friends. Dan Dugmore and Russell Kunkel had been part of her *Living in the U.S.A.* band. Keyboard player Bill Payne was a member of the group Little Feat, which had temporarily broken up when Lowell George suddenly died of a drug overdose on June 29, 1979. Guitar players Mark Goldenberg and Peter Bernstein were from the Los Angeles new wave group the Cretones, and background vocals were provided by Ronstadt's friends, including Nicolette Larson, Andrew Gold, Kenny Edwards, Rosemary Butler, and Waddy Wachtel.

The band she assembled for this album achieved "a great trashy drum sound," she said. Stripped down to bare basics, Ronstadt's music struck a new attitude. It had an aggressive — almost cynical — bite to it. She admitted, "There is definitely violence in the new stuff. I'm looking around at the new music, and searching for a helmet or a hard hat!"

She was certain that she was making the right moves with her new punk haircut, and her stronger rock and roll stance. "I didn't think I sang 'Different Drum' or 'Heat Wave' particularly well," she explained. "I was really on the fence about those two, but the public certainly didn't respond the same way. I'm sure the songs on *Mad Love* are the right songs for me."

Musician and songwriter Will Grega recalls seeing Ronstadt hanging out in the rock clubs near the campus of the University of Southern California (USC) in early 1979. "I was working at a place called Mike's Munchies, on Exposition Avenue and 21st Street in downtown L.A. The house band there was the Cretones. They were there every weekend — Thursday, Friday and Saturday nights. It was a restaurant with a stage. You walked through, you got your sandwich, and you sat in a booth. There was an upstairs dining area, with barstools overlooking the stage. That's where Linda Ronstadt liked to sit, up there on one of the stools, where she could watch everything down below. She would come in on weekends, and she would check out the bands — especially the Cretones. She liked what she saw, and that's how she got hooked up with them. One night she even got up on stage and sang with them. It was an incredible event!"

She was actively searching for material for her next album. Ultimately, most of the songs on her *Mad Love* album were drawn from two songwriters: Elvis Costello, and Mark Goldenberg of the Cretones. The trio of Goldenberg compositions she recorded — "Justine," "Cost of Love," and "Mad Love" — were all included on the Cretones' debut album, *Thin Red Line* (Planet Records, 1980).

"Elvis Costello, who I think is writing the best new stuff around, wrote three of the songs," said Ronstadt, who claimed that she had been crazy about him ever since she recorded "Alison." What did Costello think about her version of the song? "I've never communicated with him directly, but I heard that someone asked him what he thought, and he said he'd never heard it, but that he'd be glad to get the money. So I sent him a message: 'Send me some more songs, just keep thinking about the money.' And he sent me the song 'Talking in the Dark,' and I love it. I also recorded 'Party Girl' and 'Girl's Talk.' "

The *Mad Love* album also included an unlikely song from Neil Young, "Look Out For My Love," which was originally from his 1978 album *Comes a Time* (Reprise Records). The Young version sounds like it was an outtake from the 1972 *Harvest* album, complete with acoustic guitars and sung in a folk ballad fashion.

Since the essence of new wave rock was taken from the guitar and drums sound of pre-1967 rock and roll, it made sense to include two songs from that era. On the *Mad Love* album, Linda offered her own blistering versions of two hits from the '60s music charts: Little Anthony and the Imperials' "Hurt So Bad" (1965) and the Hollies' "I Can't Let Go" (1966).

While she was grappling with her decision about what direction she should head, Linda considered possibly changing her producer, Peter Asher, and her recording engineer, Val Garay. She explained, "Peter, Val and I pretty much felt we had exhausted the possibilities within the confines of the style in which we had made records. I wanted to change. And I wondered if I should change producer and engineer for the new album. When I approached Peter about this, he had to talk to me wearing his manager's hat. He never jealously guarded his role as producer. He encouraged me to think freely of all the possibilities. Then I realized that the desire to stretch was on all our minds, and it seemed to me that to take that step as a team — I would wind up with a much more solid and authentic version of what I wanted. It was the best decision I'd ever made. To adopt a new musical style, just for the sake of it, is like putting on a chicken suit — it looks ridiculous. At the same time, I wanted to change, yet the thoughts of changing producer and engineer made me sweaty under the armpits. We had worked together for so long. But we all wanted to flex our musical muscles on this one."

Linda felt the most comfortable with the Elvis Costello songs that she recorded on the *Mad Love* album. "I love Elvis Costello," she exclaimed. "Elvis Costello just touches my heart. The first thing that you associate with him is anger. But there's also tenderness and a great deal of humor. I've seen him perform, and I was just mesmerized. I saw him at Hollywood High. I was in the back row and I had to stand on my seat through the whole thing. I mean, I wouldn't stand on my seat for anybody.

"I like to take his songs and switch the gender around, because his gender assignments are very flexible," she explained when the album was released. She especially liked the results of the song "Girl's Talk." According to her, "You remember high school girls' talk? It's always gossipy and it's scandalous and it's naughty, *and* there's always some real hard kernel of truth in it. Girls' talk is something you can use to defend yourself, and you can use it to attack with — a flexible kind of weapon. I love that first line in the song: 'There are some things you can't cover up with lipstick and powder.' "

The final recording session for the *Mad Love* album was on January 10, 1980, and the following month it was in the record stores. The whole package was something of a surprise to her legion of country/rock fans. Even the album cover was something of a departure, with Linda depicted in a close-up black and white shot, gossiping on the telephone, obviously illustrating the song "Girl's Talk." The album title and Ronstadt's name appeared on torn pieces of paper, placed at an askew angle, contrasting her slick late '70s image.

From the opening notes of the title track, *Mad Love* kicks off with a decidedly different beat. Russell Kunkel's drumming is crisp and pulsing, Dan Dugmore and Mark Goldenberg's guitar playing wails, and Ronstadt's singing has an accusatory snarl to it. The music, the singing, and Linda's domineering stance in the songs were totally unique.

Costello's "Party Girl" comes the closest to sounding like the typical Ronstadt ballad, but the vantage point of the singer in the song isn't that of the heartbroken victim. This time around she turned the tables to become the girl who can deliver anything but time to the latest object of her affections.

While she comes across a bit strident on several of the cuts, "Hurt So Bad" stands out as an excellent rocker that might have appeared on any of her previous albums. Even with her pleading vocals, and Danny Kortchmar's screaming guitar solo, she keeps the song harmonic and focused. It is interesting to listen to the Cretones' version of "Justine" and "Mad Love," and then to switch back to Linda's interpretation of the same songs. Her singing is more sharp and direct, while their performance has a blasé vagueness to it. "Girl's Talk" is indeed the perfect vehicle for showing off Linda in the setting of girl group giddiness, while maintaining the domineering stance that she takes throughout the album.

When the LP was released, Linda was prepared for the backlash that such a stylistic "about face" would cause among her fans and critics. "I don't know how this album will sell," she admitted in early 1980. "I'm sure I'll be attacked: 'Linda's sold out, trying to be trendy, gotten away from her roots.' But, well, can't worry about what the critics say."

As could be expected, the reviews were mixed. Some people loved it and relished the change, while others abhorred it. On the positive side of things, *The New York Times* called *Mad Love* Ronstadt's "most exhilarating record in ages," and *Billboard* claimed that *"Mad Love* ranks as Ronstadt's most endearing album since *Heart Like a Wheel* and . . . it gives [her] a firm grip on the '80s." Even the usually snide rock publication, *Creem,* exclaimed, "It's so hot it's cool . . . these are ten unusually fine and intelligent rock love songs, and they're sung with feeling . . . she really seizes this moment, and it's about time!"

On the down side, *Rolling Stone* found that "The care and reverence of the performances and arrangements, rather than enhancing the material, unwittingly insult it . . . though *Mad Love* isn't a major exhibition, it's certainly a fascinating failure." *Us* magazine complained that "something essential is missing . . . she either doesn't quite understand what she's singing or that she has absolutely no feeling for the lyric." In their year-end issue, *People* magazine proclaimed *Mad Love* one of 1980's ten "worst" albums. According to their review, "If Lawrence Welk arranged songs by the Clash, they couldn't be any less convincing than Linda's ungainly paean to punk."

Regardless, buoyed by three hit singles, and a lot of curiosity, *Mad Love* hit Number Three on the album chart, and was certified Platinum in May 1980. The singles "How Do I Make You" and "Hurt So Bad" both landed in the Top Ten, and "I Can't Let Go" broke the Top 40 that summer. This gave Linda her seventh consecutive Platinum album (excluding the reissues on Capitol Records), and her seventh and eighth Top Ten hits.

Critics-be-damned, Linda Ronstadt had another hit on her hands. However, the unkindest cut came not from the press, but from her punk poet idol himself—Elvis Costello. As conspicuously published in *Rolling Stone* magazine, Costello denounced Ronstadt's *Mad Love* album as a complete "waste of vinyl."

Linda was too busy hitting the concert trail to be bothered by a bad review, or Costello's snitty swipe. Elvis Costello never had a million-selling recording in his life, and the inclusion of his songs on Ronstadt's *Living in the U.S.A.* and *Mad Love* albums was the closest he would ever come to large-scale commercial success.

In addition to playing a month-long tour of huge venues across America in the spring of 1980, Linda was also in the news for her sudden forays in political activism. On March 29 she performed in front of a huge anti-nuclear rally in Harrisburg, Pennsylvania, on the steps of the state Capitol. However, her most controversial appearance came in Cedar Rapids, Iowa, on April 21 when she headlined a concert at Five Seasons Center.

Originally, the concert date was just going to be another stop on her *Mad Love* tour, but by the time it was over, Linda had the Federal Election Commission conducting a very public investigation of her political alliances. In the March 25 issue of *The Cedar Rapids Gazette,* it was announced that Linda would be donating her proceeds from the concert at the Five Seasons Center to Gary Hart's senatorial bid in Colorado. Jerry Brown's presidential aspirations had already been dashed against the rocks, so Linda decided to shift her financial support to Hart (one of Brown's classmates at Yale).

According to Hart's campaign finance director, Susan Smart, Hart was pleased to have Ronstadt in his corner for the upcoming elections. Said Smart at the time, "We're delighted she's willing to do this for us. We don't have a firm figure on how much money it might involve. Senator Hart probably asked her if she would help out, but then she might have offered to do it. People shouldn't be concerned they're going to hear speeches about Hart. They come to hear Linda. The ad in the paper there carried a disclaimer it was for the Hart committee. She wanted to do something for the campaign, and the tour was unable to come this far west. If it could have been held in Colorado, I'm sure that's where it would have been. It's not unusual for a concert to be held for a candidate in another state."

When questioned, Mike Gebauer, who managed the Five Seasons Center, explained that the cash was Linda's to spend as she pleased, and that the event was not officially a "fund raiser" per se. "Ronstadt can do anything she wants with the money," he said at the time. "We haven't got anything to do with that. She apparently has determined that the proceeds from this one will go to Hart. I'm not sure of the exact figure, but I think she's being paid $50,000 for this one. Beyond that, it is a common practice for the performer to get a percentage of any money brought in over our total expenses. At this point it's impossible to say what that might be."

Problems started brewing before the concert, when Hart's opponent in the election, Republican candidate Howard "Bo" Callaway, accused the Hart organization of "sloppy" dealings in securing Ronstadt's financial support. According to Callaway, the money had not been raised along the proper guidelines drawn up by the Federal Election Commission.

Hal Haddon, who was Hart's campaign manager, made a public statement claiming that Senator Hart could not and would not accept the money that Ronstadt raised. Haddon cited the failure of the concert promoter to properly follow the official Federal Election Commission procedures. Unfortunately, that did not close the case.

After the commission conducted an investigation, they found that Linda had announced to donate her proceeds from the concert, after she had been paid her advance, and that she and her promoter were at fault. They also dismissed the matter as having been done quite innocently, but she did risk a $5,000 fine for going over her allotted $1,000 personal donation limit.

The concert held on April 21 went quite smoothly, although the reviewer for *The Cedar Rapids Register* claimed that there were problems with the sound system. Yet, the review that appeared in the paper admitted that "the crowd of 7,013 at The Five Seasons Center approved of it all, ignoring the glitches and cheering the lustier moments of rock spirit that emerged."

The Cedar Rapids Gazette, reviewing the same show, noted, "Linda Ronstadt appears to be the new record-holder for the most standing ovations given a performer in one 90-minute concert at the Five Seasons Center. She received too many to count." According to that review, "The two songs that brought down the house were 'Hurt So Bad' . . . [and] 'Silver Threads and Golden Needles.' "

Although she was the undisputed "Queen of California Rock" that spring, by summer she had packed her bags and headed to New York City. She was about to make her theatrical debut, and she temporarily put her rock and roll career on hold. In a matter of months, she went from punk to *The Pirates of Penzance*. If this didn't confuse her fans, nothing would!

Linda's move to New York City had been brewing for quite some time. She had been popping in and out of Manhattan to visit friends, to make guest appearances on "Saturday Night Live," and to hang out at the rock clubs since the mid-'70s. She had come to enjoy the energy that the Big Apple had to offer. Her decision to move was hastened by the fact that *Us* magazine had published the address of her Malibu beach house the year before, and the hordes of sightseers who showed up unannounced drove her crazy.

The press had put a real strain on her relationship with Jerry Brown, due to their 1979 African fiasco. Now the media had turned her home into a tourist attraction. In 1980 she regarded her relationship with Brown to be on a "just friends" basis, and her love of L.A. was likewise starting to wane.

"I don't think it's an accident that everybody is starting to drift there," she explained. "Just like it wasn't any accident people started drifting to the West Coast when they did. The business goes in a cycle: New York, L.A., England, London, and back to New York. And as long as I've been in the business, that has never stopped."

Contemplating her shift in coasts, Ronstadt claimed, "L.A. is real comfortable, but things tend to get a little bit too mellow. L.A. doesn't have any cafe society. California sound? It reflected the comfort, but it also reflected an empty sort of disillusioned hollowness." She also felt that moving to New York would add some new sparkle to her lovelife. "I like 'em in ties and three piece suits," she said, admitting that she was actively looking for a new love.

"The thing about New York is that there are so many different top-quality things," she explained. "One time I was in New York and I went to see Baryshnikov dance, and it put something that I badly needed to have back in perspective — which was what a show looks like from the audience's point of view. Because when I go on the road, I have so much stage fright that I tend to ignore the audience completely, and of course, if I think of them I go, 'Ooohhh! They're looking at me!' You can go to New York and see the best ballet, you can see the best jazz, and you can see the best everything . . . And you don't even have to spend any money to be entertained. I love seeing beautiful buildings, and there are beautiful little visual jewels everywhere to see. My favorite thing to do is walk around with somebody that can see things like that. Danny Aykroyd is a great example of that. I mean those guys are like mental photojournalists — Billy Murray is the same way. They're just always gathering data. And I think that the 'Saturday Night' show was really enormously responsible for this sort of renaissance thing that's happening in New York. I think that 'Saturday Night' brought a lot of different kinds of artists together. And it created a focal point. All those people were really into hanging out, so it was something to do. There's a purpose around hanging out."

Linda became very friendly with all of the original cast members of NBC-TV's "Saturday Night Live." On one occasion she had even appeared on the show totally unannounced. It was the week that the U.S. government announced that it was putting a ban on the dietetic artificial sweetener, saccharin. To make fun of the ban, which killed Ronstadt's favorite beverage, Tab, a brief skit was written as a lament to the death of saccharin.

In the skit, Gilda Radner played her established character of Jewish American "Princess" Rhonda Weiss, and she sang a song called "Goodbye Saccharin," backed up by her J.A.P. trio of girlfriends, the Rhondettes (Jane Curtin, Laraine Newman, and Linda Ronstadt). The song expressed the disbelief that a long-time friend as "sweet" as saccharin could do something as vile as giving cancer to laboratory rats!

Linda had a hard time learning the words to the satirical song, until she realized that she would soon have to face life without her favorite diet soda. "I was on 'Saturday Night Live,' " she recalled, "and had to sing a song about saccharin. I just couldn't remember the lyrics, and finally I thought about how miserable I'd be if there weren't any Tab — and I got the song!"

Although she was being romantically linked in the press to singer Brett Hudson and to New York writer Pete Hamill, she claimed that she was "just friends" with both men. Only thirty-four at the time, she publicly proclaimed that, "I just can't get serious about a man under forty." Brett did accompany her to New York City while she was rehearsing *Pirates,* but they soon went their separate ways.

Moving to New York City certainly improved her dating possibilities. According to her, "New York doesn't care about stars, it's just being female in the street. If you had your hair in rollers, mayonnaise smeared all over your face and a rhinoceros on a leash, you'd still get hit on. It's just hard to walk down the street in New York, unless you have a man with you."

How did Ronstadt end up in New York City, playing Mabel in the 1980 production of *Pirates of Penzance*? She recalls that reading the Colette novel *La Vagabonde* made her dream of one day appearing in a musical. "It touched off something I'd always been fascinated with — the idea of being in a little theater, being a music-hall girl," she claimed.

It was *The New York Times* music critic John Rockwell who first recommended that she get in touch with producer Joseph Papp. She remembered: "I wanted to get involved in something that could utilize some of the areas of my singing that I wasn't able to utilize in the pop music field. I wanted it to be within the context of something that I thought would be high quality, with people I thought would be high quality, so that I could learn from them. But not where I had to be the center of attraction, or where I would have to have full responsibility for the show. So when I spoke about this to John Rockwell, he said, 'There's one guy in town you gotta meet, and his name's Joe Papp.' And I'd never heard of him."

Papp knew Linda could sing, but when they met he wanted to know if she could act. "I don't know," was her reply. They resolved to stay in touch with each other, and over the course of time, Papp and director Wilford Leach decided to mount a production of Gilbert and Sullivan's *The Pirates of Penzance,* to be presented in Central Park during the summer of 1980.

Said Papp, "I remember sitting around and saying 'I wonder if Linda Ronstadt could sing in that higher key?' So I called her in California. And she said, 'I'll be in tomorrow.' "

When Papp phoned Ronstadt's Malibu home, it was Jerry Brown who answered the call. "Jerry picked up the phone," recalled Linda, "and he just somehow vaguely knew Gilbert and Sullivan. He told me it was *H.M.S. Pinafore,* because that was the Gilbert and Sullivan *he* knew. And *H.M.S. Pinafore* was the one — coincidentally — that my sister did when she was twelve and I was six. So I knew all the songs. I called them right back and said, 'God, I hear you're going to do "Pinafore." I know all the songs!' And Joe said, 'No, it's not "Pinafore," it's "Pirates of Penznace." ' And I'd never heard of that. So I hopped on a plane and flew back to see what the music was like, to see who the people would be. I was real embarrassed. I had a little patch of pink in the back of my hair, and I had real, real, real short hair, and I said, 'I know I don't look very Victorian, but I *can* look that way.' They showed me

In 1980 Ronstadt moved to New York City to star on Broadway as Mabel Stanley in Gilbert and Sullivan's The Pirates of Penzance. *Rex Smith (left) portrayed Frederic, and Kevin Kline (right) played the Pirate King.*

(Photo: Martha Swope/Mark Bego Archives)

the music. I don't know how to read music, so they taught me a couple of the songs, and I started to sing them, and I had this funny little voice that I hadn't used in a long time, and there was a funny stretch where air would come out, but no voice — like a dotted line. But I knew I could do it!"

After she sang "How Beautifully Blue the Sky" from the score of *Pirates,* Papp knew that Linda would be right for the role of doe-like and innocent Mabel. She recalls that her rapport with Joseph Papp was one of the crucial elements that made him offer her the role, and for her to accept it. "I met Joe Papp, and I liked him right away," she claimed. "The stereotype is that New York theater people are real precious and they think California is a fairy world full of lotus eaters and cuckoo brains. But we had a real good rapport. When he called me with this idea I just said, 'You bet!' "

With that, the deal was set. Although she had earned an estimated $10 million in 1979 as a rock star, she agreed to perform in *Pirates* for the standard salary of $400 a week for the initial Central Park run of the musical.

To sing the part of the winsome Mabel, Linda needed to utilize a higher register than she had developed during her years as a rock star. When she began rehearsals for *Pirates,* in the summer of 1980, she started taking nightly voice lessons to hit the "upper extension" that defines a "coloratura soprano." According to her, "I spent the first twelve to thirteen years of my life trying to be a boy soprano, and the next bunch of years trying to be one of the Ronettes. So, I'm like a boy soprano singing falsetto."

It was a bit of a vocal stretch to progress from singing the growling "Mad Love" to master the lilting lyric control of "Poor Wandering One." Amid rehearsals Ronstadt admitted, "I'm having problems. I'm not going to pretend I'm not having problems with it. I mean, I didn't know how to breathe for this type of singing. So I went to my voice teacher and said, 'Please, how do I do this?' "

One of the most appealing aspects of playing the role of Mabel was the fact that Linda did not have to carry the weight of the play on her shoulders. Although she portrayed the ingenue in the story, and was responsible for several solos amid the light opera, she was one of six major characters in the production: Kevin Kline as the Pirate King, Patricia Routlege as Ruth, Rex Smith as Frederic, George Rose as Major General Stanley, and Tony Azito as the Police Sergeant. All had previous theatrical experience.

Kevin had won a Tony Award for his portrayal of actor Bruce Granit in the 1978 Broadway production of *On the Twentieth Century.* Rex, who was a rock singer like Ronstadt, had been seen on Broadway in the long-running musical *Grease*. George had won a Tony as Best Actor in a Musical for portraying Alfred P. Doolittle in the twentieth anniversary production of *My Fair Lady*, and had played Captain Hook in the 1979 Broadway production of *Peter Pan* with Sandy Duncan. Tony had appeared in the Lincoln Center production of *Threepenny Opera*.

Ronstadt's inclusion in the cast was obviously going to be great for drawing a crowd, but she was the cast's theatrical novice. Instead of making her feel out of place in the cast, she found that the rest of the company made her feel quite comfortable and welcome. Linda commented during rehearsals, "I have no feeling that the people here are resentful or in any way disturbed by my presence here. I have the feeling that they're really on my side, they want me to succeed, and they're real patient about the fact that it's gonna take me a while to learn some of the basic things about staging that they all cut their teeth on ages ago."

During rehearsals, Linda amazed her co-stars with her vocal skills. "When we first went through the score," recalls Kevin Kline, "and Linda sang 'Poor Wandering One,' I started to cry. She was that good!"

Mastering the songs that Mabel sings was just one part of the challenge for Linda. She admitted that her own onstage stiffness during rock and roll concerts had always been one of her major problems. "I've been known to go entire tours literally without saying a word on stage," she said before the play opened. "We'll see what happens. I'm trying to learn how to march around the stage." This time around there was no microphone stand for her to nervously grasp mid-performance.

As the central "lovers" in the plot, Linda and Rex were key figures in the cast. "We're the straight men," explained Ronstadt. "This show is crammed with professionals who play off us. I do have the prettiest songs to sing, but it's not the focal point of the show. If we're wobbly, the rest can march on."

Having Linda in the cast was an important element in bringing a young rock and roll age audience to the park, yet in the original 1879 production of *Pirates of Penzance*, the character of Mabel only had one major solo song to sing. To stretch her time in the spotlight, an additional song was added: "Sorry Her Lot," which was borrowed from Gilbert and Sullivan's other opera of the same era, *H.M.S. Pinafore*. Oddly enough, it was a song that Linda remembered singing when her sister was performing *Pinafore* in Tucson when they were both children.

According to the production's director, Wilford Leach, "Gilbert and Sullivan, in its day, was popular theater. It wasn't refined and distanced. Popular theater now is pop singers, and that's how we got interested in Linda and Rex. I think two of her songs, 'Poor Wandering One' and 'Sorry Her Lot,' are going to be outstanding numbers, and they're done very simply, unadorned, straightforward. We're saying this piece, like certain Shakespeare we've done, has been covered up by tradition. Let's go back to the original text and music and peel away some of the tradition. If people enjoy it, that's more than enough."

Linda looked forward to the play's opening, on July 28, at the open-air Delacorte Theater in the southwest corner of the Great Lawn in Central Park. "It's a very mixed-bag musical, but I think it's gonna work well," she said prior to opening night. "It's gonna draw a stratified audience — my fans, Rex's fans, Gilbert and Sullivan fans, people who just come to the park, and probably a lot of rubberneckers — great! The audience is part of the experience. It's like a big prank on everybody."

Generally, Joseph Papp's New York Shakespeare Festival mounted two or three productions each summer in Central Park, presented for free to the public. The annual festival had been established as a tax-exempt cultural event, beginning in 1954, which, according to its provisional charter, was created "to encourage and cultivate interest in poetic drama . . . and to establish an annual summer Shakespeare Festival." In addition to presenting the best of Shakespeare's works, it had been expanded to encompass other "classics" of the English language as well.

When *The Pirates of Penzance* opened, it was a huge success. "It should prove the most popular summer event in town," claimed Douglas Watt in his review of the show in *The New York Daily News*. And indeed — it did! In his review, Watt found that, "A great deal of attention naturally focused on the appearance of pop idol Linda Ronstadt and, to a slightly lesser extent, pop singer Rex Smith in the romantic leads of Mabel, the principal Stanley's daughter, and Frederic, the pirate apprentice. Both acquit themselves well, but in different ways. Whereas he is the much stronger actor, she is the superior singer, and with training could be a truly accomplished one. Even so, she manages the coloratura passages and other ornamentations of Mabel's role with surprising panache and has no trouble at all in looking adorable."

The Central Park production of *The Pirates of Penzance* was the perfect way to introduce Linda to the legitimate theater. Surrounded by a supportive cast of co-stars, she proved her mettle and drew crowds and rave reviews as well. From the opening week of the production, talk circulated about transferring the play to Broadway.

The play's opening night was quite a heralded event, which drew a star-studded audience. The crowd that first evening in Central Park included Mayor Ed Koch, Jackie Onassis, Mike Nichols, Neil Simon, Marsha Mason, Madeline Kahn, and Estelle Parsons. Several Broadway producers were also present, including Lee Guber and Morty Gottlieb, in addition to a very proud Joseph Papp.

The Central Park run of the show was completed on August 24, and plans were quickly made to transfer the production to Broadway the following January. The one major cast alteration was the addition of Estelle Parsons as Ruth, the pirate nurse. Estelle, who won an Academy Award for her appearance in the film *Bonnie and Clyde* (1967), had starred on Broadway in *And Miss Reardon Drinks a Little,* and appeared in Joseph Papp's production of *Threepenny Opera.*

Just after completing the Central Park version of *Pirates,* Ronstadt was lamenting to the press about how lonely she was, in spite of her vast success. "I'm lonely and I'm bored," she proclaimed in September 1980. "But I'm 34 years old, and headed off on the road again without any real strong commitment to anyone. What I actually need is something a lot stronger than just the blush of romance. I need a real man, and real movie-type love affair. You know, it really is lonely at the top. That's not just a cliche — and I'm living proof of it. I make a million dollars, or whatever the hell it is, each year, and I have a home in Malibu and a big career — but what do I have personally? I make the press every time I even say so much as 'Hello' to Jerry [Brown] and I've even gone so far as having a guy live at my home with me [Adam Mitchell], who's a strictly platonic friend, just to keep myself from being too lonely."

Ronstadt was so encouraged by her reception in the New York Shakespeare Festival production of *Pirates* that she was already discussing further musical theater projects with Joseph Papp and director Wilford Leach. While plans were being formalized to move the Gilbert and Sullivan hit to the Uris Theater in the Broadway theater district, Ronstadt, Papp, and Leach were bantering about plans for further classic revivals.

In October 1980 it was announced that they had decided to mount a production of Bertolt Brecht and Kurt Weill's *The Seven Deadly Sins,* starring Linda in the role that was originally created by Lotte Lenya. "We like working together, and wanted to do something else," said Leach at the time. "In *The Pirates of Penzance,* Linda plays a Lillian Gish-type role. But there is a side of her that is very spunky. We talked about works that had wonderful music that could show her spunkiness. Linda will be in *The Pirates of Penzance* until the end of June [1981], then she is going on a concert tour and will do a record. We'll start *The Seven Deadly Sins* in October [1981]. It's hard to describe what the production, which is totally sung, will be like. It won't be like the original production staged by Balanchine. We will use film and dance and mime."

Also in October 1980, Asylum Records released the album *Linda Ronstadt: Greatest Hits, Volume Two.* It contained her eleven biggest hits from 1976 to 1980. The LP followed her recording career from "Someone To Lay Down Beside Me," off of the *Hasten Down the Wind* album, through the three singles released off of *Mad Love*. It was certified Gold in December, and peaked at Number 26. Although *Greatest Hits, Volume Two* became her first Asylum album since 1975 that didn't make it into the Top Ten, it ultimately sold a million copies and became her eighth consecutive Platinum album.

While her rock and roll records were selling briskly, Linda was busily preoccupied with her newly launched theatrical career. The planned 1981 production of *The Seven Deadly Sins* did not come about, but the Broadway run of *The Pirates Of Penzance (Or, The Slave Of Duty)* hit "the great white way" in all of its swashbuckling glory. The cast began working in front of audiences at the Uris Theater in December 1980, although the "official" opening night was January 8, 1981. At first the cast had to get used to the acoustics of the large, modern theater. One night during the 1980 Christmas season, the pit orchestra had attended a holiday party and showed up for work inebriated. Their timing was off, and they hit several discordant notes during the first act. When Linda made her first entrance, singing "Poor Wandering One," the orchestra made a mistake, and Ronstadt started to giggle at their bungle. She then began to uncontrollably laugh, and couldn't stop. Startled by her laughter, Rex Smith began to laugh as well. The song was destroyed, and as the curtain came down on the first act, the audience was booing.

When she got backstage, Linda was alternately crying and laughing. She insisted that she couldn't continue the performance, it had become such an out-of-control mess. Director Wilford Leach insisted that before the second act could begin, she had to first go out in front of the curtain, apologize to the audience for the disastrous display during "Poor Wandering One," and sing the song over again. She did so, taking all the blame for the song, without mentioning the tipsy musicians. With Rex Smith by her side, she sang the song as it was meant to be performed, and the evening was saved.

Mitchell Weiss, who at the time was the assistant general manager of the New York Shakespeare Festival, recalled that there were several acoustic mishaps to overcome. "There were quite a few 'previews,' " he said, "because there were some sound problems at first. That was during the days before they knew how to properly amplify a theater. *Pirates* was one of the first shows to have a rock and roll sound man doing the sound. He did some concerts that Linda knew about, which is why they gave him a chance."

The sound man who was brought in was Don Ketteler, who had worked with the rock group Kiss, and with Meatloaf. He had also

worked at the rock club the Bottom Line, running the sound board.
Ketteler explained at the time, "The problem is to make Gilbert and
Sullivan's fairly intimate sound audible everywhere, and still seem to be
coming from the stage — a matter of psycho-acoustics."

When the play did open, it did so with a grand flourish. "When
it was opening on Broadway, we already knew it was a hit," said Mitchell Weiss, "so Joe Papp wanted to make sure the whole place was fes-
tive. There were helium-filled balloons everywhere. Linda Ronstadt's
dressing room, which was a two-room suite, had to be redone in all
pink. She had a pink rug, pink furniture, pink everything."

Weiss remembers that one of the projects that he assisted Papp
with was the selection of opening night gifts for the cast members. "We
had fun with it," he said. "There were some really 'hot' gifts given.
Kevin and Rex — one of them got an actual pirate's sword, authenti-
cated from the 1700s, and the other got a pirate's dagger. Wilford received a coin from a treasure chest, found off the island of Penzance. Joe
wanted to get Linda something — because of her voice — that had
something to do with a bird: something very elegant. She ended up
with a Lalique sculptured singing bird."

According to Mitchell, "Everyone involved with the show was
very impressed with Linda, because she wasn't on a big 'star trip.' She
was the biggest star in the production, yet she didn't play any competition games. She didn't demand press interviews, she didn't demand
this — she didn't demand anything. She was there to do something unusual, and to make a career change for herself. When she went to
Broadway, she didn't take a lot of money. She did not demand a star's
salary. She agreed to go pretty much even with Kevin and Rex and
everybody else. She didn't say, 'I'm the one who's selling the tickets!'
— even though she was."

The initial production had been a local summer hit in New York
City when it played Central Park, but the Broadway opening really
made big news, covered in the national media by everyone from *Time*
magazine to *Rolling Stone*. Suddenly, the whole country was talking
about Linda Ronstadt's transformation into an accomplished Broadway
star.

Linda had indeed come a long way, from the tentative rock star
who was experimenting with Gilbert and Sullivan's material to a full-
blown Broadway attraction. At first, she explains, "I couldn't quit tap-
pin' my foot in time to the music and shakin' my ass on-stage." She
quickly got out of the habit of shaking her rear end and got down to the
business of winning audiences.

"If you go to the theater only once this year, this is the show! One
of the most joyously creative productions in all musical theater,"

claimed Jack Kroll in *Newsweek.* "The beginning of a full-blown love affair that may just last for years!" said Frank Rich in *The New York Times.* "One of the most enchanting musicals to be seen on Broadway for many a year!" heralded Clive Barnes in *The New York Post.* And Joel Siegel of ABC-TV found *Pirates* to be "more fun than F.A.O. Schwarz at Christmas time!" Linda and her fellow cast members had a huge hit on their hands.

Time magazine trumpeted the fact that "a new old musical, *The Pirates of Penzance,* captures Broadway!" The same article said of Linda, "Ronstadt, 34, looks as innocent as a fawn and is able to hit high notes that her rock fans probably never knew existed."

Reveling in his directorial success, Wilford Leach explained, "The play has always been done in such a rigid, lifeless way that people don't realize how funny and vigorous the material is on the page. We wanted to do the play, rather than people's idea of it. We decided to scrape off the encrustations of tradition, but remain faithful to the script." And, revealing the motives behind casting Linda Ronstadt and Rex Smith, Leach stated, "We weren't out to do a rock version of Gilbert and Sullivan, I wanted pop singers to make us re-hear the lines."

The production indeed had so much vitality and excitement in it that the bitter cold January weather couldn't keep crowds from lining up for tickets. Surmising the key to the popularity of the show, *Time* claimed that, "This updated version of Gilbert and Sullivan's *The Pirates of Penzance* has something few other musicals can boast of: absolute, unqualified, irresistible fun."

When *Pirates* went to Broadway, Linda Ronstadt wasn't the only woman to have a rock and roll background. One of her character "sisters" was Karla DeVito, who sang behind Meatloaf and Laurie Beechman (a Broadway veteran who had just released her own rock album called *Laurie and the Sighs*). DeVito was Ronstadt's understudy, and was called upon to fill in for Linda on more than one occasion.

In fact, four days after the show opened, Linda took ill with an acute sore throat and laryngitis. Karla had to step in for Ronstadt on January 12. That night, Joseph Papp met with the press and announced, "I'm hoping Linda will be back tomorrow. She is being treated by Dr. Wilbur Gould. He treated Rex Smith, who was out of *Pirates* Sunday afternoon. We were lucky we opened the show. Colds and sore throats have been rampant."

Unfortunately for Linda, on the night of January 12, several of the "second night" critics were present in the audience and were forced to review Karla's performance, not Linda's. After leaving the show in late spring, Ronstadt stated, "I would have died before I let my understudy take over on-stage. Not that I begrudged her a chance to shine before an audience, but it was my part!"

According to Ronstadt, she really loved the character of Mabel. She found her to be "basically earnest, curious and innocent, and no dummy; she's smarter than you think. It's a facet of my own personality, not one I wear every day, but it felt authentic. When I walked onstage, Mabel did things." Whether or not she was actually "possessed" by the fictional "spirit" of Mabel, Linda was entranced by her.

On February 1, 2 and 8, 1981, Linda and the cast of the show went into the Columbia 30th Street Recording Studio in Manhattan and recorded the original cast album of *The Pirates of Penzance*. Produced by Peter Asher, and released in May of 1981 by Elektra Records, the resulting two-record set LP contained nearly two hours of music and dialogue from the show. According to George Rose, "Usually show records are done in one day, but there were many problems with this one, and we all wanted it to be perfect."

Recorded in three eight-hour days, the album brilliantly captured the excitement of the Broadway production, with Linda's solos — "Poor Wandering One" and "Sorry Her Lot" — among the highlights. Although it was popular with Ronstadt fans and theatergoers, the album only lasted on the LP chart in *Billboard* for three weeks, peaking at Number 178.

In the spring of 1981, when the Tony Award nominations were announced, Linda Ronstadt was nominated in the category of Outstanding Performance by an Actress, Musical. Kevin Kline and George Rose were both nominated in the category of Outstanding Performance by an Actor, Musical, for their respective roles in *Pirates,* and Tony Azito was nominated in the category of Outstanding Performance by a Featured Actor, Musical. Wilford Leach's direction and Graciela Daniele's choreography were also nominated for Tonys, as was the production, under the category of Outstanding Reproduction of a Play or Musical. That year, the other "revivals" up against *The Pirates of Penzance* were *Brigadoon, Camelot,* and Elizabeth Taylor's version of *The Little Foxes*.

Linda's fellow musical actress nominees were Lauren Bacall in *Woman of the Year,* Meg Bussert in *Brigadoon,* and Chita Rivera in the short-lived *Bring Back Birdie* (the sequel to *Bye Bye Birdie*). Although it was Bacall who walked away with the Tony, Ronstadt had the distinction of having her debut Broadway performance counted among the year's best. Wilford Leach and Kevin Kline both won Tonys in their categories, and Joseph Papp won a Tony for the production itself.

For her first Broadway project, Ronstadt had won critical raves and had received the confidence to go on to tackle more challenging projects. Several other female pop stars were enviously watching her progress from the wings. One of them was Cher, who had been trying for years to be taken seriously as an actress.

Kevin Kline, Linda Ronstadt, and Rex Smith at the New York premiere of the movie version of The Pirates of Penzance. *(Photo: Bettina Cirone/Star File)*

Recalls Cher, "The night before [the West Coast production of] the show closed, I saw Linda Ronstadt do *The Pirates of Penzance.* She did it in Los Angeles for one night only. Watching her I thought, 'If Linda can do this, what am I doing wasting my time? If [movie] studio people won't take me seriously, then I'll go to New York to try my luck." Inspired by Ronstadt, Cher flew to New York City, auditioned for Joe Papp, and was recommended to Robert Altman for his Broadway production of *Come Back to the Five and Dime Jimmy Dean, Jimmy Dean.* Had it not been for Linda, Cher may never have had the nerve to finally make the transformation from pop star into an Academy Award-winning actress.

In June 1981, Linda left the Broadway company of *Pirates,* and the role of Mabel was officially handed over to Karla DeVito. Karla released her debut solo album *Is This a Cool World Or What?* (Epic Records) that summer, and for a while performed with Rex Smith in the show. When Rex left the cast, Robbie Benson took over the role of Frederic. Karla and Robbie fell in love and were married shortly afterward. So, although Linda may not have found love amid her run on Broadway in *Pirates,* her understudy did. (In September 1981, Maureen McGovern took over the role of Mabel.)

One of Linda's commitments when she left the show in 1981 was a concert tour of Japan. On August 10 she was in the recording studio in Los Angeles, working on her next solo album, *Get Closer.*

While the cast album of *Pirates* captured the sound of the show on vinyl, the following year, Linda recreated the role of Mabel in the movie version of the play. Although she swore she would never become a movie actress (*FM* had been enough for her), she flew to London in the dead of winter to bring Mabel to life on film. Working with Papp, Leach, Smith, Kline, Rose, and Azito had been so rewarding that she couldn't pass up the opportunity to rejoin them one last time to recreate their Broadway roles. To add to the box-office appeal of the film, Angela Lansbury was added to the cast, in the role of Ruth.

The movie was made entirely on the lot of Shepperton Studio Centre in London, although the music was recorded in America by Peter Asher before filming commenced. Each of the principal actors agreed to work for next to nothing, just so their work could be captured on film.

Linda found the process of filmmaking less than enjoyable. During the production of the movie version of *The Pirates of Penzance,* Linda complained, "Moviemaking is like working in a factory gluing fenders on cars. Three minutes and stop, three minutes and stop. I said I wouldn't do it if they paid me, so — they didn't pay me — and I did it! I haven't talked to anyone who wasn't wearing a costume in a month and a half!"

Spending February and March of 1982 in the London movie studio, Linda occupied her time off-camera by reading books. Her passion at that point was Henry James, and his *Portrait of a Lady*. She enjoyed it so much that on one of her rare days off she went into downtown London and returned with three more volumes by James: *The Awkward Age, The Spoils of Plynoton,* and *What Masie Knew.*

The filming of *Pirates* was done on a tight budget, with Joseph Papp in firm control of the production. There were offers from Hollywood studios, but they wanted major cast changes to improve the box-office sales. One studio wanted to replace Kevin Kline with John Travolta. That's when Papp decided to do it his way. The film was originally budgeted at $9 million, although there were additional costs, and the production ultimately cost closer to $12 million to complete.

There was also a tight time factor. The final day of filming Kline's scenes came within two hours of his catching a flight to New York City, to begin shooting *Sophie's Choice* opposite Meryl Streep. He finished *Pirates,* and the very next day he was on the set of *Sophie's Choice.*

Ronstadt was also in a rush. Her *Get Closer* album wasn't getting any closer to completion, and she was also due in the recording studio to begin the *What's New* album with Nelson Riddle. At the time, she was more excited about the prospect of starting *What's New* than she was about finishing *Get Closer.* "Rock and roll is structured for guitar players, and the singing line is secondary," she commented. Her work in *Pirates* had made her more aware of her vocal strengths. She also found that she had lost some of her previous "chest tones" she used in the 1970s to sing rock. On her 1981 tour of Japan, she discovered that since hitting the coloratura soprano range, her voice had changed a bit. "I couldn't belt as hard," she said, when she returned to singing rock and roll.

While she was busy working on the *Pirates* movie, Linda was hit by two tragedies at once. Her mother, Ruthmary Copeman Ronstadt, had been fighting a losing battle against lung cancer. Linda was on the set of the movie when her mother died. A couple of days later, her "Saturday Night Live" pal, John Belushi, also died.

Linda had gone back to Tucson before the filming of *The Pirates of Penzance* began, and spent some time with her mom. When her mother took a turn for the worse, the film schedule was rearranged so that she could fly to Tucson to see her. She then quickly returned to London.

"She still knew me," Linda recalled of her final visit, "but she was in a lot of pain." Returning to London, Linda dove back into the film. "One day my father called me and told me my mom was dead. I couldn't even cry because it would mess up my make-up." That was March 4, 1982.

A few days later, John Belushi succumbed to a fatal dose of drugs at the Chateau Marmot Hotel in Los Angeles. Ronstadt said in disbelief, "First my mother and then my friend in the same week. I felt as if somebody had put a bucket over my head and was hitting it with a hammer."

The film version of *Pirates* premiered at the Public Theater in New York City on February 18, 1983. The debut screening was star-studded, with all of its principals in attendance, including Ronstadt and Peter Asher, Angela Lansbury, Kevin Kline, Rex Smith, George Rose, Tony Azito, and the proud producer himself — Joseph Papp. Other celebrity spectators included Lauren Bacall, Christopher Reeve, Morgan Fairchild, Placido Domingo, Neil Sedaka, and model Julianne Phillips.

The result of the film was entertainingly effervescent. Instead of trying to transpose the musical to a lifelike set, the action took place on a stylish and colorful recreation of a small town on the coast of Cornwall, in the 1880s. The scenes on the pirate ship were filmed with an obvious backdrop simulating the sea coast, and the English Channel was depicted as too blue to be real. In that way, the production captured the cartoonish bafoonery of the characters.

When Linda Ronstadt, as Mabel, appears from behind one of the huge paper maché rocks that line this faux sea coast, the close-up camera shot that captures her is magnificent. With her doe-eyed look of innocence, she makes the most of the scene — which she totally steals from the rest of the cast. Not since Bambi's first scene on the screen has an actor or actress personified vulnerability so magnificently. Opening her mouth and announcing " 'Tis Mabel!," she proceeds to show off the glorious upper register of her famed soprano.

The movie version of *Pirates* was an excellent vehicle for Ronstadt to demonstrate her innocent presence and her incredible vocal control. Her only undoing came on her four lines of spoken dialogue, which were delivered with a painful stiffness. On stage, her discomfort was masked by her distance from the audience. In the movie scene where she pleads with Frederic to console her father, she comes across as almost mechanical. However, when she sings, all is forgiven.

The film version of *The Pirates of Penzance* differs slightly from the stage production. Many excerpts of music and dialogue were cut to keep the film moving along at a fast pace. George Rose's showstopping "I Am the Very Model of a Modern Major-General" and the Smith/Lansbury/Kline rendition of "Now For the Pirate's Lair" both sustained large lyric deletions. Likewise, Ronstadt's second solo from the stageshow, "Sorry Her Lot," was also cut from the film. There was no way in which the film could not come across as slightly "stagey" and unrealistic. The cuts in the script didn't necessarily help the film.

There is something "magical" about a theatrical production that is almost impossible to transpose to the screen. Sitting in a Broadway theater, a viewer can choose a segment of the stage to focus on. In a film, the camera makes the decisions for the audience. While close-ups magnified the solo performances, the wide-angle production numbers suffered a bit. Still, the film was a significant success in terms of capturing a creative milestone in Ronstadt's singing career.

Reviews for *The Pirates of Penzance* movie were decidedly mixed. Although everyone loved Ronstadt's ultrasonic trilling, the film itself left several reviewers with a cold feeling. "The dash and pizazz of the Broadway production were absent, lost in a tangle of bad camera angles and clunky directing," deadpanned *Rolling Stone*. According to *People*, "Linda Ronstadt can sing gloriously. This film version of Gilbert and Sullivan's operetta, which Ronstadt did last year on Broadway for producer Joe Papp, makes that clear. Sadly, it also reveals Linda cannot as yet walk, talk, smile, gesture or otherwise act convincingly in front of a camera . . . What should be gossamer — and was on-stage — is rendered all too solid and earthbound on-screen." Yet, *Us* magazine recommended it, exclaiming, "The Broadway pop version of Gilbert and Sullivan's venerable operetta jumps onto film with its high spirits — and original cast — virtually intact!"

The mixed reviews did not diminish Linda's love and admiration for the character of Mabel Stanley. "I've always had this fascination with innocence," she claimed. "Mabel is very earnest and innocent, but in a knowing way — she's no Goody Two Shoes. It's not ignorance, though a lot of people get innocence and ignorance confused. Actually, Mabel is a lot like Snow White, who's one of my heroines. She sang in the same range that I sing in as Mabel — that little American soprano voice, up in the treetops."

After the premiere, the cast split up for the last time and went their separate ways. Rex Smith was busy that television season, hosting "Solid Gold" with Marilyn McCoo. Kevin Kline and Angela Lansbury went back to their movie careers, and Linda returned to the recording studio.

The *Pirates* experience — in Central Park, on Broadway, and on film — had been great for Linda. It gave her a new sense of confidence to try her wings in other areas than her rock and roll recording career. It also inspired her to seek arenas of musical expression that personally interested her, and encouraged her not to make decisions simply because they seemed commercially sound.

Through *The Pirates of Penzance,* she made several lifelong friends. When Rex Smith recorded his fourth album for Columbia Records, entitled *Camouflage* (1983), Linda lent background vocals on the song

"Real Love." That song was written by Mark Goldenberg and was the first cut on the Cretones' 1980 album *Thin Red Line*. Thus it was the fourth song from the Cretones' debut LP that Ronstadt recorded, following the three that she performed on her *Mad Love* album.

After she completed her Broadway run in *Pirates* in 1981, Ronstadt had begun recording the follow-up album to *Mad Love*. Entitled *Get Closer*, the album encompassed the back-to-basics rock and roll formula of the *Mad Love* album, and combined four cuts recorded along those lines — with the traditional pop/rock mixture that had made her famous in the 1970s.

Ten of the cuts on the album were recorded from August 1981 to August 1982. Two additional songs were left over from Ronstadt recording sessions in 1977 and 1978. The album was released in September 1982, and was certified Gold in November. It was her first new studio album to miss a million-selling Platinum certification since *Heart Like a Wheel*. This raised the paramount question: "Had Linda lost her audience by going 'new wave,' and then suddenly shifting gears to perform Gilbert and Sullivan light opera?" In 1977, when she was riding the peak of her success, her *Simple Dreams* album was Triple Platinum for sales in excess of three and a half million copies in the United States alone. When *Get Closer* was released in 1982, it was every bit as solid an album as *Simple Dreams*, yet it sold only 800,000 copies and peaked at Number 31 on the album chart.

Get Closer had all of the elements that had made Ronstadt's million-selling albums — from *Heart Like a Wheel* to *Mad Love* — a success. She had used all of her favorite musicians: Andrew Gold, Kenny Edwards, Bill Payne, Russell Kunkel, Dan Dugmore, Waddy Wachtel, Bob Glaub, and Danny Kortchmar. She had songs by Dolly Parton and Kate McGarrigle; sang a duet with John David Souther; and had several of her singing star friends harmonizing with her (including James Taylor, Dolly Parton, and Emmylou Harris). She had lamenting ballads ("The Moon is a Harsh Mistress"), new versions of 1960s pop classics ("Tell Him"), and she included a bit of country and western ("My Blue Tears"). She even ended up with great reviews. There was no reason why this album shouldn't have become a huge Platinum success — yet it didn't.

"Linda Ronstadt's voice has never sounded better than it does on *Get Closer*," said *Rolling Stone*, pointing out that, "she uses her voice like a daring rock and roller." *People* magazine claimed, "She still has the best white pipes around and the most dependable transmission this side of Aamco . . . she demonstrates her amazing range from torch bearer to temptress . . . her album is titled *Get Closer*, but Linda Ronstadt's vocal range has never reached farther." And *Stereo Review* exclaimed that,

"There aren't many pop singers who can do as many things as well as Linda Ronstadt can! Her new Asylum album, *Get Closer,* almost seems designed to demonstrate that."

On *Get Closer,* Linda chose to cover several pop and rock hits from the 1960s: The Exciters' "Tell Him" (1962), Billy Joe Royal's "I Knew You When" (1965), Ike and Tina Turner's "I Think It's Gonna Work Out Fine" (1961), and the Knickerbockers' "Lies" (1966). Two of the most effective ballads on the album were Jimmy Webb compositions, "The Moon is a Harsh Mistress" and "Easy For You To Say."

When the album was completed in 1982, it was decided to unearth two previously unreleased songs that Linda had recorded in the 1970s. "Sometimes You Just Can't Win," which she sings with John David Souther, was recorded in June 1977, originally intended for inclusion on her *Simple Dreams* album. "My Blue Tears," which Linda sings with Dolly Parton and Emmylou Harris, was recorded on January 18, 1978. Produced by Brian Ahern, it was one of the first songs recorded for the aborted Ronstadt/Parton/Harris album.

Linda's fans could not have asked for a more well-rounded pop/ rock/country album from her. Several of the cuts, including "Get Closer," "I Knew You When," and "Lies," have all of the rock and roll punch of the songs on her *Mad Love* album. Although *Get Closer* failed to become a huge commercial success, in January 1983 Linda was nominated for two Grammy Awards. The single "Get Closer" was nominated for Best Rock Performance, Female; and the album was nominated for Best Pop Performance, Female. However, she didn't win either award.

After Linda turned the song "Get Closer" into a Top 40 pop hit, Lever Brothers licensed the song for use in its television commercials to advertise Close Up toothpaste. The lyrics were changed to "Get Close Up," and although it wasn't Linda's voice that was heard on the advertisements, people still think of Ronstadt when they brush their teeth with Close Up!

Get Closer was to become Linda Ronstadt's last pop/rock album for seven years. She had to make a decision at that point in her career: was she going to get further into rock and roll music, or was she going to do something totally new? In 1983 she made the decision to explore several different avenues of musical expression, and she hasn't taken a backward look since.

On her three albums with Nelson Riddle, Linda sang several lush and romantic ballads from the 1930s and 1940s.

(Photo: Mark Hanauer/Mark Bego Archives)

A Sentimental Journey

7

I t was during the summer of 1980 that Linda Ronstadt became reacquainted with the lush and timeless music of the first half of the twentieth century, when jazz, big bands, and beautifully orchestrated ballads were popular. She was at the Long Island home of record producer Jerry Wexler when a song by Mildred Bailey hit the turntable. "She sounds very pure and sexy at the same time — a sexy Snow White," commented Ronstadt. All of a sudden she decided to rekindle her long-forgotten love affair with the music of Billie Holiday, Frank Sinatra, and Peggy Lee.

While she was still working on *The Pirates of Penzance,* she began going through her friend Pete Hamill's extensive record collection and taking note of the songs that touched her the most. She was soon obsessed with the idea of recording an entire album of pop and jazz standards written by the likes of Sammy Cahn, George and Ira Gershwin, and Irving Berlin. It reminded her of the 78s that her father used to play on the record player when she was a child, and how he used to sit at the piano and sing "What'll I Do" to her.

After she completed the Broadway run of *Pirates* in the summer of 1981, she went into the recording studio with Jerry Wexler and made her first attempt at capturing on tape the mood and the feeling that these classic recordings evoked. Wexler and Ronstadt worked together in a four-day recording session which yielded several songs accompanied by a small jazz combo. She was literally possessed by the songs that she had chosen, such as "What's New?" and "Lover Man (Oh Where Can You Be)."

Unfortunately, when she heard the "playback" on the studio monitors, Linda hated the results. She refused to allow them to be released. Contractually obligated to produce a new album, Ronstadt reluctantly began recording the *Get Closer* album instead. According to Bryn Bridenthal, vice-president of Asylum Records, "Others thought she sounded wonderful, but she didn't think so, and it's her record."

"An expensive rehearsal session" is how Linda later described the abandoned jazz sessions that she recorded with Jerry Wexler. "The tracks weren't right, the way they were recorded wasn't right, the way I sang them wasn't right. 'What's New' and 'Good-Bye' I couldn't sing at all. But I could sing them in the shower, so I knew there was something wrong with the arrangements," she said. Upon her command, the tapes were scrapped. "Doing that killed me," she later confessed, but she knew that the recordings were not up to the standards she envisioned them possessing. "It just wasn't right, but I couldn't get rid of the tunes. They're the most wonderful songs."

Although she was discouraged by her first attempt at recording an entire album of standards, her friends continued to encourage her. The most supportive advice came from Andrew Gold, J. D. Souther, Steve Martin, and John Rockwell. "That gave Peter [Asher] and me the confidence to go back and try again," she said.

"Peter was not very familiar with this kind of music," she recalled. "It was my idea to get Nelson Riddle to do the arrangements. Nelson was one of the few guys who really, legitimately interpreted jazz to an orchestra without losing its flavor and its authenticity. He knew how to do that without turning things into sugar water."

Although he had come out of the big band era of the 1940s, Nelson Riddle hit his stride when he connected with Frank Sinatra in the 1950s and arranged a series of immensely popular albums for "the chairman of the board." Linda remembered the first time that she became familiar with Nelson's masterful arrangements:

"In 1972, when I met J. D. Souther, he sat me down in the living room one night and said, 'Now listen — we're *really* going to listen to this.' And we listened to Nelson Riddle. It was great. I just flipped out. I said, 'This is gorgeous!' One of the great things about Nelson's arrangements is that they are so unobtrusive. They don't make you think of the arrangements — they don't dominate the record. What they do is *evoke* like crazy. When you listen, you simply surrender yourself to the feelings it evokes."

Ronstadt proudly proclaimed that she had "One For My Baby" on her jukebox at home. "For years I just said, 'Wow, listen to that. Just Frank and the piano.' And all of a sudden I realized there is a *whole orchestra* on it. Nelson got it in and out so subtly that all it did was paint pictures for you, instruct your mind to see all those visions. But you're not aware of it. That's really brilliant. Yet, when you really listen critically and say, 'What are the horns doing there? What are the flutes doing? What is the string section doing?' you just go crazy, because it's so beautiful. It's so subtle and so complex."

"One For My Baby" was one of the songs contained on the Gold, Number One album *Frank Sinatra Sings For Only the Lonely,* which was arranged and conducted by Nelson Riddle in 1958. Included on that album were unforgettable versions of "Spring is Here," "Blues in the Night," "Good-Bye," "Guess I'll Hang My Tears Out To Dry," "Gone With the Wind," and "What's New?" The album was one of Linda Ronstadt's favorites.

Riddle was a teenage trombone player who left his home in southern New Jersey to travel with a band that passed through town. Throughout the 1940s, he gained a solid reputation as an arranger and a conductor. In the '40s and '50s, he worked with several of the hottest popular singers of the era, including Nat "King" Cole and Peggy Lee. He arranged Judy Garland's *Zing! Went the Strings Of My Heart* and the much heralded *Ella Fitzgerald Sings the George and Ira Gershwin Songbooks.* However, it was his work with Sinatra that made him into a musical legend in his own right.

In April 1953, Frank Sinatra began a ten-year association with Capitol Records. He had just completed a long-running contract with Columbia Records that dated back to his 1943 hit "All Or Nothing At All," which he had recorded with Harry James. His first Capitol recording was the two-sided single "I'm Walking Behind You," backed with "Lean Baby." Axel Stordahl did the arranging, and Voyle Gilmore was producer. There was a gap of several months before Sinatra re-entered the recording studio, and by then Stordahl had taken a job conducting and arranging for the television series "Coke Time With Eddie Fisher" (Coke referring to "Coca-Cola").

Axel Stordahl suggested that Sinatra try Billy May as his new arranger. Unfortunately, Billy May had a previous commitment that conflicted with Sinatra's scheduled recording dates. Finally, Voyle Gilmore suggested that they get into contact with Nelson Riddle. It became one of the most significant "chance" unions of the decade.

In 1953, "record albums" were just beginning to be actively marketed. Although the format of the ten-inch "long player" had been developed in 1948, the record business at that time was still dominated by 78 R.P.M. (revolutions per minute) singles. The single recordings and the albums had nothing to do with each other; they were considered to have appealed to totally different markets.

The first ten-inch album that Sinatra recorded was called *Songs For Young Lovers*, which was produced by Gilmore and arranged by Riddle. They decided that all eight songs contained on it should have a unifying feeling and a common sound to them. The album, recorded on November 5 and 6 of 1953, included "My Funny Valentine," "A Foggy Day," and "Little Girl Blue." The *Songs For Young Lovers* album was such a hit that the following spring, Riddle and Sinatra recorded a second eight-cut album entitled *Swing Easy*. Again, the song selections and the arrangements were all unified, but the album had more of a jazzy feeling than its predecessor. When Riddle and Ronstadt began working together in the 1980s, their albums also followed this pattern, with *What's New* containing mainly sentimental songs, and *Lush Life* introducing a bit of "swing" to Linda's nostalgic repertoire.

Nelson Riddle's work with Sinatra had direct bearing on his later work with Ronstadt. For his recordings with Linda, he used the same basic formula. According to him, "I look for the peak of a song and build to it. We're telling a story. It has to have a beginning, a middle, a *climax*, and an ending."

Linda was reluctantly recording rock and roll for her *Get Closer* album when she began working with Nelson Riddle in 1982. She was still obsessed with the work Nelson Riddle had done in the 1950s with Frank Sinatra when she and Peter Asher lined up a meeting with the famous arranger and conductor. Since she had disastrous results when she attempted to record an entire album of "standards" the previous year with Jerry Wexler, this time she had a new scheme up her sleeve. *Get Closer* was going to feature several different musical styles, and she thought that Nelson Riddle could arrange one song for her as an experiment to include on the album.

A meeting was set up between Ronstadt, Asher, and Riddle, in early 1982, at the West Hollywood recording studio where Linda was working on *Get Closer*. According to Riddle, "I didn't know very much about Linda's work. In the back of my mind I started to scheme a bit. I don't like to do single arrangements. I like to do albums."

At their first meeting, Nelson was taken by Ronstadt's singing. He described her voice as possessing "strong, sure, pure tone, a naiveté and a freshness and a little-girlishness which were very appealing." They talked for a while and discussed the kind of material that Linda wanted to do. Riddle was impressed, and he announced to her that he would work with her — only if she agreed to do an entire album, and not just one song.

"As soon as he said that, I handed him the songs, and we ran into the other room to the piano," she recalled. "We got along great!"

Ronstadt had most of the songs picked out that ultimately were included on the *What's New* album. They were songs that she had fallen in love with, and she believed in the lyrics. "It's like falling for a man," she claimed. "You can't not do it. He might be married or maybe not even like you very much and make a complete fool out of you, but you have to have him. When you fall in love you have no choice, and I literally had no choice with these songs. I was hijacked."

Riddle's career had reached new heights in the 1970s when he won an Oscar for his score of the 1974 film version of *The Great Gatsby*. However, in 1980 his career suddenly hit an impasse when he fell ill with cirrhosis of the liver. He fought for two years to regain his health, and in 1982 he was wanting to return to the recording studio so that he could continue creating the music he loved.

"I like a glass of vodka," he explained of his health, "but I never drank so that I was inebriated. I had a weak liver, and I suppose I was one of those guys who should never have had *anything* to drink." Having recovered, Riddle claimed, "It taught me that just to swing your feet over the side of the bed in the morning is its own reward. Nobody knows how long you're going to be around, so you might as well enjoy it."

For their first meeting together, Riddle brought along the original sheet music for "Guess I'll Hang My Tears Out To Dry." It was the same sheet music that he had used when he recorded the album *Frank Sinatra Sings For Only the Lonely*. Having heard Ronstadt's singing key, Riddle crossed out the words "Frank's key," which was written in the corner. "You can't do that, that's historic!" Linda exclaimed. Already she felt that she was working in Sinatra's shadow.

The significance of the music, and the fact that several people told her she was crazy for attempting this project, made her wonder if she had gotten herself into something over her head. Nevertheless, Ronstadt, Riddle, and Asher began recording the *What's New* album on June 30, 1982, at the Complex recording studio in Los Angeles.

When she began listening to the playback of the first sessions, Linda was still frightened that she didn't sound good enough. " 'What's New?' was the first thing we recorded," she said, "and I thought it sounded pretty good — but I have a hard time listening to my own singing, so I'm never quite sure if it's good or not. I say, 'Oh, there's a million things wrong with my voice.' But we took it exactly as we recorded it. We didn't change anything."

According to Linda, she and Peter were too used to listening to rock and roll to realize how good the first sessions actually were. "After we recorded the first three songs with Nelson, I didn't think they were good enough," she explained. "We kept trying to make the orchestra synch up with the bass and drums, like rock and roll — everybody on the same backbeat. But the backbeat just isn't the dictator of this music like it is in rock and roll. So Peter and I were in there tapping our feet and frowning and saying, 'There's a flam here, there's a flam there!' Randy Newman was in the neighborhood and came by to visit us. He's had a lot of experience conducting orchestras and recording with them. Randy just laughed at us and said, 'You know what you're doing? You just listen to the *flow* of it.' As soon as we figured that out it was a little bit easier."

Riddle, on the other hand, was knocked out by what he heard coming out of Linda's mouth. "She's got a strong, beautiful voice and really unbelievable power. God, when she belts out 'What's New?' you really believe it," he said.

Although three of the songs that Linda recorded for the *What's New* album were also contained on the LP *Frank Sinatra Sings for Only the Lonely,* Ronstadt ended up with all-new arrangements, tailored to her own voice. Explaining his personal recipe for unforgettable arrangements, Riddle explained, "I just did it as I felt it now. The same principles guided me that have always guided me, that is, to give the singer room to breathe. When the singer rests, then there's the chance to write a fill that might be heard. I don't know what kind of arrangements I wrote for Linda. It is probably as mysterious to me as it is to you. One goes on instinct." As instinctively correct as he was in the 1950s, Nelson and his arrangements again proved winning in the 1980s. Beginning with *What's New,* Riddle crafted three of the most gloriously successful albums in Ronstadt's highly varied recording career.

When it was completed, Ronstadt was exceedingly proud of the *What's New* album. Prior to the album's release she proclaimed, "This record is the most important thing I have ever done, the best songs I have ever sung, and the best singing I have ever done. I feel it's my life's work in a way. I don't know what my fans will think of it. I don't care too much. I hope they like it, but if they don't, there is nothing I can do about it."

"It's a bold move," Peter Asher admitted at the time. "I had mixed feelings about how the record would sell, but not about whether she would do it well."

Nelson Riddle also realized that Linda was running certain risks by recording an album of material culled from the 1920s, 1930s, and 1940s. "Linda deserves a lot of credit for having the courage to do such an album," he said, "to fly in a sense, in the face of the times."

Even her record company expressed its doubts about finding a market. "I was told that there would be no commercial audience for this, and it would probably be the end of my career if I put it out," Ronstadt recalled. "I just wanted to make people dream, make them slow dance around the living room, sit down on the couch and make out."

When the *What's New* album was released, in September 1983, its success was indeed a calculated risk. Her last rock and roll album, *Get Closer,* had sold only 800,000 copies in America, and it was clear that Ronstadt had to try something different. But was this too different? The results were phenomenal: by November it was certified Gold, and by December it was Platinum. It hit Number Three on the *Billboard* LP charts, and by the following spring it had sold over two and a half million copies, becoming the third most successful album of her entire career.

What's New became the first of Linda's totally thematically uniform albums. It has even more of a cohesive quality than her all-new wave *Mad Love* album. All of her albums from that point on have had a unified direction and a flow to the material they contain.

Just as he had done with Sinatra's *Songs For Young Lovers* album in 1953, thirty years later Nelson Riddle provided lush arrangements that surrounded Ronstadt's voice and created an exquisite setting in which her singing could be the focal point. The vocal control that she displayed on the *What's New* album was obviously strengthened by her coloratura training amid the run of *The Pirates of Penzance.* Although the "chanteuse" Linda Ronstadt who is heard on *What's New* isn't as high a soprano as the winsome Mabel Stanley, portraying Mabel helped to instill confidence in Linda. The clear and sustained notes that she holds on "Someone To Watch Over Me," "Good-Bye," and the song "What's New?" bear witness to this newly instilled confidence.

The song choices on her first Riddle-arranged album really made this the strongest of their trio of collaborations together. The element of surprise also worked in her favor. Everyone who had ever been touched by Ronstadt's music in the past expected a certain degree of quality from this album, but no one suspected that she was going to be this good!

What's New contained one classic song after another: Bing Crosby's "I Don't Stand a Ghost of a Chance," George and Ira Gershwin's "I've Got a Crush On You," and Irving Berlin's "What'll I Do" (which Riddle had used as the theme for *The Great Gatsby* in 1974). The album not only appealed to Linda's established fans, but expanded her audience across all demographic barriers. For her younger fans, it provided them with a wealth of new songs that had been missing from the record charts for years. For those record buyers who were older, it brilliantly resurrected several truly great songs from a bygone era.

"It wasn't meant to be dedicated to older people," Linda explained, "but I'm gratified by their response. They went through a lot, you know, with the sacrifices they made during the war years, and in the '60s, we all grew up with such a defiant posture against the generation that preceded us — just spoiled ingratitude. We told them, 'Forget your values, your expressions, your hairstyles, your clothes, your music.' "

When *What's New* was released, it drew a wave of rave reviews. *Time* magazine called it "a ravishing album of standards by a lovelorn rock and roll girl." *Stereo Review* referred to it as "an almost sinfully pleasing album . . . with Riddle's expert help she gives a series of musically accurate, professionally crafted, and totally charming performances." And *People* declared it one of the ten best albums of the year.

The album was still high on the charts when Linda announced that she was planning to do more albums with Nelson Riddle. "I'm dying to do another one with him," she claimed. "I've already started to pick out the songs."

In the fall of 1983, and again the following spring, Linda Ronstadt, accompanied by Nelson Riddle and his forty-seven-piece orchestra, hit the road for an immensely successful series of concerts. Their touring encompassed a list of varied venues, from Radio City Music Hall in New York City, to the New Orleans World's Fair Amphitheater, to the Copa Room at the Sands Hotel in Atlantic City, New Jersey.

The very idea of appearing at Radio City Music Hall — the nation's ultimate art deco theater — along with the legendary Nelson Riddle and his orchestra was almost overwhelming for Linda. The only member of her previous touring band was pianist Don Grolnick. What went through her mind as she prepared to make her first non-rock and roll entrance at Radio City? "God," she pondered, " 'Where is the nearest subway?' I was really scared. But I really wanted to do it. It was like a dream to me."

Her fascination with the material, and the confidence that Nelson Riddle had in her, made her feel exuberent while performing on this particular tour. She explained at the time, "The songs are so good, and I feel so good singing them. I've been in the business almost 20 years and suddenly find myself with a lifetime supply of wonderful songs. I don't have to go out and struggle through a show that's made out of ten hits I'm real tired of. I'm not really thrilled with the idea of singing 'You're No Good' the rest of my life. It's a good song, but you can't really compare it to Gershwin.

"A Gershwin song is like a hand motion in ballet. It expresses 97 different emotions. In a rock and roll song, you get one or two. There are a lot of good rock and roll songs, and they're nothing to sneeze at,

Linda enlisted famed conductor / arranger Nelson Riddle, and together they recorded three historic albums of American jazz and pop standards. What's New, Lush Life, *and* For Sentimental Reasons *have become Ronstadt classics.*
(Photo: Scott Weiner/Retna Ltd.)

but most rock and roll is written for guitarists. Standards were written for singers. 'Honky Tonk Women' is a great record — but it's not a great song. "The 1940s were absolutely the Golden Age of the popular song," she said. "Today we're in the Golden Age of record making in terms of technical production. But back then it was songwriting at its best. The songs are so romantic. Where people used to tell me, 'I took acid to your "Different Drum"' they now tell me that their child was conceived to the *What's New* album!"

When *What's New* was released, the Cinemax cable TV network produced, filmed, and broadcast a promotional video of four of the songs. The half-hour show, which was done as part of their "Album Flash" series, was so successful that a full hour-long concert program was planned for early 1984. Several of the same people who worked on the "Album Flash" project with Ronstadt were also used on this program, including director David Lewis and producer Robert Lombard.

The fact that Linda's *What's New* stageshow was quite elaborate (including a costumed background vocal group and a three-dimensional backdrop) posed certain cinematographic challenges. "I was notified a week before New Year's," recalled Robert Lombard, of receiving the "green light" on the Ronstadt concert special. "We started right away to scout locations. Our first choice was the Casino on Catalina Island. It was gorgeous, but out of the question, because it wouldn't accommodate the huge show that had been designed. We kept looking and finally decided on the Arlington Theater in Santa Barbara, where we shot two live concerts on the ninth and tenth of March."

The special was entitled "Linda Ronstadt in Concert with the Nelson Riddle Orchestra," and it debuted on May 27, 1984. Since Linda and the orchestra were all costumed in 1940s clothes, and the theater was from that era, the live audience was asked to dress in the style of that decade as well. According to Peter Asher, "While some came in ordinary tuxedos, others arrived in double-breasted suits. The most extreme couple: he in a '40s American officer's uniform, she in an old-fashioned wedding dress. They looked terrific."

The television special, created from those two concerts in Santa Barbara, opened with Linda singing the song "I've Got a Crush On You" to a simple accompaniment. Her hair was done in a 1940s pulled-back style, and she was wearing a black dress with an elaborately embroidered collar. She was filmed in black and white at the beginning, but as she hit a crescendo in the song, the curtains on the stage parted to reveal Nelson and his orchestra, and as in *The Wizard of Oz* everything was suddenly in color. The effect was wonderful. In the middle of the second song, "What's New?," a second set of back curtains stretched open to reveal an additional horn section. Behind them was a back-lit set that simulated the 1940s Manhattan skyline.

In addition to several of the songs from the *What's New* album, the special also debuted some of the songs slated for Linda's second album with Riddle, which had yet to be recorded. Those songs included "Falling in Love Again," and Fats Waller's "Keeping Out of Mischief Now." "Falling in Love Again" was featured on her 1984 *Lush Life* album; the Waller tune, however, was not (although she announced in this special that it would be).

For the song "Falling in Love Again," Linda addressed the audience for one of the first times in her career. In her little Minnie Mouse-like speaking voice, she told the audience that her mother warned her "not to cry for the moon," and that one should be careful what they wish for or they could end up sorry. With that, a huge crescent moon was lowered from above the stage. She took a seat inside the moon, and it was hoisted up into the stratosphere of sparkling lights that twinkled like stars behind her.

In the middle of the show, a small curtain-backed platform was pulled onto the stage, resembling the intimate stage of a 1940s jazz club. Clad in formal chiffon "prom" dresses, three singers calling themselves the Step Sisters stepped onto the small stage and began their rendition of the Andrews Sisters' song about gold-digging: "Daddy." Mid-song, Ronstadt, wearing a white prom dress and a wrist corsage, joined the girls as though she was the fourth Step Sister. For three subsequent numbers, the girls were accompanied by Red Young in a white tuxedo jacket, and together they sang "Mr. Sandman," "I've Got a Guy in Kalamazoo," and "Choo Choo Cha' Boogie."

After the other singers left the small stage, Linda sang a sorrowful version of "I Don't Stand a Ghost of a Chance with You." She then rejoined Riddle to sing "What'll I Do" and "Good-Bye." After the curtain closed, Linda and her pianist, Don Grolnick, came out from behind the curtain and began the encore song, "Desperado." Before the song was over, the curtains parted and the full orchestra and the Step Sisters joined in. Including the 1973 song was an interesting idea, which Linda would later claim was not very successful.

Nelson Riddle commented on the inclusion of "Desperado" by stating, "It seems to be a gesture toward her rock fans. Many of these kids are just stretched out of shape with all this new/old material submitted to them. It means that the concert ends on a note of reassurance."

After years of going on concert tours as "one of the boys in the band," Linda was thrilled to have the female companionship of the Step Sisters (singers Liza Edwards, Elizabeth Lamers, and Rita Valente). According to her, "The girls and I love to get dressed up and paint our faces. We see books about old movie stars and paint our mouths that way, or get a '40s roll in our hair." She said that they would get "into character" by pretending that they were going to entertain a 1940s audience: "We have the same bunch of girls backstage, and go through this ritual. We put on our make-up and then I go on stage with exactly the same person. I don't want anyone to come up to me, because it's liable to blow my concentration."

During one of the shows, Linda announced from the stage, "I've heard a rumor that Frank Sinatra's been doing my tunes." The audience laughed wildly at that line. Linda thought it was funny until she got backstage and discovered that Sinatra had been in the audience that night! "If I'd known he was here, I'd have left," she said in shock, when she found that he truly had been there that night, and had left mid-show.

One of the things that she liked the most about this particular stageshow was the fact that the music gave it much more scope than her rock and roll concerts possessed. "The funny thing is, people sometimes think there is less emotional range in this show than in the rock show, but it's just not true," she said. "I only had one volume with the old show: loud. This music is so much more satisfying on an emotional level, because it's so much more complex."

The concert tour ended in July 1984, and by August she and Nelson Riddle were back in the recording studio, working on their second album. Again, Peter Asher produced and George Massenberg was the recording engineer. This time around they recorded a dozen songs and varied the tempo of the selections. Not only were there lush ballads, like on the *What's New* album, but there were also some "swing" tunes as well.

The first side of the album included mainly lamenting love songs like Hoagy Carmichael's "Skylark," Rodgers and Hart's "It Never Entered My Mind," and the Frank Sinatra standard "I'm a Fool To Want You." The second side featured Duke Ellington's jazzy "Sophisticated Lady," a bouncy version of Rodgers and Hart's "You Took Advantage of Me," and swinging renditions of the 1930s standards "Can't We Be Friends" and "Falling in Love Again." The album ends with the ultimate smoky jazz club rendition of Billy Strayhorn's "Lush Life" (that is, if one could fit a forty-seven-piece orchestra on a smoky jazz club stage!)

The *Lush Life* album was released in November 1984, and it sold briskly throughout the Christmas season. By January it was certified both Gold and Platinum, and it peaked at Number 13 on the LP charts. Like *What's New* before it, *Lush Life* won Nelson Riddle a Grammy

Award in the category of Best Instrumental Arrangement Accompanying Vocal(s).

The reviews for the album were all favorable, with several publications, including *Rolling Stone,* favoring the varied pace of *Lush Life* over the more somber *What's New.* In their review of *Lush Life, Stereo Review* questioned the validity of reinterpreting the classic material, and then conceded, "It presents a greater challenge to Ronstadt to make something new, interesting, and — most important — emotionally valid out of material that has had classic if not 'definitive' interpretations in the past. On the whole, she succeeds superbly. Thanks to her authentically contemporary musical sensibility and voice (and Riddle's masterly arrangements), her performances ring true on their own terms." *USA Today* called the album "a toast to love of the most romantic kind," and *People* proclaimed that "Linda has fun with her latest adventure in musical time travel, *Lush Life.*"

When she finished the recording sessions for the *Lush Life* album, she was on a dead run. The sessions were completed on October 5, 1984, and she was already a week late for the beginning of rehearsals for her latest theatrical excursion: portraying the role of Mimi in Puccini's famed opera, *La Bohème.*

Although it had been previously announced that Linda would return to the musical theater in Brecht and Weill's *The Seven Deadly Sins,* there was a change of plans after the filming of *The Pirates of Penzance.* Linda became enchanted with the character of Mimi, the frail Parisian seamstress dying of consumption in *La Bohème.*

During the summer of 1983, Linda spoke about the future roles she would like to play. "I want to play Snow White, she's my favorite character in literature," she proclaimed. "I first got interested in *La Bohème* when I saw the silent movie with Lillian Gish. Lillian Gish was the real Snow White. After I saw the movie, I got the record. And I thought, 'Hey, this is pretty good.' I called up Beverly Sills and told her I had discovered this opera and wanted to play Mimi. And Beverly said, 'My dear, every soprano in the world wants to play Mimi!' I felt as if I were a teenage kid who had just discovered Chuck Berry."

Wilford Leach announced in early 1984 that Linda was going to star in a revolutionary new interpretation of *La Bohème* that autumn, at Joseph Papp's Public Theater. The show was to be scaled down to fit in an intimate theater setting, with the libretto undergoing a new English language interpretation, and Leach directing. "Linda has a big thing for Lillian Gish's silent movies," Wilford explained. "She did a silent movie of *Bohème.* We modeled *Pirates* after Lillian Gish — the looks, the way she holds herself. We were talking about pieces we thought were beautiful. Linda said, 'I think I can do this if I work real hard.' "

With that, the production was put into motion, aiming at an October premiere. Linda immediately resumed taking voice lessons with her New York vocal coach Marge Rivingston. However, her *What's New* tour with Nelson Riddle took up much of her time in the first half of the year, and the recording sessions for *Lush Life* absorbed another large piece of time, from August 24 to October 5.

Whereas the character of Mabel Stanley was a coloratura soprano of ultrasonic highs, and Linda's rock and roll voice utilized her lower registers, the role of Mimi demanded a third range that was decidedly in between the two. As Ronstadt explained, "It's not that Mimi is so high, it's so middle. And there's this idea that I've been systematically working on my voice. It takes 20 years to make an opera technique. I can't do it in six months. Opera singers develop daily habits over the years — exercises, warming up — which I don't have. And let's say I'm on tour and do have a day off to work. I'm in the middle of Ohio, and where is my teacher?"

When she arrived in New York City to begin rehearsals in October, Linda began working with Marge Rivingston again. According to Rivingston, she felt that the role was believably within Ronstadt's command. "Singers hear sound within themselves, resonating in their bones," explained Marge. "People outside hear the same thing, except it's resonating through the air — it's a softer sound. While opera singers hardly ever have a chance to experience themselves from 'the outside,' rock singers are tuned to their own voices. They spend hours on end in recording studios hearing playbacks of themselves."

Nelson Riddle also voiced his vote of confidence for Ronstadt. "Linda has marvelous projection," he said, "and you'll hear in the new album *{Lush Life}* how that biting sound has modulated. She's beginning to find a real softness and sweetness. Yes, her voice may be frail for Puccini, but perhaps she can capitalize on that frailty, make it work for her."

The plot of the opera takes place in the 1830s in Paris, and is based on Henry Murger's series of autobiographical stories, which appeared in the journal *Le Corsair* between 1847 and 1849, entitled "Scenes de la Vie de Bohème" ("Scenes From Bohemian Life"). The story focuses on several struggling artists — painters and poets — trying to make a living by plying their crafts.

For this particular production, which was mounted at the Public Theater in Greenwich Village, the setting was transposed to Paris in the 1890s. According to Wilford Leach, "We're not doing second-rate opera, we're doing a first-rate popular show, a fresh reading of the familiar. It's basically still the 1830s, and basically still Paris, but it could be the East Village. It's as if we got the text and music in the mail

and said, 'This is wonderful; let's do it.' The idea is to do it almost like
a play. The aim is to focus on the melody and the story."

The story that *La Bohème* tells is both beautiful and tragic — a
story of love and friendship and sacrifice. When it was first proposed to
Linda, she listened to a full recording of the opera and recognized some
of the songs. "My father used to sing me the tunes in the car," she said,
"but I'd never heard it all the way through. To me, *Bohème* was like an
old Buddy Holly song that everyone had forgotten."

She said she always knew that her voice could make more kinds of
sounds than she had tried: "If I'd been born at the beginning of the
19th century, I'd definitely have been an opera singer; but when I was
a teenager, I loved Little Richard so much, all I ever wanted was to
sound like him. I've been doing rock and roll for so long, and those
songs don't tell my story anymore. I love them, but they are like old
friendships — or love affairs — which didn't turn out to be what they
felt like at the time. You sing the same word over and over again and it
doesn't mean anything anymore."

While Linda was busy in Los Angeles, recording her *Lush Life*
album, the New York Shakespeare Festival was still without a Rodolfo
to play opposite Ronstadt's Mimi. Finally, they decided on country and
western singer Gary Morris. Not only did he have the voice to carry off
the part of Puccini's poet, but he was a handsome teddy bear of a man
who would be the perfect counterpart for Linda's portrayal of the frail
seamstress.

"It's a marvelous production," Morris said in November 1984,
days before the show opened. "I got involved because the production
company here put out an 'open call' to record labels, looking for someone to play the lead role of Rodolfo in this production, and I think there
were several names submitted. There were 200 to 400 people audition-
ing for the role. My name was submitted, and it was probably one of
the most unfamiliar names, to these people, anyway. Basically, because
my management and my record label persisted with saying, 'Please go
sing the audition!' They had the audition set up. It evolved that I got
the role. I was one of the last people to audition. As late as September,
they still hadn't found anybody to play Rodolfo. I came in and auditioned, I think the 17th or something like that. Three days later they
called me and said I was Rodolfo if I wanted it."

Although he had placed nearly a dozen singles in the country and
western Top Ten (including "Why Lady Why," "Velvet Chains," "The
Love She Found in Me," and "The Wind Beneath My Wings"), he was
unknown by pop music fans. His recording of "The Wind Beneath My
Wings" was awarded the 1984 Song of the Year trophy by the Academy
of Country Music, yet he was still a bit of a newcomer in the eyes of Linda's multifaceted audience.

When rehearsals for *La Bohème* began at the Public Theater in October 1984, Gary found Linda very charming to work with. "She's wonderful. She's very professional, very articulate and warm, and caring and lots of things that I didn't perceive or wouldn't ever have perceived of a rock and roll star to be so warm . . . Everybody in the cast loves her," he said.

In a very real sense, both Gary and Linda had taken a dive into the deep end of the opera pool. Morris had never even seen an opera in his entire life at the time that he accepted the role of Rodolfo in *La Bohème*. In fact, he had never seen a Broadway show either! According to him, "Not to sound flip, but working with Linda didn't frighten me at all. She's as much out of her element doing this as I am!"

Interviewed at the Public Theater before the opening of *La Bohème*, Morris confessed, "We've got to get her to sing another country song before this [show] is over. We've talked about it. She said, 'Yeah, I'll do something with you.' We might do something that'll be on my next album as a matter of fact." The Ronstadt/Morris country duet has yet to have taken place. But judging by Linda's track record, anything is possible.

" 'What am I doing?' I ask myself," said Ronstadt amid the rehearsals. "I've been singing five, six, seven hours a day in this new voice I don't know what to do with. Sometimes I feel like someone let all the air out of my tires, but after a few days, I seem to come back a little stronger than before — like you do when you're lifting weights."

Wilford Leach claimed that he liked the way the rehearsals were shaping up, even if Ronstadt felt that her voice was a bit strained. "I like that break at the top of Linda's voice," said Leach at the time. "What she does is perfectly pure, though it won't remind you of opera singing. It's why I also like Americans doing Shakespeare. They give it a raw energy. My interest is in theater, not second-rate performances of opera. But what we are doing is Puccini. It's his plot and his music — not an arrangement of it — though we have moved the action to Puccini's day in the 1890s. I think Puccini might have liked Linda in the part. He was as full of life as she is."

Rather than using a direct interpretation of Puccini's lyrics, the 1984 Public Theater version of *La Bohème* featured all-new lyrics, sung in English, and twentieth-century phrases. The new lyrics were sung in a modern style, in spite of the 1890s Parisian setting. It was quite literally a pop opera, with the music — which is usually played by a full orchestra — being performed by a twelve-piece pit band. The show itself was presented in a very intimate setting, with an audience of several hundred people surrounding the small stage on three sides.

There was no dialogue in the two-hour show; everything was

sung. The amount of lyrics she had to sing, and the key that she had to sing them in, soon took a toll on Linda's voice. It was decided early amid rehearsals that she could not sing all eight weekly performances of the show. At first the plan was for Ronstadt to sing four performances a week, and the other four would be performed by Patti Cohenour. Likewise, it was decided that Gary Morris would perform only four shows a week, and he would alternate with actor David Carroll. Before the show officially opened, the strain on Ronstadt's vocal chords was too great, and the decision was made that, upon the recommendation of her throat doctor, she would perform only three shows a week to preserve her voice. A third "Mimi," Caroline Peyton, performed one show a week.

Unlike Mabel in *The Pirates of Penzance,* the role of Mimi is not a two-song ingenue featured part. In this opera, Mimi and Rodolfo carry the show. Obviously, the inclusion of Linda in the cast was the reason for the excitement about this particular production. And, because of Gary Morris' stature in the country music world, the performances to catch were those which featured both recording stars as the doomed lovers.

Before the previews of *La Bohème* began, in November 1984, every single Ronstadt performance was sold out, through the conclusion of the show's run, in the end of December. Joseph Papp admitted that if it hadn't been for Linda's involvement in the show, in any capacity, the production might not have been mounted.

Explaining details about the production, Gary Morris said that he liked the way the show was presented in an intimate atmosphere, as opposed to having a large theater audience. The way in which it was done, the performers and the audience could look each other directly in the eye.

"The way it's done here, it's really brought to the people," said Morris, "as opposed to thrown out to a mass of people. It's brought down — not musically — but the way we set it here in the Public Theater. And that's really the brain child of Wilford Leach, the director here, whose idea it was to do this in a small house — scale it down so that people could feel like they were in a living room watching this happen. It's really, really been effective. You see tears in the crowd. It really runs the gamut of emotions. We'll make them laugh, think: angry, sad, and all in a two-hour production. It really makes you want to come back for the curtain to see what's actually transpired in the house. I've never been in theater, so I've never gone through that. When you do concerts, you try to move people in different ways emotionally, but you can't do it as effectively as you can here."

Having been one of the fortunate people to have seen this production of *La Bohème* with Linda Ronstadt *and* Gary Morris in the lead roles, this author admits that it was one of the most ambitious and successful theatrical productions mounted in New York City the entire year. Although neither of the country/pop singing stars was trained as an operatic singer, in Act Four, when Mimi dies in Rodolfo's arms, there wasn't a dry eye in the house. Ronstadt's onstage shyness worked totally in her favor. She was portraying the true character of Mimi, the impoverished seamstress who felt that her life was being pulled by the tragic tides of life. Her performance was totally believable, and Gary Morris' singing was nothing short of incredible. However, everyone did not agree with this opinion.

In spite of the fact that all of the performances were sold out, including a special black-tie benefit night of Ronstadt and Morris at $500 a ticket, the press virtually trashed the show. "Papp's pop *La Bohème* turns Puccini into pap . . . Musically the whole venture is a mess — from Miss Ronstadt upward. And even she is not terrible — just robustly mediocre . . . Ronstadt appeared a remarkably healthy Mimi — she even died looking like a sham-faced advertisement for vitamins — but at least her voice was in reasonably poor estate. She is never going to be a [Maria] Callas!" proclaimed Clive Barnes in *The New York Post*. Frank Rich in *The New York Times* found Linda "lackluster and anxiety-inducing." According to Rich, "Miss Ronstadt battles her way through the role, giving us the fragrance if not the beauty of the gorgeous melodies. Yet even her minor victories so deplete her energies that she never does get around to characterizing the impoverished seamstress: Fragile and almost expressionless from the start, Miss Ronstadt's Mimi might as well leap right from her first aria to the deathbed finale."

It was projected that the Papp production of *La Bohème* could have been extended or have been transferred to a Broadway theater. Unfortunately, that was not to be the case. The show closed on schedule, and it was never released as an album. The only memento from the show appears on Gary Morris' *Hits* album (Warner Brothers Records, 1987). Recorded at the Grand Ole Opry in Nashville, the aria "Your Little Hand" shows off Morris' grasp of the music, and gives a sample of the fresh 1980s interpretation, adapted by David Spencer.

In addition to continuing his country recording career, Gary Morris took his acting experience into new arenas after *La Bohème* closed. In 1986 he joined the cast of the short-lived TV series "The Colbys" as blind singer Wayne Masterson. In 1987 he took over the role of Jean Valjean in the Broadway production of *Les Misérables*. He may still convince Linda to record a country song with him sometime in the future.

In 1985 Linda returned to the recording studio to begin work on her twenty-second album. Her third consecutive LP with Nelson Riddle and his orchestra, *For Sentimental Reasons*, was originally planned as a two-record set, with one album of American standards and one album

La Bohème *proved an ambitious vocal challenge for Linda. Clockwise from upper left: cast members David Carroll, Gary Morris, Patti Cohenour, and Ronstadt.*

(Photo: Martha Swope/Mark Bego Archives)

composed of the Brazilian songs that were popular in the 1940s. Unfortunately, while they were working on their third collaboration, Nelson Riddle's health suddenly took a turn for the worse.

Explained Ronstadt, "While we were working on the album, I could tell by his coloring that Nelson was very ill, though I had no idea he only had a few weeks left. The record was originally going to be two volumes. We had talked about going to Cuba and Brazil to do a second disc of Afro-Cuban band music, and some bossa nova songs with Antonio Carlos Jobim. But then Nelson became so ill that we had to scramble to do what we did."

Midway through their recording, Nelson's mood took a sudden swing toward somber. "One morning he came in with the charts for 'Round Midnight,' " she recalled, "and I was shocked at how dark they were. He looked me in the eye and said he had had a bout of confronting his mortality."

In a phone conservation with New York City disc jockey Jonathan Schwartz in 1985, Riddle claimed that he could tell that he was going to die. "I can feel all my energy slipping through my fingertips," Riddle told Schwartz. A month later, Nelson Riddle was dead.

All of the arrangements for the third Riddle/Ronstadt album were completed before Nelson's death. Riddle had conducted eight of the eleven cuts intended for the album. However, at the time of his death, there were three more arranged but not yet recorded. Following Riddle's written arrangements, Terry Woodson conducted Nelson's orchestra on "Straighten Up and Fly Right," "Am I Blue," and "I Love You For Sentimental Reasons."

According to Linda, Nelson was dissatisfied with the way that "I Love You For Sentimental Reasons" was coming out. After Nelson died, Ronstadt consulted Tim Hauser of the group Manhattan Transfer about arranging for a male background vocal track behind her, like those that could be found on old Glenn Miller recordings. Explained Linda, "It's the kind of thing for older black male voices, mature black male voices, going the segue between the Mills Brothers and doo-wop, or between the Delta Rhythm Boys and doo-wop. It's four-part harmony, it's pretty complex, it's vibrato-y. It's a vocal style that's valid that I'd like to explore a little bit."

She liked the way that particular song came out, and developed a sudden fascination for the vocal groups of the 1940s and early 1950s. "I've been working with Gene Puerling of the Hi-Lo's," she explained in 1986. "He was the real state-of-the-art modern harmony arranger. Brilliant, brilliant guy. He's singing with me now; we're doing his arrangements on stage. It's just so amazingly fun. I just woke up one morning and I wanted to hear those chords! It's like when you wake up in the morning and you kind of have a yen for pomegranate juice instead of orange juice. It's so neat, it hits your brain in a certain way, like a big spray of water in your head."

A second song that was recorded after Riddle's death, "Straighten Up and Fly Right," also included an additional voice on it. James Taylor performed a harmony vocal on the Nat "King" Cole swing classic, behind Linda's singing. "I Love You For Sentimental Reasons" and "Straighten Up and Fly Right" were the two lightest treatments of any of the songs on the *For Sentimental Reasons* album. The rest of the cuts *were* all decidedly more somber.

Talking about the musical differences between *For Sentimental Reasons* and her two previous Riddle collaborations, Linda said, "Although Nelson was wonderful at covering the vocal cracks and crevices between vocal phrases, on this album, a lot of the songs have long rubato sections."

For Sentimental Reasons was released in September 1986 and was certified Gold in December. Although it sold less well than its two predecessors, it was a welcomed third edition of the historic Ronstadt/Riddle teaming. Not only was it released as a single album unto itself, but it was also marketed as part of a packaged trilogy, along with *What's New* and *Lush Life.* The three-album package was entitled *Round Midnight,* and it was a perfect way to link all three of the separate LPs. (In addition to the three-record and three-cassette packages, *Round Midnight* was also released on two compact discs, encompassing all of the thirty-two songs that Linda and Nelson worked on together.)

After the *For Sentimental Reasons* album was released, Linda announced that she was going to close the book on the jazz and pop standard recording phase of her career. "I don't think I could do it anymore without Nelson," she announced with sadness in her voice. "He was irreplaceable. Nobody put jazz in the pop orchestra the way he did. Where other arrangers simply laminated various elements, he achieved a brilliant synthesis."

According to Linda, "The mythographer Joseph Campbell invented a wonderful phrase, 'following your bliss.' He wrote that doing what made you feel blissful was really the only guideline for how to live your life and stay out of trouble. That's what I was doing on my three albums of standards with Nelson Riddle. There was no more blissful musical experience than singing those songs with Nelson's arrangements."

In its review of the three Riddle and Ronstadt albums, *USA Today* compared the albums. "*For Sentimental Reasons* is Linda Ronstadt's third collaboration with esteemed pop arranger Nelson Riddle . . . So what's new?" the review asked. "Her voice. It leads these performances more than on her two previous volumes, the ballads-only *What's New* (1983), and the brassier, occasionally up-tempo *Lush Life* (1984) . . . *Sentimen-*

tal Reasons is the most confident record of the three, but it also has the perhaps inevitable feel of a coda."

During the four years that Linda was taking a sentimental journey through the musical styles of the past, her unpredictable career moves and her personal life kept her in the spotlight. She made a controversial concert tour of segregated South Africa, turned down an invitation to sing on the mega-star single "We Are the World," and lent her talents to several charities of her own choice. In the boyfriend department she went from a long-term relationship with Jerry Brown into a long-term relationship with multimillionaire moviemaker George Lucas. When she turned forty in 1986, the press made the most out of speculating whether or not she was destined to remain a lifelong bachelorette.

Politically, she put herself in a favorable light in the summer of 1982, when she performed before a crowd of 500,000 people in Manhattan's Central Park at one of the Rallies for Nuclear Disarmament. Singing a duet with her was James Taylor, and together they shared the stage with Bruce Springsteen, Jackson Browne, Gary U.S. Bonds, and Joan Baez. She also performed in Tucson that year, to raise funds at a benefit for newspaper columnist Jeff Smith, who had been paralyzed in a motorcycle accident.

However, the following year, she knew that she was going to open up a whole can of worms when she agreed to a series of concerts at the Sun City Super Bowl in South Africa. Although she was assured that she would be playing to integrated audiences, the only black faces in the crowd were those of the uniformed guards and ushers who were working at the concert.

Her opinion at the time was: "The last place for a boycott is in the arts. I don't like being told I can't go somewhere. Like when they told Jane Fonda she couldn't go to North Vietnam. Of course she should have gone to North Vietnam."

Linda wanted to see for herself whether all that she had heard about South Africa was true. "I've been to black Africa," she explained at the time. "I wanted to see what this would be like. I'll be criticized a lot when I get home. But I don't think it's fair. You can't not go to a country because there are some evil people in it. I'd love to get the chance to come back, but who knows?

"This place looks so normal and peaceful," she said while there. "But there is obviously trouble lurking just out of sight. And sometimes it comes into sight."

Linda is just one of those people who has to see things for herself and draw her own conclusions on her own terms. While she was there, she got the picture: something is rotten in Johannesburg. She hasn't returned to South Africa since then, although she did earn a very quick and easy $500,000 for six concerts.

She later explained that she couldn't understand what good a "cultural boycott" would do. "I never got that one. I don't think art should ally itself with politics. Nobody would say anything if I had played Russia, or Israel. No one takes a poll on racial opinions when I play Boston. And what if Paul Simon had been intimidated? We never would have gotten a beautiful record *(Graceland)*. To me, the best reason not to play South Africa is: it's expensive and dangerous. You can't make any money there."

In 1984, while she was appearing in *La Bohème* in New York City, Linda performed at the Police Department of the City of New York's 72nd Annual Night of Stars Benefit. She sang two songs, "I've Got a Crush On You" and "Desperado," at the Shubert Theater to help raise money for the widows and children of policemen killed in the line of duty. She had a couple of reasons for personally wanting to help out that night: "Well, the first thing is that my brother Peter is the chief of police in Tucson, Arizona, where I grew up. The second thing is — well, I just like to do what I can for the police. I mean, when you *need* a policeman, you *need* a policeman!"

Linda said that she had the flu the night the 1985 charity song "We Are the World" was recorded. She also claimed that she is more into doing her own charitable work instead of feeling obligated to follow a pack of her peers. "I do shows for a mental health facility in Tucson that helps migrant workers," she said. "I support People for the American Way [an anti-censorship organization], because there are people out there who are truly dangerous — burning books and everything. We've got to protect our civil liberties."

During this same era, in addition to her special with Nelson Riddle, Linda also appeared on three television shows of note. She was one of the guests on the hour-long Showtime cable special "Randy Newman at the Odeon." A concert performance taped at New York City's Odeon Restaurant, the show was first broadcast on December 8, 1983. She also appeared on "The Muppet Show," and was one of the non-Motown guest stars on the Emmy Award-winning television special "Motown 25 — Yesterday, Today, Forever."

The Motown special was an exciting event, as it featured reunions of several of the greatest groups of the 1960s, including the Supremes, Smokey Robinson and the Miracles, and the Jackson Five. In her segment, Linda sang duets of "Ooh Baby Baby" and "Tracks of My Tears" with the man who wrote the pair of hits — Smokey Robinson.

Ronstadt admitted that she is not in love with performing on television, but every once in a while she is inspired to make an appearance. "Television is something I don't do," she explained, "but Peter Asher called to say the Muppets had asked me on their show — and said I wouldn't have to sing my hits. I said, 'If they'll let me sing "I've Got a Crush On You" with Kermit [the frog], I'll do it.' And they did, and it worked out great!"

Linda's choice of singing material in the mid-'80s (like "When Your Lover Has Gone" and "I'm a Fool To Want You") only added to the public's image of her as the loneliest girl in town. "I don't think I'm lonelier than most people," she argued. "I think probably not even as lonely as the average wife of a business executive. I'm sure that they're left alone and are a zillion times more lonely than I am. People like to think I'm lonely because of the songs I sing. But I don't write those songs, and what else are you going to sing about? If you wake up in the morning and you sew a button on, and it was a sunny day, and you went down the street and had coffee with your neighbor, you're probably not going to write a song about that. But if somebody dumps you, you're going to write a song."

Linda still moves friends in and out of her L.A. home to keep from feeling like she is alone. In 1986 she explained, "Nicolette Larson was my roommate for a year or so. She had gotten a divorce and needed a place to throw her stuff. We were both on the road a lot, so we understood each other very well. I have another roommate, Danny Farrington, a guitar maker. He's just a pal and pays all his own expenses. Right now, we have two little ballerinas from the Joffrey Ballet staying here. I've become a huge ballet fan. It's not an open door but I like to help out friends. And I can still maintain my privacy. The house is big enough for that."

She continued, "I can be alone when I want to be. I close my door. If I want friendship, I go in the kitchen. If I've got a date and want to sit on the couch and neck, I ask everyone to beat it for the night and they will."

This explanation of her lifestyle evokes a picture of her dressed up in her Cub Scout uniform, playing "den mother" to her friends. According to her, domesticity is not one of her strong points. "I can't cook at all," she said. "I hate to cook. I live on peanut butter and jelly. If you look on the shelves, you'll find peanut butter and rice crackers. We graze at my house. We do not sit down for formal meals. I consider myself lazy. I must have a schedule or I'll sit around in bed and read all day. If I have a good book, I'm happy. I don't like going out much. I have piles of stuff all around, although I keep promising myself to put some order into the house. I have a small hill of electronic equipment that I still need to organize. And I can never find a record."

On July 15, 1986, when Linda turned forty, she was very nonchalant about her birthday, claiming, "It's no big deal. Sometimes I do wonder how I've survived in this business for such a long time. I think the closeness of my family has a lot to do with it."

That year seemed to be the one that the press chose to really pounce on her perpetually single status. *People* magazine delivered one of the cruelest blows, when they put her on the cover (March 31, 1986) alongside Donna Mills, Sharon Gless, and Diane Sawyer and asked in blaringly big headline letters, "Are These OLD MAIDS?" The cover story asserted that a Harvard/Yale study showed that the majority of single women over thirty-five can totally forget about ever getting married. The article inside spoke about several single celebrity women, including Bernadette Peters, Diane Keaton, Anjelica Huston, and Teri Garr, as well as the women on the cover. *People* gave Linda a four-percent chance of ever walking down the aisle. Another one of the subjects of the article was Linda's idol: Lillian Gish. The ninety-ish silent screen legend had her own explanation for never having wed. Said Gish, "Actresses have no business marrying. I have always felt that being a successful wife was a 24-hour-a-day job. Besides, I knew such charming men, and I didn't want to disillusion any of them."

Linda said, "If you want to get married, you'd better have a lot of reasons to justify it. And if you are not married, you shouldn't have to justify *that*. Staying single is not a crime. I wish people would stop planning a family for me." There is something about the concept of it that repels her. "You have to adapt to the person you're living with," she argued, "even to the extent of consulting them about the color of the carpets you want. I'm not that sort. I value my own outlook on life."

In the 1980s, Linda's steady beau was cinematographer George Lucas, who is most famous for the *Star Wars* trilogy of films. Ronstadt learned a lot about relationships and the press when she dated Jerry Brown in the 1970s. Therefore, she was rarely photographed with Lucas and did not make public statements about their relationship.

Linda and George were vastly supportive of each other's individual careers. When he was working in London on his 1986 film *Labyrinth,* she went with him to the EMI Elstree movie studios. When she recorded her *Trio* album with Dolly and Emmylou, and wanted a video of the first single, George filmed it for her. When she recorded her 1989 album *Cry Like a Rainstorm, Howl Like the Wind,* it was produced at George's Skywalker Ranch. They were both fiercely devoted to each other and protective of their privacy. Like the song she sang on her *Lush Life* album, it seemed that Linda had finally found her own "Someone To Watch Over Me."

Linda Ronstadt fulfilled a lifelong dream when she toured the United States with the Mariachi Vargas de Tecalitlan and presented her stage show, Canciones de mi Padre. *In the summer of 1988 the show marked her triumphant return to Broadway.*

(Photo: Max Goldstein/Star File)

Viva Ronstadt!

8

"**I** feel like the luckiest girl in the world. I'm not stuck doing anything. I'd like my records to pay for themselves, but I don't really care if they make a lot of money. But it's funny how people assume I'm not singing rock and roll because that isn't what they're personally hearing me do now. I'm around all kinds of music all the time. I hang out with rock and rollers; we make music. Whether it gets on vinyl isn't always important. I was never tired of what I was doing. There were just other things I wanted to do, and there's only so much time."

With those thoughts in mind, Linda Ronstadt plotted her course for the second half of the 1980s. Her position as the most famous and most adventurous singer in American music was never so evident as it was from 1985 to 1988. She performed live with a ballet company, sang in Spanish with Ruben Blades, recorded with avant garde composer Phillip Glass, sang country and western/folk songs with Dolly Parton and Emmylou Harris, performed with Placido Domingo in Central Park, returned to Broadway, recorded an album of traditional Mexican songs, scored a huge hit single by singing the theme song to a feature-length children's cartoon, and performed in a movie tribute to legendary rock star Chuck Berry.

In 1985, Linda began to ease into a Hispanic mode when she sang a duet with Panamanian recording star Ruben Blades on his Elektra album *Escenas* (*Scenes*). The soft story/song that they performed together is a Blades composition called "Silencios" ("Silences"). In the ballad, Blades and Ronstadt sing about a pair of lovers whose love has died. Together they sit in silence, drinking coffee and staring into space. Silence is all that passes between them. Neither love nor hate is any longer felt by them, and only habitual companionship links them. Their duet was one of the album's strongest cuts.

The *Escenas* album was written and produced by Ruben, and the music was performed by him and his group, Seis del Solar. The other guest appearance on the album is by Joe Jackson, who plays the synthesizer on the song "La Cancion del Final del Mundo" ("The Song of the End of the World"). Linda's performance on this album marked her third recording in Spanish, and gave her further confidence in singing in the language that she had heard as a child but never learned to speak fluently.

Ronstadt's budding interest in ballet and the classics led her to participate in two separate classical/dance-oriented projects. When dancer Cynthia Gregory had a couple of dance pieces choreographed using music which Linda had recorded with Nelson Riddle, Linda agreed to make a series of special onstage appearances with Gregory — singing while the ballerina danced. Linda loved the idea of having Cynthia dance to her music, but she felt self-consciously static standing on stage while the fluidly kinetic star ballerina gracefully danced. Complained Linda, "The only thing that could make it perfect would be if I could sing from the pit, so no one would be looking at me."

Her second classically-oriented project encompassed recording two songs on the Phillip Glass album *Songs From Liquid Days* (CBS Records, 1986). Glass is somewhat a combination between a classic composer, a new age artist, and an electronic visionary. He has written operas, musical theater pieces, and dance pieces — all unified with a distinctly repetitive sound pattern which, according to *Newsweek* magazine, "has been likened to an 'errant auto burglar alarm.' "

In an effort to move into a different plane of creative development, Glass asked several pop and rock lyricists to write words he could set to music. The writers he approached included David Byrne, Laurie Anderson, Suzanne Vega, and Paul Simon. The music that he composed sounds something like the soundtrack to watching bubbles rise in a glass of Perrier. There is a strange repetitiveness to his music, which only enhanced the freeform stream-of-consciousness lyrics that the writers delivered to him.

To bring the songs to life, Glass asked several vocalists to sing on the album, including Bernard Fowler, Janice Pendarvis, Douglas Perry, the Roches, and Linda Ronstadt. "Bizarre" is about the best word to describe the two Ronstadt performances on this album. Singing to Suzanne Vega's lyrics on "Freezing," Linda ponders the feeling that she would have if she were to sit on the grass stark naked. The answer: "Freezing." Singing Laurie Anderson's lyrics on "Forgetting," Ronstadt vocalizes about a man dreaming of his former lovers walking across the floor of his room. Both songs are unsettlingly strange, yet somehow mesmerizing. To complete the project, Linda performed the two new age/classical songs live in concert with Glass, in New York City, Los Angeles and San Francisco, in December 1986.

Essentially paving the way for Linda's *Canciones de mi Padre* album, in 1986 Paul Simon released *Graceland,* an album which combined American pop/rock sensibilities with authentic and simulated South African music. At first, people flipped out in a negative fashion, feeling that he was ripping off a society which America had chosen to culturally boycott. However, ultimately Simon created a harmonic musical exchange which brought the music of Africa to the top of the fickle American record charts, and put the spotlight on African culture in a new and innovative fashion.

According to Paul Simon, "People tend to look at all aspects of South African life through the prism of politics, but really, this was primarily about music. That was a hard thing to explain sometimes. Not to deny the political implications, but they are *implications*: for me, music is a universal language through which we all connect. Art has a moral position, inevitably, and showing the life of the country through its music makes it easier to understand the humanity of the situation. I mean, I don't know *anybody* who is pro-apartheid except for Afrikaners. I have a tremendous fear of a civil war-type bloodbath there on a personal level now, because I know people black and white, their children. So I guess this album is meant to be a very small statement, an introduction to people we only know through newsreels; now we'll know them on a more personal level."

Simon invited Linda Ronstadt to sing the song "Under African Skies" with him on the *Graceland* album. When she agreed, he added to the song a stanza that was about Linda's growing up in Tucson. "Under African Skies" was one of the most successful songs on the album and became one of the hit singles released from it. *Graceland* became the cross-cultural statement that Paul Simon intended it to be, and it won the Best Album Grammy Award in 1987.

Paul Simon remembered being quite impressed with Linda's professionalism in the studio. "I showed her the track, sang a sketch of the melody, and asked her if she wanted to sing with me. Working with her is just a pleasure. She's a great singer, comes right in, knows her tune. She's more of a perfectionist than I am, and I am known as a perfectionist."

Concurrent with all of these guest performances, in 1985 Linda decided that the timing was right for reviving a project that had been several years in the making: the *Trio* album with Dolly Parton and Emmylou Harris. The three women were all such close and supportive friends of each other, and they had made such beautiful music together the last time they were all in the recording studio. However, there always seemed to be one scheduling conflict after another that stood in the way of their reuniting. Linda realized that it was going to be up to her to start the ball rolling again.

Emmylou explained, "Linda called in November of '85 and asked if I had thought about doing the project. I had a lot of time available in '86 because I wasn't going on the road much. So I called Dolly. We met in Nashville to pick a producer and the time when we would record. We picked some of the songs. Linda thought it should be done acoustically. Dolly and I agreed. The other album we wanted to do [in 1978] was sort of rock and roll. But we decided to do an acoustic album of really sweet stuff that really shows off the fact that we love to sing together — not to put a lot of production on it. We wanted it simple. We started on Dolly's birthday, the 19th of January [1986]."

According to Ronstadt, "We planned and rehearsed it in Nashville and ended up recording it in Los Angeles. Emmylou dug up a lot of the material, and there are some Dolly Parton originals, as well as songs Dolly learned from her mother. Most of the songs predate bluegrass. Unlike bluegrass, the music is quiet, intimate parlor music intended to be appreciated by the people playing it."

The timing was perfect for this particular project. Dolly recalls that their first attempt to record together was a case of "too many chiefs and not enough Indians. So we had a powwow between the three of us and said, 'Why don't we wait until we can do it properly. Let's weed these people out and get rid of some of the aggravations." Separate managers and dueling record labels were among the snags that had tripped up the three singers when they began their ill-fated 1978 album attempt. Parton had just ended a long-term recording contract, and Harris had recently fired her manager. Suddenly, their path was clear.

"Now I'm in between labels," announced Dolly in March 1986. "I worked with RCA for 19 years, and now I'm not on a label so I could make the right kind of deal with this *Trio* project. Emmylou is on Warner Brothers, but that is also a part of Elektra, which Linda is on . . . Emmylou don't even have a manager at the moment — she's in between managers."

"It's just called *Trio*," explained Emmylou, "because that's such a pretty word, and basically that's what it's all about. We picked songs that we felt would work. I believe that the 'mountain music Dolly' is really the point of reference for this album. Linda and I came together on our love for Dolly's music. We both have recorded Dolly's songs. There is definitely a real ethnic feel to a lot of the material. Two of Dolly's songs were just right for the album."

Without record company interference, and without any outside input, the three women made their own decisions about material. "Through the years," said Dolly, "we noticed that every time we got together, we'd always tend to sing real country songs. Linda and Emmy'd say, 'Oh sing us that ol' song "Your Mama Said," or one of those old country songs.' It always seemed that the simpler the song was, the better we'd sound. So, that just seemed to dictate what we should do: a simpler, traditional album."

The original rehearsal sessions were held in Dolly's Nashville living room. According to her, "I contributed a lot with the old mountain songs, like 'Farther Along' and 'Rosewood Casket,' songs that my mother had loved and always sang. I helped out on the actual phrasing — that old traditional way of phrasing, and some of the harmonies. You know, the fact that I was so authentic for this music, and it's just so much a part of me — they depended on my gut feeling on the delivery, and the way they should be sung. We love to sing together because we are friends. Linda and Emmy are very intelligent and knowledgeable musically about harmony parts — more so than I am. I can sing all day, if it's got a melody and good harmony, and if it's a simple song. But when you get into a song that has really *unusual* chord structures and things, I just get lost. Then it'd be like, 'Linda, what am I supposed to sing? *What's* my part?!' We were all real supportive when it came to those points: they helped me, and I helped them with certain phrasings they liked and thought was real honest."

Linda found that the song "Telling Me Lies" captured the same essence as the traditional country songs that they enjoyed singing together. Although "Telling Me Lies" was written by Linda Thompson and Betsy Cook in 1985, it had the same quaint Appalachian feeling to it that drew them to "Rosewood Casket."

Ronstadt explained, "In a sense we were singing something that would date from 1907 to 1987. We wanted the music to be able to span that time without any real problems, and this song ["Telling Me Lies"] sums all of that music up in a way and brings it to today, which I really liked. It's kind of like time travel in a song. Emmy found it. Linda Thompson — oddly enough — is a friend of mine. But Emmy is an admirer of her voice and her songs — as I am. I was thinking more in terms of old, old, old songs . . . and Emmy is the one who had the insight to realize that Linda Thompson is a traditional singer. Even when Linda is writing contemporary songs, stylistically her contemporary songs contain so many traditional elements that there's no way she could escape it."

The recording sessions were spread throughout 1986, beginning in January and finally finishing in November. Several personal matters were resolved in the lives of the three singers simultaneously with the scattered recording dates. "When we were doing this album," Parton revealed, "one of the big things was — and I don't think Emmylou would mind my saying this — she was going through some real bad times over custody of a child. She'd just married again, and there were a lot of problems, and she was just broken at heart because she was having to go back and forth to the courtroom and things like that. So we were trying to comfort her and there were times when she was all upset when things weren't going right, and then some days things were looking better and she'd be all excited. We were trying to encourage her and give her strength. Then there were some problems in Linda's family at the time, some tragedy, and so she was in a bad place. We were real supportive of one another. We're real friends."

Two of the key people that Ronstadt, Harris, and Parton brought to the project were producer and recording engineer George Massenburg and consultant John Starling. Massenburg had been working with Ronstadt on her albums as a recording engineer since *Heart Like a Wheel* in 1974. "He was just marvelous!" Emmylou declared of Massenburg's work on *Trio*.

Speaking of Starling's role as "musical coordinator," Ronstadt explained, "He really helped out on suggesting a lot of songs. He came to Nashville when he first got started, so we could have an overviewer who wouldn't be a producer or manager. He was someone who wouldn't mind if we threw out half his ideas for the sake of the ones we kept."

Explaining the "organic" sound quality of the album, Ronstadt said that there were some initial problems in the mixing stage of the album's creation. "The way we first tried to record it was flat, without any echo or any electric enhancement. I kept listening to it and going, 'It sounds a little dead, doesn't it?' I was in the studio with the engineer [George Massenburg], because I mixed it, and I was saying to the engineer, 'Why does it sound so flat?' And he says, 'Well, I was trying to make it sound acoustic.' So I said, 'But we used electric instruments [referring to the recording equipment] — just mix it like an electric record. Mix it for what it is.' As soon as we did that, we threw on all the EQ and extra echo and fun stuff. It really just blossomed."

All of the musical instruments on the *Trio* album were acoustic, with the exception of the electric piano and the electric bass on the song "Telling Me Lies." According to Linda, "We had the help and support of all those people who were rooting for — and wanted — a good acoustic record, and had always had it in their dreams to see an all-acoustic record featuring traditional material without any attempt to make a commercial record."

The choice of musicians was as important as the choice of material. "The basic band is Kenny Edwards on acoustic bass," said Emmylou. "We had Mark O'Connor, David Lindley, and Albert Lee on various and sundry acoustic instruments. We used Russ Kunkel on drums. Ry Cooder is on one track. Billy Payne plays piano. John Starling was the musical coordinator and chief inspiration. He was the one who would say, 'Mark, why don't you try crosspicking on this? David, why don't you play mandolin? Albert, why don't you play acoustic?' He was the one who optimized all of that talent. He got the best combinations of what everybody did. I played guitar on a few things. I'm playing on the first track; the first thing you hear is me. I played on 'Dear Companion' and 'The Pain of Loving You.' George swears I'm playing on 'Wild-flowers.' I remember being out there, but I thought I got fired from that. But George [Massenburg] says there is a guitar on there and it sounds like me. I'll take credit! On 'Dear Companion' I start; then auto-harp, fiddle, crosspicking guitar, mandolin, and bass join in. 'Rose-wood Casket' has some beautiful riffs by Albert. There's dulcimer, mandolin, acoustic guitar and bass. We're talking really basic stuff. 'Wildflowers,' a song that Dolly wrote, has full band, autoharp, cross-picking guitar, and mandolin."

According to Linda, "We knew the musicians and how they play, so we knew exactly who to get for each little stylistic thing. We know that if you want odd instruments like dulcimer and autoharp, you call David Lindley, because he's got every instrument in the world. And he brought them *all!* It was so amazing — we walked into the studio the first day, and there was a whole room where David had all his instru-ments spread out: Hungarian saws, Swedish harpolecks, hurdy-gurdies and fiddles, mandolins and banjos, plus every kind of steel guitar you can imagine. We just walked around going 'plink-plonk' on all of them — it was just like being in a musical museum seeing them all spread out like that."

As a songwriter, Dolly Parton contributed two of the songs on the album. She composed "Wildflowers," which was a new song that she had written, and from her back catalog came "The Pain of Loving You," which she wrote in 1971 with her former singing partner, Porter Wagoner.

"I *love* Porter Wagoner, and he's represented on this record," said Emmylou, who is amazed that he is no longer considered "cool" by rec-ord buyers and radio programmers. "I don't understand how people could feel that," she argued, "because if they ever heard 'If Tear Drops

Were Pennies and Heartaches Were Gold' by Porter and Dolly, it would break your heart. I can't imagine anyone in the world hearing that and not deciding it's the most wonderful thing they've ever heard. But, they don't play it on the radio anymore, and they should. Maybe if they play us, they'll go back and start playing some of those old Dolly and Porter things."

Linda claims that she and Dolly tried to pin Emmylou down and force her to write a song for the *Trio* album, but to no avail: "We squeezed Emmy, and gave her Indian burns and strangled her and held her upside down and shook her and did whatever we could to get some songs out of her. But Emmy is just not one to be made to write for schedule. She won't do it. She's such a good writer, her stuff would've been so good for this record. Maybe the next one."

While the performances on the *Trio* album created an image of three girls sitting on the porch of an Appalachian house, strumming guitars and singing, the songs themselves were culled from an eclectic list of sources. "Hobo's Meditation," which Linda sings lead on, was written by Jimmie Rodgers during the Depression. "I've Had Enough" was composed by Ronstadt's friend Kate McGarrigle, and "To Know Him Is To Love Him" was written by Phil Spector and released in 1958. "To Know Him Is To Love Him" became a huge Number One pop hit the year it was released, when Spector recorded it with his former vocal trio, the Teddy Bears.

In the studio, Linda, Emmylou, and Dolly found that each had their own strengths, which added to the success of the project. "One of the things that Emmy's great at is playing rhythm guitar," explained Linda. "So we would kind of lay down the groove or the feel for the song. That was always the pulse of everything. Dolly is pure vocal embellishment. She ties little bows and ribbons, she's like Chase silver when she sings."

"I was good at ordering pizza and Mexican food from all of the local restaurants!" laughed Dolly. According to her, they had a great time working on the album: "We were friends and we got a chance to be girls. We were always talking about the new make-up or the new clothes. One day they brought in Tina Turner wigs for all three of us. We had fun doing it rather than feeling like this was something we had to do. We weren't on an ego trip. We had a chance to sit around and talk about cramps and our family problems. It made it a lot more fun than working with the guys."

On one of their recording dates, George Lucas sent the threesome roses to the studio. Emmylou's were pink, Dolly's were white, and Linda received red. When it came time to plan the release of the album, George directed a video of the first single, "To Know Him Is To Love

Him." It was filmed at Linda's house and depicted the three women cutting out Valentine hearts and singing around the fireplace.

Although George Massenburg was the official "producer," Ronstadt, Parton, and Harris called all of the shots in the recording studio. "It was the girls' record," he admitted. "These are three women who have taken great control of their lives and their careers and will not accept the old ideas about their place in music and in the world."

While the recording sessions were being wrapped up, the trio of singing legends previewed their new album on the telecast of the Country Music Awards on October 13, 1986. Showing off their three-part harmony, Linda, Emmylou and Dolly sang the song "My Dear Companion" on stage at Nashville's Grand Ole Opry. The performance, which was broadcast on CBS-TV, set the stage for the forthcoming release of the album.

Emmylou said that she had been intending to record "My Dear Companion" for several years, but had never found the right opportunity to do so. She had been carrying it around since 1979, just waiting for the right moment to record it. "I was doing [her album] *Blue Kentucky Girl* with the Whites — Sharon and Cheryl," Harris explained, "and they'd come over to record. I said to them, 'This album's perfect, except that it's missing something. I need a real sweet, beautiful acoustic song, something that's heartbreaking.' They said, 'Well, we just heard this song by Jean Richie called "Sorrow in the Wind," ' and they sat down and taught it to me. We went in and recorded it immediately. Later, when Jean Richie heard about it, she sent me a tape of songs, and 'Dear Companion' was on it with her and a man singing. It was so beautiful, I thought, 'God, this is the best thing I've ever heard!' and I kept it on my 'material cassette' since 1979 . . . So, when Linda called and said, 'Let's get together and talk about this album [*Trio*],' it was the first song I put on my tape. It was the first song we listened to, and it's the first song we decided to do."

Even the album package for *Trio* held a striking unity to it. Dolly Parton, Emmylou Harris, and Linda Ronstadt have such different individual images and tastes in clothes that there was a need to set a visual tone to the photos used on the album package. The cover shot depicted the three women as present-day darlings of the rodeo. All of their outfits were embroidered with flowers, appointed with cowgirl flair. Dolly wore a fringed crimson skirt and matching vest; Linda was outfitted in a black skirt, fringed top, and kerchief around her neck; and Emmylou was clad in black jeans, a black shirt, and pink embroidered jacket.

The black and white photo of the threesome, which was used on the back of the album and the inside of the compact disc package, represented the 1907 target era of the material that they sang on *Trio*. All three were photographed in white lace-accented dresses, as if they were performers at the '07 church social. That photograph was Linda's idea. "In my brain, I zeroed in on 1907 for what we were doing," said Ronstadt. "It was my idea to have us in the Victorian dresses, because stylistically what we had in common was from the early part of the century. We have different figures and we all have different styles of dressing and we didn't want to look like three people who'd never met each other."

The album kicks off with the Dolly Parton/Porter Wagoner composition "The Pain of Loving You," which establishes the sound and the predominant subject matter of the album. The song shows off the tight harmonies of the three singers, and like the majority of the tunes on the album, it deals with heartbreak. The song features a brief vocal solo turn by Emmylou, and an acoustic guitar solo by Albert Lee.

With regard to the beautiful harmonies throughout the album, Linda explained, "I sang the melody, with Dolly on top and Emmy underneath." The three-part harmonies are prominent on *Trio*, with all three singers taking solo turns on different songs.

Linda stands in the solo spotlight on "Hobo's Meditation" and the impressive "Telling Me Lies." "Wildflowers" is a big Dolly showcase, and Emmylou carries the majority of "My Dear Companion." The last two songs on the album, "Rosewood Coffin" and "Farther Along," are traditional mountain songs, which receive fresh arrangements. "Rosewood Coffin" was arranged by Avie Lee Parton, Dolly's mother, while Emmylou Harris and John Starling came up with this particular treatment of "Farther Along."

As cohesive and appealing as Linda's three albums with Nelson Riddle, *Trio* sets a mood and a musical approach that is carried throughout. The performances are all flawlessly executed, and all three singers are shown off with maximum vocal success. There are no synthesized effects or attempts at 1980s commerciality — just eleven exquisitely sung songs, presented with emotion and purity.

The reviews for *Trio* were glowing. "Stunningly beautiful on every cut!" exclaimed *Billboard*. And *Country Music* magazine declared, "It is impeccable. The voices are so pure and so clear that even the most hard-bitten of us can't stifle images of mountain streams and sunshine on wildflowers."

"A gorgeous sampler of female harmony singing and thrilling instrumental solos" is how *Stereo Review* described it. "It's a connoisseur's delight . . . exquisitely rendered country music . . . emotionally charged singing," said *The New York Times*. And *The Cincinnati Enquirer* swore that "*Trio* sounds so natural and unhurried you forget you're listening to an extraordinary recording. Instead, you get the impression you're eavesdropping on a very private conservation . . . If this record

In 1986 Ronstadt paired with James Ingram to sing the Top Ten duet
"Somewhere Out There."

(Photo: Elliot Landy/Star File)

were a play, it would be titled 'A Trio of White Chicks Just Sittin' Around Singing About Heartache, Heartbreak and the Hereafter!' "

When *Trio* was released, in March 1987, it was an immediate success. It debuted at Number 38 on the *Billboard* pop album charts, and quickly climbed to the Top Ten. It peaked at Number Six on the pop chart, and hit Number One on the country music chart. By July it was certified Platinum. The album stayed on the hit charts for over a year, and four Top Ten country hit singles were released off of it: "Telling Me Lies," "To Know Him Is To Love Him," "Those Memories of You," and "Wildflowers."

On March 2, 1988, *Trio* won a Grammy Award as the year's Best Country Performance By a Duo or Group With Vocal. This marked Linda's third Grammy Award.

Compact discs had a multimillion-dollar "boom year" in 1987. When the *Trio* album was released, it hit Number Three on *Billboard* magazine's compact disc chart. The album ended up on Warner Brothers Records, and it was one of the biggest hits that the company had in 1987. When "Telling Me Lies" was released as the second single from *Trio,* the decision was for it to be the first country single ever released by Warner Brothers as a compact disc single. It was only the third compact disc single in the company's history, following CD singles by Paul Simon and Fleetwood Mac. The single was a limited edition promotional CD, sent to radio stations.

Simultaneous with release of the *Trio* album, Linda Ronstadt was riding the crest of her first Top Ten pop hit single in seven years. It was the duet "Somewhere Out There," which she performed with James Ingram. The tune was the theme song from the 1986 cartoon film feature, *An American Tale.* The two singers also filmed a beautiful video version of the song which received a great deal of television airplay. The single version of the song peaked at Number Two on the pop chart in *Billboard.* Her previous Top Ten hit in that magazine was "Hurt So Bad" in 1980, which only made it to Number Eight.

The song "Somewhere Out There" was nominated for a Grammy Award in 1988, in the category of Best Pop Performance By a Duo or Group With Vocal. *Trio* was also nominated for a Grammy as Album of the Year. Although Linda did not win awards in either of those categories, she and Dolly and Emmylou shared the glory when *Trio* received a Grammy as the year's Best Country Performance By a Duo or Group.

On July 4, 1987, Linda Ronstadt was one of the singers featured in the Washington D.C. mega-concert to "Welcome Home" the Vietnam veterans. Linda teamed up with James Ingram to sing their huge hit "Somewhere Out There." Also on stage that day were the Four Tops, Frankie Valli, Neil Diamond, Kris Kristofferson, Stevie Won-

der, Anita Baker, Richie Havens, John Fogerty, and Crosby, Stills and
Nash. The concert was simulcast on the HBO cable TV network, with
several edited rebroadcasts over the next month. The money raised from
the "Welcome Home" event went toward housing, education, counsel-
ing, and legal and medical services for Vietnam veterans and their families.

Also in 1987, Linda returned to rock and roll, and to the movie
screen. She was one of the performers to appear on the film *Hail! Hail!
Rock 'N' Roll,* which was a concert film/tribute to Chuck Berry. In the
concert footage, which was a big onstage sixtieth birthday bash for
Berry, Linda Ronstadt performed "Back in the U.S.A." Other rock
stars in the movie and featured on the soundtrack album included Ju-
lian Lennon, Etta James, Eric Clapton, and Robert Cray. In interview
footage, Jerry Lee Lewis, Bo Diddley, and Little Richard are seen discussing the decade of the 1950s — when they put rock and roll music
on the map.

There was talk throughout the year of Linda Ronstadt, Dolly Parton, and Emmylou Harris mounting a concert tour, to bring the music
of their *Trio* album to the stage. However, scheduling problems arose.
According to Linda, "We had dates set. But then Dolly had her TV
show and it just got to be too much piled on her. That's the risk. It was
almost impossible just to find time to do it in the studio."

Ultimately, television appearances supplanted an actual tour.
When Dolly Parton signed with ABC-TV to create and produce her
own hour-long, prime-time variety series, all of her time was suddenly
booked. The threesome made a guest appearance on "The Tonight
Show," wearing their *Trio* album cover outfits and singing "Those
Memories of You" and "To Know Him Is To Love Him." In the interview segment with Carson, the three continually finished each other's
sentences, and laughed and joked about their obvious camaraderie.

When Parton's "Dolly" show debuted on September 27, 1987, it
seemed to be an immediate hit. In the Neilsen ratings, "Dolly" was the
Number Five rated show for its debut week. However, the ratings took
an immediate nosedive after that. The show had several artistic problems, and Dolly's production company never did find an acceptable formula on which to base the show's choppy format.

During the fall of 1987, one of the most successful segments of
"Dolly" from the entire season was the one which featured Linda Ronstadt and Emmylou Harris as guests. Their segment together was for-
matted like an at-home sing-along, with the three women laughing and
talking and harmonizing as if they were in Parton's Nashville living
room. Again, the threesome wore their *Trio* album cover costumes,
with Linda sporting her 1987 Louise Brooks-style bobbed hair-do.

Costumes and hairstyles have been an important part of Linda Ronstadt's career in the 1980s, whether it was the virginal look of Mabel Stanley, the Gay '90s Parisian frocks of Mimi, the shoulder-padded look of a 1940s big band singer, or the frisky cowgirl outfits that she sported on the *Trio* album and television appearances. In late 1987, Ronstadt again went through a visual metamorphosis. This time around she donned long black braids, and in her own chameleon-like fashion, she took on the look of a Mexican *señorita*.

Making her most revolutionary musical departure since she tackled *La Bohème*, Linda dove into still another cultural history tour on her next album — *Canciones de mi Padre* (*Songs of My Father*). Choosing to record an entire album of traditional Mexican *corridos* (story songs), *rancheras* (cowboy songs), *danza habanera* (dance songs), and *huapangos* (celebratory songs), she fulfilled a life-long desire to sing the songs of her heritage.

"I've been singing these songs since I was born. Singing rock and roll has been the most radical departure for me," she claimed. "I've always wanted to do a Spanish album. My father and grandfather and all my relatives used to play these songs when I was a little girl."

The evolution of *Canciones de mi Padre* began in 1985, when she was invited to perform at the annual Tucson Mariachi Festival. As she recalls, "The people who were organizing the festival knew that my family sings in Spanish and thought I would be interested, and they called my dad and said, 'Would she like to do this?' And I said, 'You bet!' because it meant I would get a chance to meet Mariachi Vargas [de Tecalitlan] and Ruben Fuentes."

She decided that if she could get Fuentes, who is an authentic Mexican folk singer, to help her learn several traditional songs, she could perform at the festival. As the plans for the festival began to unfold, Linda immediately began dreaming about recording an all-Mariachi album in the tradition of her idol, Lola Beltrán.

"I wanted to ask Ruben to do a record," she said, "but I had to wait, because he's a big-deal guy. I didn't know if he'd go, 'Well, this chick, I have to deal with her, this American.' But I met him. It was so funny. I had hurt my back. I hurt it so bad I was in bed three months — you know at my age everybody gets into a back injury — but this was just two days after I had hurt it. It was at the point where I was crawling. I couldn't get out of bed and couldn't walk, and I'd been two days in my nightie."

In addition to being bedridden, Linda recalled that when Ruben Fuentes visited, he walked into her Malibu home when her room was at the height of disarray. At the time she had a houseguest, the child of one of her friends, and they were in Linda's bedroom, which was strewn with glitter.

"The little child who had been staying with me was playing with me and was cutting out Valentines," said Ronstadt. "She was only three or four, so I had pieces of paper kind of glued in my hair and pieces of glitter stuck everywhere, and the carpet of my bedroom was absolutely full of glitter. But he called, and I was so kind of out of it from being sick, I had completely forgotten about it, and I said, 'Oh, gee, you've flown all the way from Mexico City.' He had somebody that was translating for him on the phone . . . I called my best friend, Patricia Casado, who owns the El Adobe restaurant in Los Angeles, which is the only restaurant I ever eat in . . . and Patricia and her mother came over to translate. And Ruben walked in and here was this mad woman with this child and glitter everywhere!"

Fuentes informed Linda that he had retired from performing, but for her he would make an exception, because of her obvious love for Mexican music. Not even the fact that Linda was flat on her back and covered with glitter could have dissuaded him from recognizing her sincerity. They immediately hit it off, and he asked her to show him a list of the songs that she had in mind. He was surprised to see that her desired repertoire comprised songs that dated back to the beginning of the century.

When he asked her where she learned of these songs, she announced, " 'I learned them from my father.' I told [Ruben] that they were really the only Mexican songs that I knew, and I really loved them. He said, 'They're very difficult to sing. Have you ever played them before?' I said, 'Not really. I've just kind of sung them, you know, singing along with my father or singing along with my brother, but I've never really sung lead.' "

She got up and demonstrated her vocal range on the songs. "So then I had to lie down, and I was trying to pick keys, going 'La, la, la, la, la, la,' " she said, claiming that she suddenly noted, " 'This might be the key of a song I've never sung before!' So he sort of got a sketch of where the keys were, and he went home and wrote some arrangements and sent them back on tape for me."

Using Fuentes' arrangements, and encouragement from her father, Linda practiced several Mexican songs in preparation for the Tucson Mariachi Festival. Finally, she reached a point where, in her words, she was "passable." When she got to the festival, she later confessed, "I was really nervous. And my dad was really cute. He went up to Ruben and — 'cause Ruben didn't know me or know what I was going to do — and said, 'Have some compassion for her.' He said it in Spanish. 'She's only learning. She doesn't quite know how to do it yet.' So, I got up on stage. I was scared to death and I dragged my dad up afterward, too. If I was going to be humiliated, we were all going to be humiliated. So he came out and sang something. We liked it. It worked out nicely, so I thought, 'Well, I'd love to make an album.' "

When she decided that she really wanted to make an album of Mexican songs, everyone tried to talk her out of it. She had wanted to do it ever since Joan Baez recorded *Gracias a la Vida,* her 1978 album of Latin American folk songs. "I told the record company I wanted to make an album all in Spanish," she recalled, "and they said, 'Joan Baez did it and it didn't sell. Can't you just do a few Spanish songs?' I really wanted to do traditional songs, but I knew that they really wouldn't fit in the middle of a bunch of American pop songs." Even her long-time producer Peter Asher tried to talk her out of it, but she was immovable in her determination. "The only negative comment I've heard is that it's not a good career move. I couldn't give two hoots about career moves at this point," she exclaimed.

"As usual," Linda continued, "I had absolutely no consideration for the audience. I mean, I never do. It's actually less selfish in a way to do it that way, because I only consider myself and I only want it to be what I think is good. I do these songs because I think they're beautiful and because I love them, and I want to hear them done correctly. And, if I please myself first and the audience seems pleased as a result of it — I'm delighted."

With that, she began to make plans to record her twenty-fifth album. It was produced by Peter Asher and Ruben Fuentes, arranged and conducted by Ruben Fuentes, and assisted and coordinated by José Hernández. Since Linda does not speak Spanish, she not only had to have the songs interpreted to her, but she had to be specifically instructed as to how to sing them.

"Even though I had sung these songs when growing up at home," she said, "I still had to practice 15 to 20 hours for each just to get the pronunciation, not to mention the intricate Indian rhythm, which just isn't the same as our African-based rock and roll. One called 'the sweep' is a flowing rhythm in between the beat, like swing. You can't write it and you can't count it — you have to feel it. There are very, very precise little techniques you have to use. Ruben will stop me and say, 'Listen, you have to sing this phrase a little longer and get the big breath here for that jump into falsetto.' It's like going off the high dive. If I do exactly what he says, I can do it."

Explaining the difference in her widely varied material, Linda said, "The attitude for rock and roll was defiant. The songs I did with Nelson were straightforward — they were my Dutch personality. They were my mom. She didn't have any kind of artifice, and I just assumed her attitude: 'This is what I think. I feel this.' But with *these* songs, it's a complete release of that other part of my heart. It's just my dad!"

Comparing the traditional Mexican songs to rock and roll, Ronstadt said, "That stuff is O.K. [referring to rock], and it was part of my development. I tried to choose the best of what was available, but soon the best of what was available wasn't half as good as the most mediocre Mexican song which I sang when I was nine years old and enjoy a million times more, now that I'm grown up and sing better. Contemporary music comes from a consumer economy, where you throw away something six months later because it's outlived its style. It's empty and boring and doesn't interest me anymore. But the lyrics and melodies of Mexican music are based on an agrarian economy, where if you have a tool or a shirt or any useful object, you have to maintain it. Because if you lose it, you can't get another. And that's what the music is like. It evokes a range of distilled emotions and an amazing strength made by hundreds of years of singers who have refined the technique and are rallying behind you.

"So maybe I won't make as much money doing this," she admitted. "I don't care. I never did it to start with for the money. I really didn't. I never sang rock and roll for the money. I just sang because I wanted to sing. And I wanted to sing with the best musicians I could find and get to be the best singer I could get to be. Not the best singer in the world, but the best singer I could be. I've never tempered my ambition. I will never be a *better* singer than Lola Beltrán, nor does it disturb me even slightly, because I have her as a model to look to, and it'll be great fun to have that for the rest of my life, to follow her example. I always loved her as a singer and she influenced my rock and roll style a lot."

As far as vocal dynamics and expressive singing, Linda's performance on the *Canciones de mi Padre* album is by far the zenith of her career. Although the material and the whole mariachi genre may not be everyone's cup of tea, between her incredible vocal control and her interpretive vibrancy she's never sounded better!

As witnessed in all of the songs on this album, traditional Mexican mariachi music speaks of life on passionate and emotional terms. Whether the emotion expressed is agony or joy, the lives lived out in the *corridos* are done so with a lust for life, because tomorrow may never come. The lyrics tell stories of dramatic happiness and/or pain, and the musical style is a return to the 1860s in Mexico.

The first recorded mariachi music dates back to 1907, when a group of American recording engineers discovered Justo Villa's quartet and captured their performance on shellac. In 1908, in the Mexican city of Tecalitlan, a group of musicians formed the Mariachi Vargas. Since that time, the tradition and the music of the original group has been carried on by a line of successive musicians (just like the Glenn Miller

Orchestra continues to exist over forty years past Miller's death). For her *Canciones de mi Padre* album, Linda Ronstadt worked with the current line-up of the prestigious Mariachi Vargas de Tecalitlan.

In 1910, when the Mexican Revolution took place, and Pancho Villa stormed Mexico City from the north, mariachi music was used to express the emotions created by love, loss, life, death, drunkenness, and the celebrations that come in between. Each song tells a tale uniquely its own.

The songs that Linda Ronstadt chose to sing on *Canciones de mi Padre* spanned several different eras and an array of emotions — from loneliness to wild partying. "It was very important to me that this record sound like it was made before World War II," she said. "The things that came later are very nice, but this is stuff that I was exposed to."

One of the highlights of the album is a touching ballad, "Dos Arbolitos" ("Two Little Trees"), which Linda sings with her brothers Pete and Mike backing her. The story that the *corrido* tells is that of two trees growing on the ranch of the song's narrator. Each tree has been provided with a companion for life, yet the singer in the song has none. "Tu Solo Tu" ("You Only You") is a *cancion ranchera* about a lover who is drinking to forget that his heart is broken. "Los Laureles" ("The Laurels") is a lively *ranchera* that likens unrequited love to a rose from Castille which cannot be possessed. "Hay Unos Ojos" ("There Are Some Eyes") is a *danza habanera* with the timing of a slow waltz, in which the singer of the song professes undying love. "Corido de Cananea" ("Ballad of Cananea") is a song from the Mexican Revolution that is a lament about being apprehended by the police and incarcerated in the jail at Cananea. One of the most effective songs on the album is "El Sol Que Tu Eres" ("The Sun That You Are"), which is a century-old farm workers' song in which the singer talks to the sun, praising its fairness for spreading equal light on everyone. On that particular song, Linda is accompanied only by Danny Valdez, who sings and plays guitar behind her on this simple *corrido* about life.

The music on the album is an exciting blend of guitars, violins, trumpets, harp, and percussion. One cannot listen to this album without thinking about a fiesta on a Mexican street and drinking salty margaritas.

When it was released in December 1987, *Canciones de mi Padre* received a great deal of media attention and almost immediately was certified Gold. Predictably, while true music aficionados unanimously praised Linda and the album, several rock and roll publications blasted her latest flight away from her abandoned rock roots.

"*Canciones de mi Padre* is Ronstadt's best record to date!" exclaimed

Newsweek. "Ultimately winning tour de force!" is how *Billboard* described it. And *People* claimed, "This whole album is a cause for celebration . . . lovingly conceived and delightfully executed, this all Spanish album is Ronstadt's tribute to her father . . . Ronstadt sounds in high spirits, her voice soaring and dancing through this melodically rich music."

The lowest blow came from *Rolling Stone* magazine, which complained, "*Canciones de mi Padre* is either a deeply felt homage to her family's Mexican heritage, or the party-gag album of the year . . . complete with a cover that makes her look like an El Torrito waitress who's been nibbling on the guacamole."

When *Canciones de mi Padre* became Linda's sixteenth Gold album and won her the fourth Grammy Award of her career in 1989 as the Best Mexican/American Performance, she knew that she had accomplished her goal. "I knew I had to learn these songs," she said, "and had to sing them, and I had to record them because that's what I do. As far as what the rest of the world wants to do, how they want to categorize it, it's not up to me to decide. My goal has been accomplished, which was just to make [the album]. The fact is that the record has already more than recouped its cost. In those two senses, I have satisfied the record company's needs, and my own needs."

The album cover depicts Ronstadt as a pensive *señorita,* gazing at the stars in the clear southern night, while Danny Valdez serenades her with his guitar. The cover is based on a painting by Jesus Helguera called "Flor Tapitia," which was done in a style similar to Diego Rivera's famed artwork of Mexico.

Just prior to the release of the *Canciones de mi Padre* album, Linda appeared in a PBS television special called "Corridos! Tales of Passion and Revolution." The hour-long program was written, produced, and directed by Luis Valdez, the famous playwright brother of Daniel Valdez. Linda was seen in two roles: as La Chata, the Mexican music hall girl singing the jubilant "Yo Soy El Corrido," and as Adelita, one of the revolutionaries singing "Soldadera" during the Mexican Revolution segment of the show. The program, narrated on-camera by Luis Valdez, was a fascinating and entertaining songfest which brought some of the most memorable *corridos* to life with song, dance, and acting. One of the best sequences found Linda singing a lusty *corrido* around a campfire the night before a revolutionary war battle. She looked and sounded wonderful, and comfortably in her element singing these traditional Mexican songs of life and death.

Just after the release of *Canciones de mi Padre,* on December 19, 1987, Linda appeared as the musical guest on "Saturday Night Live." Paul Simon was the host of the show that night. In one segment, dressed in full Mexican regalia and accompanied by a complete mariachi band, Linda performed "Por Un Amor" and "La Cigarra." In a second musical segment, Linda joined Paul to perform their duet from his *Graceland* album, "Under African Skies."

As she had done with Nelson Riddle, Linda mounted a full stage-show in 1988 — complete with sets, props, costumes, and the top musicians who played on her latest album — and hit the road. The *Canciones de mi Padre* concert tour started on February 8, with twelve stops on the original agenda. The rehearsals were held in Cuernavaca, Mexico. According to Danny Valdez, the rehearsals were held there so that "we could go right to the sources for questions about authenticity. It's been an explosion of the spirit for all of us. To bathe in one's culture is wonderful!"

The stageshow was much more than a simple Linda Ronstadt concert; it was a virtual fiesta of song and dance. It starred Linda, of course, but also featured Danny Valdez, the Mariachi Vargas de Tecalitlan, the Ballet Folklorico de La Fonda, and solo dancing stars Sal Lopez and Urbanie Lucero.

Linda — as usual — assembled the most proficient people in the business to expedite every aspect of the show. The sets were executed by Tony- and Oscar-winning set designer Tony Walton. The ten different sets included everything from a quiet Mexican village to a revolutionary war steam engine, complete with a "cow catcher" on the front which Ronstadt made one of her stage entrances upon. According to Walton, the sets were lovingly designed as a "little Valentine to her and the Mexican folk art that she loves."

Besides the traditional and graceful Mexican folk dances that the Ballet Folklorico de La Fonda performed, additional choreography was provided by director Michael Smuin, who had designed the dance numbers that Cynthia Gregory had performed to Ronstadt's music from the Nelson Riddle albums. Mexican hat dances, and the famous dance La Bamba, were performed with all of their passion and pageantry. Said Danny Valdez, "People will finally see what La Bamba really is — a slow symbolic dance of union between male and female."

Describing her role in the show, Linda Ronstadt explained, "When I'm singing, I'm either the soldier girl or the girl on the cover of the album. These characters don't talk, they sing. Then when the song ends, I step out and acknowledge the audience. It's close to a theatrical revue — more 'Ain't Misbehavin' ' than 'Sound of Music' — because it has the flavor of where the songs came from, in the early part of the century. We have wonderful folk dancers and a great band; the artistry is elegant. But really, to me, it's like telling the stories of my family. If you speak Swahili, you'll understand this show.

"The songs are presented as little vignettes that involve folkloric dancers in regional costume," she elaborated. "I want people to see how deeply ingrained these traditional songs are in the rituals of everyday life. The show begins as a concert, then moves into a vignette of the Mexican Revolution that features the image of a train which was a symbol of the revolution. Another section recreates the album cover and evokes a Mexican village in the 1920s at night. The vignettes are linked by dancing. Everything in Mexico is multilayered, like the burrito and the enchilada. This show is layered in the same way. It presents a series of images one after another of Mexican folkloric culture, visually, musically, historically, and in dance, but it is all set within the first 50 years of this century."

On July 11, 1988, Linda further explored her Hispanic roots by performing in Central Park with Placido Domingo and Gloria Estefan, in New York City's Central Park. Her appearance was part of the first International Festival of the Arts. In the show, which was free to the public, Linda performed two of her Nelson Riddle-arranged songs ("I've Got a Crush On You" and "What's New?"), three of her *corridos* ("Tu Solo Tu," "La Cigarra," and "Por Un Amor"), and a pair of songs with Placido Domingo.

From July 12 to July 30, 1988, Linda Ronstadt brought her lavish *Canciones de mi Padre* show to Broadway's Minskoff Theater, and proceeded to win the most glowing reviews of her singing career from Manhattan's hardest-to-please critics. The "limited run" show on Broadway was one of the summer's hottest tickets on "the great white way."

The *Canciones de mi Padre* show was divided into two acts with several scenes, separating the different types of *corridos*. The first scene of Act One was a straight mariachi segment. The Mariachi Vargas de Tecalitlan opened the show with the song "Fanfarria," after which a huge Mexican fan suspended at center-stage parted, and out stepped Linda Ronstadt, dressed in black embroidered suit and boots, looking like the prosperous owner of a Mexican ranch. She launched into "Los Laureles" and proceeded to show off the glorious control of her beautiful voice on such standout songs as "Tu Solo Tu" and "La Cigarra."

The second scene was a dance segment with the Ballet Folklorico de La Fonda. Sal Lopez and Urbanie Lucero were dressed in Jalisco costumes, and they performed traditional folk dances. The third scene began with the dramatic entry of Linda Ronstadt aboard a revolutionary war steam engine. Sitting on the cow catcher, and dressed like a female warrior, she launched into the songs of the Mexican Revolution.

Act Two began with two numbers by the Mariachi Vargas de Tecalitlan, and then Linda entered in the red skirt from her *Canciones de mi*

Padre album cover and a pair of long, black braids cascading down her front. This was the all-ballad segment of the show. The third scene of Act Two was a dance segment, beginning with the dance company in Vera Cruz costumes, dancing the La Bamba. The graceful movements of the dancers included the traditional tying of a piece of cloth into a bow — with their feet. The effect was beautiful. In another dance, the Jarabe Tapito (the dance company) wore sequined China Poblanca costumes, and for the final movements of it, Linda joined in the dancing, also wearing an elaborate China Poblanca dress.

The final scene of the show was done against the backdrop of a town square with tin fronts on the buildings. At the climax of the show, Linda extended a finger, and a white *paloma* (dove, or white pigeon) landed on it, followed dramatically by a white flock of *palomas*. The show ended with the whole company performing the song "Volver, Volver" ("Return, Return"), which is a lover's plea. The entire show was exquisitely mounted and performed, and it was the most confidently radiant that Linda had ever appeared on stage.

The critics loved it. "Linda Ronstadt excelled all my expectations!" claimed Clive Barnes in *The New York Post* . . . "*Carumba!* Linda Ronstadt's *Canciones de mi Padre* is absolutely terrific! It has the kick of tequila and the romantically lambent smoothness of an unlikely Mexican moon poised in a suspiciously velvet sky . . . deftly staged!" . . . "A truimphant mariachi extravaganza! A vibrant, dreamy triumph!" said *Variety* . . . *The New York Times* called it, "A lavish Broadway style review whose sumptuous visual tableaux and elaborate choreography extend Linda Ronstadt's beautiful Spanish-language album in the realm of musical theater!"

Claimed Ronstadt, "Although this project is the hardest thing I've ever done, it's also been the most rewarding. Like most other performers, I've always suffered from stage fright. But singing with a mariachi band, for the first time in my life I'm not intimidated, because I'm singing like myself. I feel completely happy and at home."

Linda had once again defied all of her critics and masterfully conquered still another arena of creativity. With the album and the stageshow version of *Canciones de mi Padre,* she had focused the spotlight on a stylistic bit of Mexican musical history, and turned it into a 1980s triumph. What more can one say but: *Viva Linda Ronstadt!"*

From pop to rock to country to jazz, Linda has proven that there isn't a type of music she can't sing. In the 1990s she promises to stretch her vocal talents even further.

(Photo: John Bellissimo/Retna Ltd.)

Still Within the Sound of Her Voice   9

Before she hit the road with her *Canciones de mi Padre* stageshow, Linda was already wearing a new hat. This time around she was trying her hand at becoming a record producer. According to her, in the past she had never wanted the responsibility of being a producer. However, through the years she had been moving closer and closer to controlling her own recordings in the studio. She already chose her own material and hand-picked her band members. Why not take the next big step and command the control board herself? In 1988 the perfect opportunity presented itself.

"I never wanted to produce," she explained. "I've had offers, but I just never wanted to. In a sense I always co-produce my own records. I think most artists are involved with [their own] production."

What was it that made her change her mind? Just by chance she had gone to see her friend and fellow musician, David Lindley, and his group El Rayo-X performing, and she fell in love with the new material that he was doing. "I wanted to buy the record!" she said. However, Lindley and El Rayo-X were without a record contract. "I could dream in sound," Ronstadt continued, "it makes a picture for me. It was selfish, really, I wanted the [David Lindley and El Rayo-X] record. It didn't have anything to do with wanting to have this career as a producer, because I don't think that's in the cards for me. I have too many records of my own to make."

However, into the studio she went. Linda used her pull with her record label, Elektra/Asylum, and negotiated an album deal for Lindley and his group on the Elektra label — with the stipulation that she was to be the producer of the project. Lindley had added so much of the authenticity and color to the Ronstadt/Parton/Harris *Trio* album that she was determined to help Lindley out. She enlisted the services of recording engineer Ed Cherney, and into the Complex recording studio in Los Angeles they headed.

"Ed knows a lot more about electronics than I do," Ronstadt explained of Cherney's expertise. "I don't know anything about electrical stuff. I know about sound, and I know about relationships of sound — which is what a producer's job is. You hear patterns and you hear the way something relates to something, if something sounds vague, or if it doesn't sound good, then you do something else. It announces itself immediately if it's good. Over the years you develop an ability to hear sound in microscopic detail. You can hear the tiniest little nuances, the tiniest little breath or gasp or intonation. You can hear texture in a vocal, for instance. We've developed our ears to hear these very subtle relationships or one instrument to another, one instrument to the track, one instrument related to the effect you want to put on it."

According to Cherney, "It's been the most unselfish project that I've ever worked on. [Linda's] so unselfish that what we're doing is making a David Lindley record, *not* a Linda Ronstadt record. In a lot of other situations it doesn't turn out that way — there's someone else imposing their will on the artist. For me it was as if we'd been working together for a long time. I literally cut my musical teeth listening to records by Linda and 'Mr. Dave' [Lindley's nickname]. It's really been quite easy for me because Linda's vision and Dave's vision are so clear that we rarely have to talk about what specifically we have to be doing or what we're looking for, it's so obvious."

Lindley agreed that working in the studio with Ronstadt behind the control board was a great experience. "It's unbelievably easy," he said. "It's very, very easy, because we have a lot of the same ideas about the way things should sound."

Producer Ronstadt concurred, "It's nice to have that common vocabulary. I know him. I know what his music sounds like."

El Rayo-X bass player Jorge Calderon echoed, "Linda really knows what she's doing. It's O.K. that she's a female producer, because she's been around so many musicians, she's cool about dirty jokes!"

The resulting album, *Very Greasy* by David Lindley and El Rayo-X, was released in August 1988. The sound quality was on a par with the most successful Ronstadt rock and roll discs. The music on the album sounds like a combination of white reggae and island ska, blended with rock and roll and a smattering of Cajun thrown in here and there. The most successful cuts are the jumping "Gimme Da' Ting," which features Linda Rosntadt singing in the background, a reggae version of Bobby Freeman's "Do Ya Wanna Dance," and a great ska rendition of the Temptations' "Papa Was a Rolling Stone." Renewing Ronstadt's fascination with Warren Zevon, a sparkling ska version of "Werewolves of London" sounds like it is being performed at a Caribbean island fete.

The salsa had barely settled from the *Canciones de mi Padre* album, and Linda Ronstadt was talking about heading to another geographic location for her next album. This time around she considered heading to Cuba to record an album called *Voces* (*Voices*), which tells the story of a third-generation Cuban/American woman who finds herself caught up in "this new culture of materialism," explained Ronstadt in 1988. "She's really questioning, and she remembers — she remembers her first love and the excitement of her first kiss. It sounds very serious, but she's very funny. She's a feisty little Latin girl, saying, 'What the hell is this?' She's used to taking charge of herself and is just confused as to what direction to take charge in." The music itself, to be sung in both English and Spanish, Linda described as "really traditional Cuban music, before there was even a word such as 'salsa.' "

Said Ronstadt at the time, "What I'd like to do is take my rock and roll band to Mexico City and do an hour show with the mariachis and an hour show with the rock and roll band. That would be great fun! Because people say, 'You're not doing rock and roll anymore!' Well, I had a huge single last year ["Somewhere Out There"]. I sang with Chuck Berry in his movie (*Hail! Hail! Rock 'N' Roll*). I live in that genre still. It's just that I'm not always doing it in front of the public, and like I say, they think when they don't see you doing it — you've disappeared: 'You don't do that!' "

In 1988 there was also talk about Ronstadt recording an all R&B album. It was then that she began discussing the possibility of singing with Aaron Neville, the lead singer of the New Orleans quartet known as the Neville Brothers. What she ultimately ended up doing was create an album that combined all of these elements — something R&B, something rock and roll and, just for kicks, a song with a Spanish title.

After weighing all of the possible musical directions that she could take next, in early 1989 Linda Ronstadt returned to the recording studio to begin work on her twenty-sixth album. Since the word "unpredictable" seems to be her middle name, no one was quite sure what to expect from her. Hardly anyone would have guessed that she would complete the decade of the '80s by returning to pop and rock and roll music. Much to the public's surprise, when *Cry Like a Rainstorm, Howl*

Like the Wind was released in October 1989, that is exactly what it turned out to be.

For her hardcore fans from the 1970s, it was a much-welcomed homecoming. And for Linda it became a masterful showcase for her to demonstrate the vast vocal expertise that she had developed during her decade of stylistic experimentation and voice-expanding development.

Cry Like a Rainstorm, Howl Like the Wind is out of the "classic Ronstadt album" mold, yet it incorporates some exciting new twists. The twelve cuts on the album all fall into three distinctly different categories: five solos, four duets with Aaron Neville of the Neville Brothers, and three songs with the eighty-voice Oakland Interfaith Gospel Choir. Although on paper it doesn't sound like these three different types of songs work together, in the context of this album they are unified by the brilliant production quality of the music, the high emotional pitch of the performances on the songs, and the brilliant dynamics of Linda's expressive voice.

The ballads are smooth and creamy, the orchestrations are lush, the rock numbers crackle with crisp excitement, and most of all, Ronstadt's vocals are buoyant and velvety smooth throughout. Her voice has never sounded better, more glorious, or more exciting. She hits and sustains an ultrasonic range of notes that she was never able to achieve on her earlier recordings. Her involvement in the *Pirates of Penzance, La Bohème,* and *Canciones de mi Padre* projects obviously extended her range, her control, and her self-confidence. She sounds absolutely phenomenal on this album, and it's great to hear her really rock out on the songs "Trouble Again" and "So Right, So Wrong."

Although her music constantly changes, some things do remain consistent in her varied career. Naturally, the production duties fell on Peter Asher, and she utilized her favorite recording engineer, George Massenburg. The musicians on the album included some of her favorites, like pianist Don Grolnick, bass player Lee Sklar, and drummer Russ Kunkel. Several of the songs included on the album represent something of a reunion, namely the three cuts that feature the guitar work of Andrew Gold.

In addition to enlisting the services of several of her musician friends, Linda also involved her boyfriend George Lucas. In fact, the entire album was recorded at his Skywalker Ranch in Marin County, California, from March to August of 1989.

To return to her old song-selection formula, Linda chose the majority of the cuts from old friends whose songs graced her albums during her Double Platinum rock and roll era. Twenty years after she worked with him in the Stone Poneys, Kenny Edwards is represented by his songwriting credit on the tune "Trouble Again," which he penned with Ronstadt alumnus Karla Bonoff. Karla's songwriting on Linda's albums dates back to *Hasten Down the Wind* in 1976. Another veteran songwriter from Ronstadt's past, Jimmy Webb, was first recorded by her when she sang "The Moon is a Harsh Mistress" on her *Get Closer* album in 1982. On *Cry Like a Rainstorm . . .* she recorded four Webb tunes and three songs by Bonoff. For a touch of classic '60s R&B, Linda chose the soul belter "When Something is Wrong With My Baby," which was written by Isaac Hayes and David Porter, and had been a huge Top 40 pop hit for Sam and Dave.

The appearance of *Cry Like a Rainstorm . . .* came at a perfect time. The year 1989 had already been an enormously successful year for several women in the music business who had their heyday in the 1970s. Bette Midler scored her first Number One single in a decade with "The Wind Beneath My Wings," Donna Summer made a surprise comeback with the Top Ten hit "This Time I Know It's For Real," Cher produced two back-to-back Top Ten hits with "After All" and "If I Could Turn Back Time," and even Liza Minnelli released the biggest album in her career, *Results,* and the international hit "Losing My Mind." When Linda took her turn at the bat, she hit an immediate "home run."

The album opens with a Jimmy Webb composition called "Still Within the Sound of My Voice." A lush ballad, the song is thematically similar to "Hey Mister, That's Me Up On the Jukebox." However, this time around, instead of singing to a stranger, she is addressing a friend or a former lover. It works brilliantly, because in the lyrics of the song Ronstadt is actually singing about her comeback. In essence she is saying: "If you are listening to this song, or watching my video, I want you to know that I'm still here singing for you." It proves to be the perfect song to mark her contemporary pop comeback.

The title cut was written by Eric Kaz, and like the majority of the songs on the album, it includes a sixty-one-piece orchestra, billed as the Skywalker Symphony Orchestra and assembled especially for the album. Beginning a cappella, with Ronstadt fronting the Oakland Interfaith Gospel Choir, the effect has the exciting dynamics of a Sunday morning revival meeting.

The three songs written by Karla Bonoff — "All My Life," "Trouble Again," and "Goodbye My Friend" — are without a doubt the most poignant ones on the album. "All My Life" is about finding the love of a lifetime, "Trouble Again" is about a love affair of the tormenting kind, and "Goodbye My Friend" is about losing a close friend to AIDS.

The most talked-about songs on the album are the four duets that Linda performed with Aaron Neville of the New Orleans group the Neville Brothers. Ever since the group appeared in a "cameo" as themselves in the popular movie *The Big Easy* (1987), a lot of national attention has been centered on them. Literally a band made up of four brothers who are in their forties and fifties, they have been working in the music business together and separately since the 1950s. On a national level, of the four brothers, only Aaron Neville has had any sort of major success. In 1966 he scored with a huge Number Two pop hit called "Tell It Like It Is." During that era he toured with soul star Otis Redding and played at several of the major black venues across the country, including the Apollo Theater in Harlem. In 1976 Aaron united with his three brothers, and together they produced a Creole-influenced dance album called *Wild Tchoupitoulas,* which became something of a cult hit. Since then they have been a permanent New Orleans fixture, performing almost constantly at a club called Tipitina's. In the summer of 1989, the Neville Brothers toured with Ziggy Marley.

Linda became interested in doing something with Aaron to help put the spotlight on his expressive voice. When it was announced that Linda and Aaron were working together in the recording studio, it was natural to surmise that Ronstadt was looking to get involved in some sort of Creole/jazz type of music. Instead, she found that his voice blended perfectly with hers, and they recorded the quartet of songs found on *Cry Like a Rainstorm, Howl Like the Wind.*

Linda first met Aaron a couple of years before at a Neville Brothers concert. "Whenever the Neville Brothers came to Los Angeles, I'd be hanging over the rail with every other musician in town," she recalled. He invited her up on stage during one of their shows to harmonize on a doo-wop medley. According to her, "I thought our voices sounded good together."

The material that Linda and Aaron perform together on her album has a wider scope than one might suspect — from the lovely ballad "All My Life" to the powerful and soulful tour-de-force of "When Something is Wrong With My Baby." It is almost as if these four songs are Linda's tribute to the 1960s duets of Marvin Gaye and Tammi Terrell.

Just to have a taste of something Mexican/Spanish on the album, Linda included the Jimmy Webb song "Adios." The lyrics tell about running away to California at the age of seventeen. It is perfect as an autobiographic ode. The background vocals on "Adios" are arranged and sung by Brian Wilson of the Beach Boys.

The majority of the songs included on this album have appeared on other people's albums over the years. "All My Life" and "Goodbye My Friend" are both included on Karla Bonoff's 1988 album, *New World.* "Trouble Again" appeared on Karla's 1980 Columbia album, *Restless Nights.* "Don't Know Much" first appeared on Bette Midler's 1983 album, *No Frills,* and "I Keep It Hid" was sung by Mary Wilson on the 1972 album *The Supremes Produced and Arranged By Jimmy Webb.*

In her own trademark way, Linda knows how to take a song, tailor it for her own voice, and put her own personal stamp on it. With every song on this album, she does just that. She has again proved herself as the most successful interpreter of classic songs in the music business.

The first single off of the album was the duet with Aaron Neville, "Don't Know Much." In just a couple of weeks it was already a Number One hit on the Adult Contemporary music charts, and a major Top Ten pop hit. Likewise, the album was an instant smash that was almost immediately certified Platinum.

The reviews for *Cry Like a Rainstorm, Howl Like the Wind* were exceedingly glowing and superlative-laden. According to *Us* magazine, "Ronstadt really cranks up on Sixties soul duets with Aaron Neville . . . nothing could be better for Ronstadt . . . under producer Peter Asher's orchestration, she puts it together perfectly." *The New York Times* claimed that *"Cry Like a Rainstorm* is Ms. Ronstadt's most consistent contemporary album since *Prisoner in Disguise . . .* with its plush orchestrations and concert atmosphere, *Cry Like a Rainstorm* blends the Southern California style of Ms. Ronstadt's 1970s albums with the more formal atmosphere of her '80s trilogy of American pop standards . . . a strong new album!" And *People* magazine proclaimed: "Good, new pop songs are around for those singers capable of finding and interpreting them this well . . . Aaron Neville, who is to New Orleans what Ronstadt is to Los Angeles — a singer laureate . . . their voices fuse like sunlight beaming through a stained-glass window."

With *Cry Like a Rainstorm, Howl Like the Wind,* Linda Ronstadt had re-established herself as the pop world's leading interpreter of songs of any origin. She had returned to pop, R&B, and rock and roll material, but she did it her way. As the decade of the 1980s ended, Ronstadt found herself at the strongest position of attainment and accomplishment of her career. She had again demonstrated that she could sing any kind of material she wanted and make it into a hit. Although commercial attainment was never her goal, she had nonetheless reaffirmed her status as a contemporary pop legend.

Anxious to promote the album, Linda and Aaron appeared as the musical guests on "Saturday Night Live" on December 9, 1989. Together they performed "Don't Know Much" and "When Something Is Wrong With My Baby." In February 1990, due to the overwhelming demand, the song "All I Want" was released as a single. Because of radio airplay, the song was already in the Top Ten in *Billboard* magazine's Adult Contemporary chart before copies of the single were even released to the stores.

When the Grammy Award nominations were announced in early 1990, Ronstadt was up for awards in three separate categories. "Don't

Know Much" by Linda and Aaron was nominated as the Song of the Year, and as the year's Best Pop Vocal By a Duo or Group. The album *Cry Like a Rainstorm, Howl Like the Wind* was also nominated as the Best Pop Vocal Performance, Female. The night of February 21, 1990, she and Aaron performed "Don't Know Much" on the Grammy telecast and proceeded to win the Pop Vocal By a Duo or Group award for that song. Linda also announced her plans to produce Aaron's upcoming solo album.

In addition to her own 1989 album, Linda also made a couple of guest appearances on the albums of friends as well. She provided all of the vocals on the Phillip Glass album *1000 Airplanes on the Roof,* and she sang the harmony vocals on the song "Hangin' on a Limb," on the Neil Young album *Freedom.*

Now that she's been a singer of Mexican *corridos,* an opera diva, a big band vocalist, an Appalachian folk troubadour, a rock star, a movie star, and a country and western cowgirl, what lies ahead for Linda Ronstadt? This is a totally logical question — with a completely unpredictable answer. Her talent certainly has few boundaries, and she puts even fewer limitations on her scope of experimentation. Where is her quest for musical adventure going to lead her next?

There has been some discussion of further albums of traditional music from other countries. Linda has openly talked about Irish music, and about an album of Latin jazz. This author thinks that an album of German songs from the Brecht and Weill songbook would be ideal to give equal billing to the other predominant part of her heritage. "I wouldn't do a reggae album," she said. "I could never sustain it. And, I'd rather hear Ladysmith Black Mambazo do South African jive than me."

Although she has appeared in three movies and headlined two Broadway shows, Linda claims that acting is not her forte. "I'm not interested," she said, dismissing further acting assignments. "It's like asking a schoolteacher why aren't they a secretary. I mean, I'd infinitely rather be a schoolteacher than a secretary, and I'd infinitely rather be a singer than an actress. Acting is boring to me. I mean, it's interesting, and I respect the people that do it, but why do I want to go and work for somebody else? I'm self-employed. I can do as I please. And when you act, man, you're talking 'meat.' You have to do everything they tell you. You have to wear what they tell you to wear, you have to paint your face the way they tell you to, you have to stand where they tell you to, and you have to act like they tell you to, and I'm not good at doing what I'm told!"

After appearing in *The Pirates of Penzance* and *La Bohème* in New York City, she isn't so sure that she'll tackle any more operas. "They were amazing experiences," she admits, "but I'm a seat-of-the-pants singer, without a trained operatic and legitimate voice. I've been told I could have sung in that style if I had started training when I was much younger. Technically, the bottom of my voice is overdeveloped, while my high voice is patterned after my brother's boy soprano. While working in those shows, I also found the experience of city life very stressful."

With regard to singing all sorts of music throughout her varied career, she theorized, "Musicians never live right in the moment — we are all derivative. Before George Jones there was Hank Williams, before the Beach Boys there were the Hi-Los, and Ray Charles imitated Nat ["King"] Cole when he was starting out. The very first time I thought of recording 'standards' was after Mick Jagger played me a jazz album of standards that featured Charlie Parker and Ben Webster. In the '60s, people drew artificial lines between what was hip and what was not. That confusion of ideology and music, I think, was wrong. I refuse to be an idealogue who memorized rules about good taste and good art. I have to go by feeling, by exploring my own roots, by following my bliss."

Several people interviewed for this book spoke of Ronstadt's penchant for recreational drugs during the 1970s, especially cocaine. Linda, however, claims that those stories are all exaggerated. "In the rock business, particularly in L.A., it's almost impossible to avoid that scene altogether," she said. "The real hard rock and rollers are dead [including her friend Lowell George]. The ones who survived paced themselves. But, yes, I am intense, and, yes, I take chances, and yes, I push it to the limit — but there *is* a limit. Look at someone like Rod Stewart. He's supposed to be the biggest drug taker, biggest chaser of women; I mean, look at that guy's face, his skin, his hair. If he were doing all those things he was supposed to be doing, his skin would be green, his hair would be falling out and he wouldn't be able to walk, let alone run around the stage the way he does. I've learned to pace myself. I just don't do things that are flat-out stupid. Security comes from knowing what you're doing. There was a time when the music just wasn't good enough. I'm doing my best work now. And being fit, in good shape, working out, makes you feel better than taking drugs. Those of us who managed to survive the '60s are so grateful to be alive, that the idea of taking things that, you know, will harm you just doesn't seem smart.

"I'm basically a very conservative person," Ronstadt proclaimed, "and I always have been. There are plenty of girls in show business who do much wilder things than I ever do, and yet they have the reputation of being the most amazing Goody Two Shoes!"

In a way, Linda feels that the press has a habit of distorting what she says. "Interviews," she explained, "in a sense, steal your soul, your privacy. If I come out with an opinion about something, or a funny, snappy remark, I can't use it again. After it has gone into print, it has become useless, a cliché." However, she was quick to admit, "The press has nobody to check its authority to control it — and thank God there isn't. I would sooner see us go down in the worst kind of decadence and horrible corruption than see the press be censored; but if the press is unwilling to take responsibility for its actions, then it will cause its own demise. It's gotten to the point where I pick up a magazine and I just don't believe a quarter of what I read. I know how much stuff has been distorted about me. It even happens in places like *The Wall Street Journal* — my hero."

In March of 1988, Ronstadt found herself in the middle of a public battle with *San Francisco Chronicle* columnist Herb Caen. In an effort to have her own house in the San Francisco area, so she could be close to her steady beau, George Lucas, she purchased a $2.55 million home in the area of the city known as Pacific Heights. When Herb Caen published the address of the house in his column, Ronstadt was madder than a wet hornet. Not only did she denounce him as a "creep," but she also claimed that his action caused her to "not like the house, and it made me not like the neighborhood, and it made me not like the city." She promptly looked into selling the piece of property — even before she moved into it!

As Linda's music has changed over the years, so has her audience. Now she doesn't find herself in rock and roll auditoriums that reek of marijuana smoke. She is more likely to appear in actual theaters, or prestigious halls like Radio City Music Hall. "They're not teenagers with terrible identity crises," she says of her 1980s and 1990s audiences. "People bring their fathers backstage to meet me!"

Although she claims that a life in show business can carry with it severe loneliness, she is happy with her life. "Wherever I go," she said, "I carry my lunch, a cassette player and a good book." Her favorite books are still history books and nineteenth-century novels.

Throughout her career, Ronstadt has been all over the world, but Tucson, Arizona — her hometown — is still her favorite place on the globe. "I still feel that city is my home. My old room is still there. I miss the desert and the stars and the quiet. I go to Tucson several times a month. My family lives there. They know when they have a good deal. And I love visiting my two nephews. They sing with me and I hate to miss anything with them."

Since her brother Pete is the chief of police in Tucson, it does put some constraints on her. "I make sure to obey the speed limit," she swears. "If I get caught, I get a double ticket and a lecture. A speeding ticket would hurt his feelings!"

According to Linda, another reason for loving Tucson is the Mexican food that she finds there: "I still go home and have such a great time eating tamales at Christmas. Tamales under a tree keeps you sane!"

For Linda Ronstadt, making music — of all sorts — is what she enjoys the most. " 'Joy' is a combination of despair, fear, fatalism, anger, triumph — it's all those things. You know [author/philosopher] Joseph Campbell? He was a very good friend of mine, the neatest man I've ever known. He said to me once, 'Life is basically intolerable.' He said music is the only way we have of dealing with it, and music is mythology. Music is an oral myth. Music is oral dreaming. It's a way of triumphing over despair. The Catholics say, 'Life is a vale of tears: Help me here in this vale of tears.' It's a myth — the metaphor of life is the vale of tears. So, if you can triumph over it, that's cause for joy!" said Linda.

As 1990 began, Linda not only celebrated with a new hit album, but a new boyfriend as well. Her new beau is Quint Davis, a Louisiana empresario who is the producer of New Orleans' annual Jazz and Heritage Festival. She has kept busy with Davis, a summer 1990 concert tour, and with producing Aaron Neville's solo album.

"Today I'm comfortable," she claims of her life and her lifestyle. "I really don't need much money to make me happy." For that reason, she feels that she is free of any constraints from her manager or her record company. If she feels like singing the Tucson phone book as her next album, and she feels that it is worthy, and she can do it well — who knows?

"I hope to be singing until I'm 80!" she proclaims. And hopefully, she'll make good her promise. Whether she's singing country and western, Mexican folk songs, American blues, pop standards, Motown hits, new wave rock, bluegrass folk songs, or Broadway show tunes — it really doesn't matter. Linda Ronstadt is America's most gifted and most successful soprano pop singer. She is a stylistic singing chameleon whose talent knows no boundaries.

Wherever it is that her eclectic taste and her highly developed sense of musical adventure leads her next, her devoted audience is sure to follow. Linda Ronstadt's brilliant and successful singing career will continue to evolve, flourish, and grow — as long as there are music lovers in the world who are still within the sound of her glorious voice.

Wishing upon a star. By constantly challenging herself, Linda Ronstadt makes all of her musical dreams come true.

(Photo: Scott Weiner/Retna Ltd.)

Linda Ronstadt
Discography

ALBUMS

1. *Linda Ronstadt and the Stone Poneys*
   (Capitol Records ST-2666)
   Released: January 1967
   (Re-released as *The Stone Poneys Featuring Linda Ronstadt*, March 1974)
   Producer: Nikolas Venet
   "Sweet Summer Blue and Gold"
   "If I Were You"
   "Just a Little Bit of Rain"
   "Bicycle Song (Soon Now)"
   "Orion"
   "Wild About My Lovin' "
   "Back Home"
   "Meredith (On My Mind)"
   "Train and the River"
   "All the Beautiful Things"
   "2:10 Train"
2. *Stone Poneys: Evergreen, Volume II*
   (Capitol Records ST-2763)

Released: June 1967
Producer: Nikolas Venet
  "December Dream"
  "Song About the Rain"
  "Autumn Afternoon"
  "I've Got To Know"
  "Evergreen (Part One)"
  "Evergreen (Part Two)"
  "Different Drum"
  "Driftin' "
  "One For One"
  "Back on the Street Again"
  "Toys in Time"
  "New Hard Times"

3. *Linda Ronstadt: Stone Poneys and Friends, Volume III*
  (Capitol Records ST-2863)
  Released: April 1968
  Producer: Nikolas Venet
    "Fragments: Golden Song, Merry-Go-Round, Love is a Child"
    "By the Fruits of Their Labor"
    "Hobo"
    "Star and a Stone"
    "Let's Get Together"
    "Up To My Neck In High Muddy Water"
    "Aren't You the One"
    "Wings"
    "Some of Shelly's Blues"
    "Stoney End"

4. *Hand Sown . . . Home Grown*
  (Capitol Records ST-2863)
  Released: March 1969
  Producer: Chip Douglas
    "Baby You've Been On My Mind"
    "Silver Threads and Golden Needles"
    "Bet No One Ever Hurt This Bad"
    "A Number and a Name"
    "The Only Mama That'll Walk the Line"
    "The Long Way Around"
    "Break My Mind"
    "I'll Be Your Baby Tonight"
    "It's About Time"
    "We Need a Lot More of Jesus (and a Lot Less Rock and Roll)"
    "The Dolphins"

5. *Silk Purse*
   (Capitol Records ST-407)
   Released: March 1970
   Producer: Elliot F. Mazer
   "Lovesick Blues"
   "Are My Thoughts With You?"
   "Will You Love Me Tomorrow?"
   "Nobodys"
   "Louise"
   "Long, Long Time"
   "Mental Revenge"
   "I'm Leavin' It All Up To You"
   "He Dark the Sun"
   "Life is Like a Mountain Railway"
6. *Linda Ronstadt*
   (Capitol Records SMAS-635)
   Released: January 1972
   Producer: John Boylan
   "Rock Me on the Water"
   "Crazy Arms"
   "I Won't Be Hangin' Round"
   "I Still Miss Someone"
   "In My Reply"
   "I Fall To Pieces"
   "Ramblin' Round"
   "Birds"
   "Faithful"
   "Rescue Me"
7. *Don't Cry Now* * +
   (Asylum Records SD-5064)
   Released: September 1973
   Producers: John David Souther, John Boylan, Peter Asher
   "I Can Almost See It"
   "Love Has No Pride"
   "Silver Threads and Golden Needles"
   "Desperado"
   "Don't Cry Now"
   "Sail Away"
   "Colorado"
   "The Fast One"
   "Everybody Loves a Winner"
   "I Believe in You"
8. *Different Drum*
   (Capitol Records ST-11269)

Released: January 1974
Producers: Nikolas Venet, John Boylan, Elliot F. Mazer, Chip
   Douglas
   "Different Drum"
   "Rock Me on the Water"
   "I'll Be Your Baby Tonight"
   "Hobo"
   "Stoney End"
   "Long, Long Time"
   "Up To My Neck in High Muddy Water"
   "Some of Shelly's Blues"
   "In My Reply"
   "Will You Love Me Tomorrow?"
9. *Heart Like a Wheel* ** +
   (Capitol Records ST-11358)
   Released: November 1974
   Producer: Peter Asher
   "You're No Good"
   "It Doesn't Matter Anymore"
   "Faithless Love"
   "The Dark End of the Street"
   "Heart Like a Wheel"
   "When Will I Be Loved"
   "Willing"
   "I Can't Help It (If I'm Still In Love With You)"
   "Keep Me From Blowing Away"
   "You Can Close Your Eyes"
10. *Prisoner in Disguise* ** +
   (Asylum Records 7E-1045)
   Released: September 1975
   Producer: Peter Asher
   "Love is a Rose"
   "Hey Mister, That's Me Up on the Jukebox"
   "Roll Um Easy"
   "Tracks of My Tears"
   "Prisoner in Disguise"
   "Heat Wave"
   "Many Rivers To Cross"
   "The Sweetest Gift"
   "You Tell Me That I'm Falling Down"
   "I Will Always Love You"
   "Silver Blue"
11. *Hasten Down the Wind* ** +
   (Asylum Records 7E-1072)

Released: August 1976
Producer: Peter Asher
"Lose Again"
"The Tattler"
"If He's Ever Near"
"That'll Be the Day"
"Lo Siento Mi Vida"
"Hasten Down the Wind"
"Rivers of Babylon"
"Give One Heart"
"Try Me Again"
"Crazy"
"Down So Low"
"Someone To Lay Down Beside Me"

12. *Linda Ronstadt: Greatest Hits* ** +
(Asylum Records 7E-1092)
Released: December 1976
Producers: Peter Asher, John David Souther, John Boylan, Elliot F. Mazer, Nikolas Venet
"You're No Good"
"Silver Threads and Golden Needles"
"Desperado"
"Love is a Rose"
"That'll Be the Day"
"Long, Long Time"
"Different Drum"
"When Will I Be Loved"
"Love Has No Pride"
"Heat Wave"
"It Doesn't Matter Anymore"
"Tracks of My Tears"

13. *A Retrospective* *
(Capitol Records SKBB-11629)
Released: April 1977
Producers: Peter Asher, Chip Douglas, Nikolas Venet, John Boylan, Elliot F. Mazer
"When Will I Be Loved"
"Silver Threads and Golden Needles"
"Hobo"
"I Fall To Pieces"
"Birds"
"I Can't Help It (If I'm Still In Love With You)"
"Different Drum"
"Some of Shelly's Blues"

    "I'll Be Your Baby Tonight"
    "Louise"
    "Long, Long Time"
    "Faithless Love"
    "Rock Me on the Water"
    "Lovesick Blues"
    "Rescue Me"
    "Just a Little Bit of Rain"
    "The Long Way Around"
    "You're No Good"
    "Ramblin' Round"
    "Crazy Arms"
    "It Doesn't Matter Anymore"
    "Will You Love Me Tomorrow?"

14. *Simple Dreams* ** +
    (Asylum Records 6E-104)
    Released: August 1977
    Producer: Peter Asher
    "It's So Easy"
    "Carmelita"
    "Simple Man, Simple Dreams"
    "Sorrow Lives Here"
    "I Never Will Marry"
    "Blue Bayou"
    "Poor Poor Pitiful Me"
    "Maybe I'm Right"
    "Tumbling Dice"
    "Old Paint"

15. *Living in the U.S.A.* ** +
    (Asylum Records 6E-155)
    Released: September 1978
    Producer: Peter Asher
    "Back in the U.S.A."
    "When I Grow Too Old To Dream"
    "Just One Look"
    "Alison"
    "White Rhythm and Blues"
    "All That You Dream"
    "Ooh Baby Baby"
    "Mohammed's Radio"
    "Blowing Away"
    "Love Me Tender"

16. *Mad Love* ** +
    (Asylum Records 5E-510)

Released: February 1980
Producer: Peter Asher
   "Mad Love"
   "Party Girl"
   "How Do I Make You"
   "I Can't Let Go"
   "Hurt So Bad"
   "Look Out For My Love"
   "Cost of Love"
   "Justine"
   "Girl's Talk"
   "Talking in the Dark"

17. *Linda Ronstadt: Greatest Hits, Volume II* ** +
   (Asylum Records 5E-516)
   Released: October 1980
   Producer: Peter Asher
      "It's So Easy"
      "I Can't Let Go"
      "Hurt So Bad"
      "Blue Bayou"
      "How Do I Make You"
      "Back in the U.S.A."
      "Ooh Baby Baby"
      "Poor Poor Pitiful Me"
      "Tumbling Dice"
      "Just One Look"
      "Someone To Lay Down Beside Me"

18. *The Pirates of Penzance* (Original Cast Recording)
   (From the Broadway production, also starring Kevin Kline, Estelle
   Parsons, George Rose, and Rex Smith)
   (Elektra Records VE-601)
   Released: May 1980
   Producer: Peter Asher
   Listing of Linda Ronstadt performances only (solo and with cast
     members):
      "Poor Wandering One"
      "How Beautifully Blue the Sky"
      "Hold, Monsters!"
      "Oh, Men of Dark and Dismal Fate"
      "Oh, Dry the Glistening Tear"
      "When the Foeman Bares His Steel"
      "All Is Prepared"
      "Stay, Frederic, Stay!"

"Sorry Her Lot"
"No, I Am Brave"
"Sighing Softly To the River"
"Finale"
19. *Get Closer* * +
(Asylum Records 6E-155)
Released: September 1982
Producer: Peter Asher
"Get Closer"
"The Moon is a Harsh Mistress"
"I Knew You When"
"Easy For You To Say"
"People Gonna Talk"
"Talk To Me of Mendocino"
"I Think It's Gonna Work Out Fine"
"Mr. Radio"
"Lies"
"Tell Him"
"Sometimes You Just Can't Win"
"My Blue Tears" (produced by Brian Ahern)
20. *What's New* (with Nelson Riddle and His Orchestra)
(Asylum Records 60260)
Released: September 1983
Producer: Peter Asher
"What's New?"
"I've Got a Crush On You"
"Guess I'll Hang My Tears Out To Dry"
"Crazy He Calls Me"
"Someone To Watch Over Me"
"I Don't Stand a Ghost of a Chance With You"
"What'll I Do"
"Lover Man (Oh Where Can You Be)"
"Good-Bye"
21. *Lush Life* (with Nelson Riddle and His Orchestra) ** +
(Asylum Records 60387-1)
Released: November 1984
Producer: Peter Asher
"When I Fall in Love"
"Skylark"
"It Never Entered My Mind"
"Mean To Me"
"When Your Lover Has Gone"
"I'm a Fool To Want You"
"You Took Advantage of Me"

"Sophisticated Lady"
"Why Can't We Be Friends"
"My Old Flame"
"Falling in Love Again"
"Lush Life"

22. *For Sentimental Reasons* (with Nelson Riddle and His
    Orchestra) * +
    (Asylum Records 60474-1-E)
    Released: September 1986
    Producer: Peter Asher
    "When You Wish Upon a Star"
    "Bewitched, Bothered and Bewildered"
    "You Go To My Head"
    "But Not For Me"
    "My Funny Valentine"
    "I Get Along Without You Very Well"
    "Am I Blue"
    "I Love You For Sentimental Reasons"
    "Straighten Up and Fly Right"
    "Little Girl Blue"
    " 'Round Midnight"

23. *Round Midnight* (with Nelson Riddle and His Orchestra) +
    (Asylum Records 60489-1-LR)
    Released: September 1986
    Producer: Peter Asher
    This is a boxed set containing all three of Linda Ronstadt's al-
    bums with Nelson Riddle and His Orchestra:
    What's New
    Lush Life
    For Sentimental Reasons

24. *Trio* (Dolly Parton, Linda Ronstadt, and Emmylou Harris) ** +
    (Warner Brothers Records 25491-1)
    Released: March 1987
    Producer: George Massenburg
    "The Pain of Loving You"
    "Making Plans"
    "To Know Him is To Love Him"
    "Hobo's Meditation"
    "Wildflowers"
    "Telling Me Lies"
    "My Dear Companion"
    "Those Memories of You"
    "I've Had Enough"
    "Rosewood Casket"
    "Farther Along"

25. *Canciones de mi Padre* * +
    (Asylum Records 60765-1)
    Released: December 1987
    Producers: Peter Asher and Ruben Fuentes
       "Por Un Amor"
       "Los Laureles"
       "Hay Unos Ojos"
       "La Cigarra"
       "Tu Solo Tu"
       "Y Andale"
       "Rogaciano El Haupanguero"
       "La Charreada"
       "Dos Arbolitos"
       "Corrido de Cananea"
       "La Barca de Guaymas"
       "La Calandria"
       "El Sol Que Tu Eres"
26. *Cry Like a Rainstorm, Howl Like the Wind* ** +
    (Featuring Aaron Neville)
    (Elektra Records 60872-2)
    Released: October 1989
    Producer: Peter Asher
       "Still Within the Sound of My Voice"
       "Cry Like a Rainstorm"
       "All My LIfe" •
       "I Need You" •
       "Don't Know Much" •
       "Adios"
       "Trouble Again"
       "I Keep It Hid"
       "So Right, So Wrong"
       "Shattered"
       "When Something is Wrong With My Baby" •
       "Goodbye My Friend"
                        • *Duet with Aaron Neville*

* Gold for sales in excess of 500,000 copies
** Platinum for sales in excess of one million copies
+ Available on compact disc

SINGLES

1. "Sweet Summer Blue and Gold" (with the Stone Poneys)
   (Capitol Records/1967)
2. "Different Drum" (with the Stone Poneys)
   (Capitol Records/1967)
3. "Up To My Neck in High Muddy Water" (with the Stone Poneys)
   (Capitol Records/1968)
4. "Some of Shelly's Blues" (with the Stone Poneys)
   (Capitol Records/1968)
5. "Long, Long Time"
   (Capitol Records/1970)
6. "(She's a) Very Lovely Woman"/"Long Way Around"
   (Capitol Records/1971)
7. "Rock Me on the Water"
   (Capitol Records/1972)
8. "Love Has No Pride"
   (Asylum Records/1973)
9. "Silver Threads and Golden Needles"
   (Asylum Records/1974)
10. "You're No Good"
    (Capitol Records/1974)
11. "When Will I Be Loved"/"It Doesn't Matter Anymore"
    (Capitol Records/1975)
12. "Heat Wave"/"Love is a Rose"
    (Asylum Records/1975)
13. "Tracks of My Tears"
    (Asylum Records/1975)
14. "That'll Be the Day"
    (Asylum Records/1976)
15. "Someone To Lay Down Beside Me"
    (Asylum Records/1976)
16. "Lose Again"
    (Asylum Records/1977)
17. "Blue Bayou"
    (Asylum Records/1977)
18. "Lago Azul" ("Blue Bayou" in Spanish)/"Lo Siento Mi Vida"
    (Asylum Records/1977)
19. "It's So Easy"
    (Asylum Records/1977)
20. "Poor Poor Pitiful Me"
    (Asylum Records/1978)
21. "Tumbling Dice"
    (Asylum Records/1978)

22. "Back in the U.S.A."
    (Asylum Records/1978)
23. "Ooh Baby Baby"
    (Asylum Records/1978)
24. "Just One Look"
    (Asylum Records/1979)
25. "How Do I Make You"
    (Asylum Records/1980)
26. "Hurt So Bad"
    (Asylum Records/1980)
27. "I Can't Let Go"
    (Asylum Records/1980)
28. "Get Closer"
    (Asylum Records/1982)
29. "I Knew You When"
    (Asylum Records/1982)
30. "What's New?"
    (Asylum Records/1984)
31. "Somewhere Out There" (duet with James Ingram)
    (MCA Records/1986)
32. "To Know Him is To Love Him" (with Dolly Parton and Emmylou Harris)
    (Warner Brothers Records/1987)
33. "Telling Me Lies" (with Dolly Parton and Emmylou Harris)
    (Warner Brothers Records/1987)
34. "Those Memories of You" (with Dolly Parton and Emmylou Harris)
    (Warner Brothers Records/1987)
35. "Wildflowers" (with Dolly Parton and Emmylou Harris)
    (Warner Brothers Records/1988)
36. "Don't Know Much" (with Aaron Neville)
    (Elektra Records/1989)
37. "All My Life" (with Aaron Neville)
    (Elektra Records/1990)
38. "When Something Is Wrong With My Baby" (with Aaron Neville)
    (Elektra Records / 1990)

APPEARANCES ON OTHER ALBUMS

1. *Harvest* by Neil Young
   (Reprise Records/1972)
   Background vocals on:
   "Heart of Gold"
   "Old Man"

2. *Dream* by the Nitty Gritty Dirt Band
   (United Artists Records/1975)
   Duet vocals on:
   "Hey Good Lookin' "
3. *Andrew Gold* by Andrew Gold
   (Asylum Records/1975)
   Background vocals on:
   "Heartaches in Heartaches"
   "Love Hurts"
4. *Elite Hotel* by Emmylou Harris
   (Reprise Records/1975)
   Background vocals on:
   "Amarillo"
   "Till I Gain Control Again"
5. *Black Rose* by John David Souther
   (Asylum Records/1976)
   Background vocals on:
   "If You Have Crying Eyes"
6. *What's Wrong With This Picture?* by Andrew Gold
   (Asylum Records/1976)
   Background vocals on:
   "Lonely Boy"
7. *Karla Bonoff* by Karla Bonoff
   (Columbia Records/1977)
   Background vocals on:
   "Home"
   "Rose in the Garden"
8. *Excitable Boy* by Warren Zevon
   (Asylum Records/1978)
   Background vocals on:
   "Excitable Boy"
9. *FM* movie soundtrack
   (MCA Records/1978)
   Solo "live" versions of:
   "Tumbling Dice"
   "Poor Poor Pitiful Me"
10. *Nicolette* by Nicolette Larson
    (Warner Brothers Records/1978)
    Background vocals on:
    "Mexican Divorce"
    "Give a Little"
    "Come Early Mornin' "
11. *An American Dream* by the Nitty Gritty Dirt Band

(United Artists Records/1979)
Duet vocals on:
"An American Dream"

12. *Radioland* by Nicolette Larson
(Warner Brothers Records/1980)
Background vocals on:
"Ooo-Eee"

13. *Bad Luck in Dancing School* by Warren Zevon
(Asylum Records/1980)
Background vocals on:
"Empty-Handed Heart"

14. *Light of the Stable* by Emmylou Harris
(Warner Brothers Records/1980)
Background vocals on:
"Light of the Stable" (with Dolly Parton and Neil Young)

15. *Roses in the Snow* by Emmylou Harris
(Warner Brothers Records/1980)
Duet vocals on:
"Gold Watch and Chain"

16. *Evangeline* by Emmylou Harris
(Warner Brothers Records/1981)
Trio of Emmylou Harris, Linda Ronstadt, and Dolly Parton on:
"Evangeline"
"Mister Sandman"

17. *All Dressed Up and No Place To Go* by Nicolette Larson
(Warner Brothers Records/1982)
Background vocals on:
"Say You Will"

18. *Camouflage* by Rex Smith
(Columbia Records/1983)
Background vocals on:
"Real Love"

19. *Escenas* by Ruben Blades y Seis del Solar
(Elektra Records/1985)
Duet vocals in Spanish on:
"Silencios"

20. *Graceland* by Paul Simon
(Warner Brothers Records/1986)
Duet vocals on:
"Under African Skies"

21. *Songs From Liquid Days* by Phillip Glass
(CBS Records/1986)
Lead vocals on:

"Freezing"
"Forgetting" (with the Roches)
22. *An American Tale* movie soundtrack
    (MCA Records/1986)
    Duet with James Ingram on:
    "Somewhere Out There"
23. *Hail! Hail! Rock 'N' Roll* movie soundtrack
    (MCA Records/1987)
    Lead vocal on the live version of:
    "Back in the U.S.A."
24. *Very Greasy* by David Lindley and El Rayo-X
    (Elektra Records/1988)
    Linda Ronstadt produced this entire album and sang background vocals on:
    "Gimme Da' Ting"
25. *1000 Airplanes On the Roof* by Phillip Glass
    (Virgin Records/1989)
    All vocals on the album
26. *Freedom* by Neil Young
    (Reprise Records/1989)
    Harmony vocals on:
    "Hangin' On a Limb"

Bibliography

Information for this book has been gathered from first-hand interviews and information contained in the following publications.

BOOKS

Dick Clark's The First 25 Years of Rock and Roll by Michael Uslan and Bruce Solomon (Dell Publishers/1981).
The Book of Rock Star Quotes compiled by Jonathan Green (Delilah Books/Putnam Publishers/1982).
Linda Ronstadt by Vivian Claire (Flash Books/1978).
Linda Ronstadt: An Illustrated Biography by Connie Berman (Proteus Books/1980).
The Linda Ronstadt Scrapbook by Mary Ellen Moore (Ace Books/1978).
The Love You Make: An Insider's Story of The Beatles by Peter Brown and Steven Gaines (Signet Books/1984).
Rock Encyclopedia by Lillian Roxon (Tempo Books/1969).

MAGAZINES AND NEWSPAPERS

After Dark
American Cinematographer
American Way
Associated Press (newswire)
Bananas Magazine
Billboard
Birmingham Post Herald (Birmingham, Alabama)
BMI
Boston Globe (Boston, Massachusetts)
Boston Herald (Boston, Massachusetts)
Boston Phoenix (Boston, Massachusetts)
Bridgeport Courier News (Bridgeport, New Jersey)
Broadside

Carlesbad La Costan (Carlesbad, California)
Cashbox
Cedar Rapids Gazette (Cedar Rapids, Iowa)
Cedar Rapids Register (Cedar Rapids, Iowa)
Celebrity
Chicago Sun-Times (Chicago, Illinois)
Chicago Tribune (Chicago, Illinois)
Cincinnati Enquirer (Cincinnati, Ohio)
Cincinnati Post (Cincinnati, Ohio)
Circus
Country Music
Country Music People
Country Song Roundup
Creem
Dallas Morning News (Dallas, Texas)
Detroit Free Press (Detroit, Michigan)
Flint Journal (Flint, Michigan)
Frets Magazine
Ft. Wayne News Sentinal (Ft. Wayne, Indiana)
Greenville Piedmont (Greenville, South Carolina)
High Fidelity
Hit Parader
Hustler
Life
Los Angeles Times (Los Angeles, California)
Mademoiselle
Melody Maker
Minneapolis Star Tribune (Minneapolis, Minnesota)
Morristown Daily Record (Morristown, New Jersey)
National Enquirer
New Castle Courier-Times (New Castle, Indiana)
New Times
New York Daily News (New York City, New York)
New York Magazine
New York Post (New York City, New York)
New York Press (New York City, New York)
New York Times (New York City, New York)
New Yorker
Newsday (New York City and Long Island, New York)
Newsweek
Ogden Standard Examiner (Ogden, Utah)
Orlando Sentinel (Orlando, Florida)
Parade